Dedication

To my parents, George and Katherine Harbeson,
for the love and adventure and strength and hope they gave us
on this all-too-short road to Wherever the Heck We Are;

To my siblings Lee Anna, Richard, Becky, and Peter the Great,
for all the support, come-uppances, and old stories
they have gleefully bestowed on me;

And to all the "Ve Get Too Soon Oldt, and Too Late Schmardt" people
of Wasilla and elsewhere in Alaska, especially the Coghlans, Turners,
Edes, Posts, and Beldens, and my Wasilla High School classmates:

Keep Smiling!

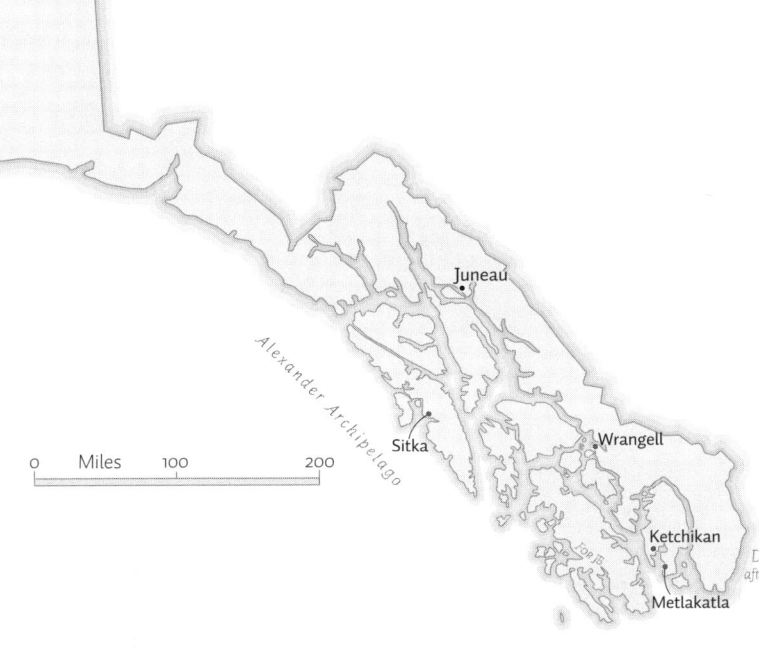

Copyright © 2010 by George Harbeson Jr.

No part of this book may be reproduced or used in any form or by any means without prior written permission of the author or publisher, excepting brief quotes used in connection with reviews.

Printed in the United States of America.

First printed August 2010.

Hardscratch Press, 2358 Banbury Place,
Walnut Creek, California 94598.

The front-cover photograph of KATY and GEORGE HARBESON was taken on their Wasilla homestead, 1963. The vehicle is a 1961 Corvair Lakewood 700 4-door station wagon (see Chapter 6); second son Richard (back to camera) stands before the door to the "basement house." The photo of a stretch of the Alcan Highway is from 1954.

Library of Congress Control Number: 2010930087

ISBN: 978-0-9789979-8-4

9 8 7 6 5 4 3 2 1

CATALOGING-IN-PUBLICATION DATA

Harbeson, George, Jr.
 Homesteaders in the headlights / George Harbeson, Jr.
  p. ; cm.

 ISBN 978-0-9789979-8-4
  1. Harbeson, George, Jr. 2. Harbeson family. 3. Frontier and pioneer life – Alaska – Wasilla. 4. Teachers – Alaska – Wasilla – Biography. 5. Wasilla (Alaska) – Biography. 6. Wasilla (Alaska) – Social life and customs. 7. Wasilla (Alaska) – History. I. Title.

F910.7.H27A3 2010
979.8/3
                    2010930087

Homesteaders
in the
Headlights

by

George Harbeson Jr.

12/4/2010

To Dee Longenbaugh,
Thank you for your review of
my book. I appreciate it!
Best Wishes,
George Harbeson Jr.

A Hardscratch Press book

Introduction

THE HARBESON FAMILY CAME TO ALASKA in 1954 when George Harbeson was hired to teach English at Wasilla High School. He was a dedicated teacher and favorite basketball coach, inspiring his students in and out of the classroom.

Turned down for medical reasons when he tried to volunteer to serve in the Army after Pearl Harbor, he was later drafted and served until he was discharged in December 1945. Thereafter, he attended teacher's college on the GI Bill, majored in English, and stayed an extra year to get his master's degree.

When I moved to Wasilla in 1963, George was an active citizen and popular teacher, involved in community affairs and politics. One of my daughter's most vivid high school memories is of listening to Mr. Harbeson read aloud John Steinbeck's *The Red Pony*, and my son-in-law still recalls Mr. Harbeson's explanation of how the mill rate works. George Harbeson's life—cut short at age 64—is the perfect illustration of how one person can make a difference in the life of a community.

Congratulations to George Jr. for writing this meaningful tribute to both his parents.

—*Katie Hurley*

Former state Representative Katie Hurley's record of public service in Alaska has spanned seven decades. A lifelong Alaskan, she has held many posts: among them, chief of staff for territorial Governor Ernest Gruening, Senate secretary for the territorial Legislature, chief clerk for the Alaska Constitutional Convention, and president of the State Board of Education under Governor William Egan. She was the first woman to win a statewide nomination for lieutenant governor and has served as executive director of the Alaska Commission on the Status of Women, as a member of the Alaska State Judiciary Council, and as chair of the Alaska State Commission on Human Rights.

Contents

Dedication/Map *of* Alaska

Introduction

CHAPTER 1 — One Man's Dream, One Woman's Reality — 11
Plowing, Planting, and Baseball [15] — *Skinning a
New Jersey Mink* [23] — *"Bound for Alaska"* [25]

CHAPTER 2 — The Territorial Years: 1954-56 — 33
Settling In [41] — *Country Living* [45] — *Growing Up Groton* [49]
White Meadow Lakes Interlude [54] — *Second Time Around* [56]

CHAPTER 3 — Fellow Travelers — 59
The Coghlans [59] — *The Posts* [65] — *The Turners* [70]
The Edes [77] — *The Beldens* [83]

CHAPTER 4 — We Become Homesteaders — 87
Prometheus' Gift [90] — *Everyday Homesteading* [93]
Barrel Stove Adventures [98] — *The Law of the Firstborn* [102]
Laundromat Lowdown [105]

CHAPTER 5 — The 1964 "Good Friday" Earthquake — 108
Work and Play and a House, Oh My [112]

CHAPTER 6 — Lug Nut Theater — 117
The '54 Chevy [122]
*Imposters – A Battery for Any Occasion – Cold-Weather Options – Can We Do
That Again, Papa? – Cousin Billy – Ditch-Diving and Other Dances
Life Was Good! – Out to Pasture – Dreams of Flying*

The '47 Jeep [135]
*Homesteaders in the Headlights – Mowing Daze – Beats Shoveling
Waterhole #1 – Night Caucus – Mud-Hole Escapade – Push-Start Miracle
The Little Jeep That Could and Did*

The '61 Corvair [153]
Corvair Potpourri – Corvair Icecapades – The Missing Mouse

Hal Post's '47 Ford Flatbed [160]
Richard Gets Run Over

The '66 Scout and More Tippage [165]
Asparagus? *In* Alaska? – *Scouting the Power Line*

Miles to Go [171]

CHAPTER 7 — Subsistence for the Soul and Stomach — 175
Fish on! [176] – *Set Nets in the Mud* [179] – *A'Hunting
We Went* [183] – *Caribou on Forward Control* [185] –
Turned Around and Upside Backwards [190]

CHAPTER 8 — The Game Is the Thing — 197
The Early Years [199] – *Batter Up!* [203] – *Home Court Advantage* [206] –
Errant Directional Inclinations [210] – *High School Commences* [213] –
The '62 Season Begins [216] – *Tales of Adversity and Courage* [223] – *Of Champions
and Moose Droppings* [227] – *A Long, Long Ride and a Rough Flight* [230] –
Get Me to the Game on Time [233] – *Host Families* [237] – *Overtime Medley* [238]

CHAPTER 9 — Encore Sports — 245
The Trials and Tribulations of Brother Richard [247] –
Faux Beer, P.D.A., and Pancakes [248] – *A Family Affair* [251]

CHAPTER 10 — The Animal Kingdom — 255
Bruce the Second [256] – *Beloved Blackie* [258] – *Snoopies* [260] –
Cats Galore [261] – *Bully* [265] – *Monkey Business* [266] – *Moosin'
Around* [267] – *Bear With Me* [269] – *Like Father, Like Son* [272] –
Froggie Stuff [275] – *Mousin' Around* [277]

CHAPTER 11 — Pastimes Quiet and Shocking — 281
Playing With Electricity [285] – *Nomads of the Night* [286] – *Bunk Mate Bugs
and BB Guns* [287] – *Model Airplane Antics* [289]

CHAPTER 12 — Flannel Boards and Grape Juice — 291

EPILOGUE — 299

Looking Back — 303

Index of People — 304

Acknowledgements — 309

About the Author — 311

Katherine (Katy) *and* George Harbeson *on the day after their wedding in November 1946, at the Montville, New Jersey, home of Katy's parents, Frank and Hazel Bartholomay.*

1

One Man's Dream, One Woman's Reality

I ONCE KNEW A MAN WITH A WEAK-SIGHTED EYE, a sore pitching arm, and a desire to make a difference in the world. He was my father. And he did make a difference.

George Stockton Rall Harbeson had an abiding and powerful faith in the common citizen and democratic ideals. Committed to improving society for all people through education, tolerance, and reason, he discovered a place where he could translate that faith into action. By his chosen profession of teaching and by example, Papa led my mother, Katherine; my younger siblings Lee Anna, Richard, Becky, and Peter; and me, through our early years in frontier Alaska.

But goals in life must face reality. Papa's reality was driven more by his wider early experience, from boyhood on a New Jersey farm to a teenage job in New York City to World War II service on the other side of the world. Mom's life was grounded in the Alaskan practicality of our family.

Eight years younger than Papa and like him reared in the Montville, New Jersey, area, Katherine Elaine Bartholomay was the daughter of Frank and Hazel Bartholomay. Frank was a stonemason and fox hound enthusiast. Katherine and her sister Mary and brother Frankie were nicknamed Chicky, Ducky, and Jake. Mom, the oldest of the three, took it upon herself to watch over her two younger siblings in their activities. She grew taller than her classmates, considered herself "big and gangly," and felt out of place; at eighteen she was five feet eight or nine, statuesque with long black hair. Photos show her with a film star appearance, perhaps a taller Hedy Lamarr. Something of a tomboy, she hated school in general but wanted to be an artist. Her life in Alaska included years of privation and often tedious work, but she also took private lessons and painted scenes of our homestead, of Cook Inlet, and family members, and experimented with carving, weaving, and other media. She never did like sports, but had enjoyed being Belle Starr when playing "Western" with friends in elementary school. She loved horseback riding, and she and her sister Mary each had a lamb for a pet.

In Montville, when Papa walked to school along the old Morris Canal bed in the mid-1930s, he saw two little black-haired girls with their hair in bangs playing in an adjacent yard. The two were Katherine and Mary, but Papa didn't know that then. About twelve years later he married the older one, Katy, as she was now called. They officially met in February of 1946. Mom graduated from Boonton High in the spring and she and "Harb," her lifelong name for him, dated that summer and fall. Papa, attending Montclair State Teachers College at the time, borrowed his brother Davis' 1930 Pontiac and took Mom to the Morris County Fair. On the way back, with his bad arm aching from throwing at coconuts in paper sacks for prizes, he stopped the car below his family's farmhouse and asked her to marry him. Papa had four days off from classes in November, and they were married in the Dutch Reformed parsonage on Changebridge Road by the Reverend Donald M. Wade. Rev. Wade, a close personal friend of the Harbeson family, later became the longest serving pastor in the more than two centuries of the church's history.

Papa had white-blond hair when young; it later darkened, but it remained unruly throughout his life. When he showed up at the wedding with his shock of hair, Don asked him if he needed a comb, but Papa said it wouldn't do any good. Papa and Mom were the love of each other's world for their entire lives—although I'm sure there were times when they wondered about that.

KATHERINE ELAINE BARTHOLOMAY, *Boonton High School Class of 1946.*

Brothers Sterne *(left) and* **George Harbeson** *change a tire on a trip through the South in the early 1940s.*

Plowing, Planting, and Baseball

PAPA'S BIRTH YEAR, 1920, WAS A LEAP YEAR. Prohibition was now in effect, and the Nineteenth Amendment giving voting rights to women was ratified in August. Domestic radios had recently appeared in stores—a Westinghouse model sold for ten dollars. The Band-Aid was invented by Earl Dickson, but it didn't catch on until a donation program sent a supply to the Boy Scouts of America. The League of Nations was formed, but the United States chose not to become a member. Howard Cosell and Leona Helmsley were born, and the Boston Red Sox traded Babe Ruth to the Yankees. Residual effects of The War to End All Wars and the 1918 Spanish Flu pandemic continued to be felt. The population of the U.S. had increased, with Papa one of an estimated 107.8 million people. And then before his tenth birthday the Roaring Twenties ran headlong into the black despair of the 1929 stock market crash and the onset of the Great Depression.

How, where, and when his lifetime goals began to gather strength and reality, I can only surmise. He preferred not to talk about himself. What I know of those early years comes from recollections that he set down decades later, and those didn't come to light until later still, when he was gone and I couldn't ask him questions. Was it born in the stacks of books from his father's once prosperous used-book store on New York City's 23rd Street? As a young boy myself, I investigated the dusty piles of rare volumes in the family's old barn and wondered at the worlds hidden between those faded covers. Did his sense of adventure dawn during long boyhood walks on the ties of the nearby Lackawanna Railroad line that stretched away to unknown lands? He waded and splashed in Valhalla Creek; its very name may have inspired his imagination.

His family struggled to coax a living from their farm during the Depression. Papa became a prolific reader and may or may not have read of Alaska. A wide selection of magazines and other publications was available to him. His high school classroom walls were hung with photographs of the "Bearded Poets"—Whittier, Lowell and Longfellow—along with portraits of George Washington and Abraham Lincoln. Mōmer Harbeson, his paternal grandmother—Mōmer an affectionate name for his grandmothers on both sides, Degenhardt as well as Harbeson—wrote poetry and paid to have it published. Reputedly a second cousin to Victorian sister poets and writers Alice and Phoebe Cary, she read poetry and Dickens to Papa and his brothers and sisters.

High school courses for Papa included Latin, American Democracy, and French, common curriculum in those days. His father, Davis Lawler Harbeson, helped him with the Latin, and with his Virgil and Caesar assignments. For his own pleasure, his father arose early and used an oil lamp for light to write translations for himself. He placed a copy in English of *Robinson Crusoe* on the table side-by-side with another copy in the language he was working on—French, German, Italian, Portuguese, Danish, Norwegian, or Russian—and referred to the English copy when necessary.

But before reading and bookish discussions came plowing, planting, weeding, harvesting, canning, repairing machinery. Traveling vendors were often the only source of needed goods and supplies. Papa's family didn't have electricity or a telephone until he was in his early twenties. He says his introduction to electricity on the farm occurred when he arrived on furlough one dim moonlit night in 1943 and walked home on the railroad tracks from the Towaco station. In the near darkness he turned onto the familiar path up the hill to the house and walked smack into a large electric light pole planted in the middle of the path. When Papa was in his sixties, he commented that counting his youth and the early years on our homestead in the 1960s, he'd spent half his life without electricity.

As with electricity in those days, medical science also held little resemblance to today's practices. Papa's memoirs give a glimpse of the medical procedures of his youth.

> *I was born at home in our farmhouse,* as were my younger siblings Sterne and Louise. We had various home remedies for our ailments. I had measles and chicken pox, but was lucky to miss diphtheria and scarlet fever. I thought I had mumps, but got them later when I was twenty-nine and student teaching. Doctor Longstreet was the doctor in the Montville area. Doc contracted polio when young, and had a wooden leg. He also had a glass eye, and was partly deaf. He drove a horse and wagon for years, then acquired a Model T. If people became sick

enough for a doctor, they sent for him. My father used to joke that when I was born, he asked Doctor Longstreet, "Between you, me, and the newel post, who does he look like?" and Doc replied, "The newel post." As it turned out, eight years later Dr. Longstreet also attended the birth of Katherine Bartholomay, my future wife-to-be.

Doctor Longstreet was a school doctor, too. He checked students' hearing with a pocket watch. One day he checked Raymond Baldwin's hearing by holding the watch out from Raymond's ear, then moving it closer and closer before discovering that the watch had stopped.

- -

PAPA HAD A BAD left eye from birth, due to the law-required medical practice of applying silver nitrate to a newborn's eyes to combat infection, or it might have been a so-called "lazy eye"—a form of amblyopia?—which wasn't corrected by wearing a patch over the good eye, a procedure developed later. His older sister Dorothy also had it. But Papa kept it to himself by reading eye charts with his good eye and pretending with the other, or memorizing the lines. He was sixteen and a high school senior before his family knew he had a bad eye. His father bought him eyeglasses, but they didn't help. I don't think he was legally blind in the eye, but he learned to compensate. He rarely mentioned it to me or the rest of our family, disguising it well, as he did with most of his ailments, including the fatal heart condition that took him at age sixty-four. This stubbornness and independence delivered him and us through difficult times, but had he relented at the end, I might have realized a belated opportunity to learn more from him.

When Papa was seventeen and recently out of high school, his older brother, Davis, got him a job as an office boy and runner with the law firm of Wright, Gordon, Zachary, Parlin, and Taylor on the 27th–29th and 35th floors at 108 Wall Street. He wore a three-piece suit with a white, blue, or pink shirt, a tie, and Thom McAn brown shoes. He commuted from the farm and worked 9 a.m. to 6 p.m. five days a week, with half-day Saturdays, for $.40 an hour—$.50 an hour for overtime, and holidays for $1.00 an hour. John Foster Dulles worked on the 28th floor and had a "bird-like" secretary named Ettinger who often advised Papa to go to college. The job took him around the city and beyond. He delivered legal papers prepared for the City Transit System, and to Mike Quill, the perennial head of the Transit Workers Union on 132nd Street. In 1940 he took his first ride in an airplane when he carried documents to the Washington, D.C., office of Thomas "Tommy the Cork" Corcoran. Corcoran was a lawyer, public servant, and controversial political figure in the New Deal era before he evolved into a corporate heavy hitter in the decades that followed. He was perhaps the main forerunner of today's lobbyists.

Papa mingled with the crowds on his train rides into the city, and in the small basement Wall Street café called The Spot, where everything cost a nickel—a Pepsi, a cup of beans or macaroni, or a hot dog, for example. He also ate at the E & B Cafeteria and at the restaurant in the old India House. Many years later, my Uncle Davis took me to lunch at one of the few surviving automats, to give me a flavor of the New York City of his and Papa's younger years.

Papa's war service as a sergeant and radioman in the 147th Army Air Communications Squadron certainly gave him a broader perspective on the world. After the Pearl Harbor attack, he and other office boys sat in the conference room of the Wall Street law firm and listened to FDR's speech. He then tried to enlist but was rejected because of his bad eye and was classified 1B in the draft. Drafted in 1942, he served for over three years. He wasn't a Marine, but I'm curious if he had any connection to the Navajo code talkers, since he was in radio operation, and in the right areas, but shortly after the islands had been taken. He certainly wouldn't have said anything, and details of the code talkers have only recently been released.

He served on Eniwetok, Saipan, and Iwo Jima at the end of his three-year stint. He told us briefly that he lacerated his right palm on Saipan coral when Japanese Zeros strafed the airstrip where he was stationed. Other soldiers dived into ditches splashed with gasoline and were burned badly. During the two weeks he spent in the hospital on Saipan, medics tended to the more serious burn cases first and delayed his treatment, which allowed infection and gas gangrene to fester in his wounds. He said the burned soldiers were released before he was, and he ended up with some permanent damage, which, like his eye problem, we never noticed during the homestead years.

He loved baseball—his first date with Mom was to see a baseball game in New York City—but his eye and arm problems affected his playing. Sometimes his elbow became so sore that he poured Sloan's liniment on it before he threw. In the summer of 1946, after the war, he pitched for a Towaco town team near his home in New Jersey. My cousin John Wilde tells of attending one of Papa's baseball games there.

> Your father's dead arm was the subject of an interesting story. When he was in college he picked up pin money pitching for a semi-pro team in Towaco. Your mother and I watched him play in Parsippany one Sunday afternoon. The field had a short porch in left field, about 250 feet. The "fence" was a corn field. Any ball hit into the corn field was a home run. Practically every batter tried to loft fly balls to left. By the seventh inning the score was something like 15–13, in Towaco's favor. Your father came in as relief. He was allowed eight warm-up pitches. Since his arm was dead, he was the most nuthin' nuthin' baller I ever saw. He was crafty, though. A batter from the opposition stood by the plate to see what kind of stuff your father had. Your father lobbed seven floaters over the plate, then he reared back and let fly with a blazing fast ball that almost decapitated the onlooker. Your father came off the mound wiping his face and yelled to his catcher, "Sorry, sweat got into my one good eye." Your mother Katy clapped her hands and said to me, "George is so clever."
>
> He couldn't have thrown another fast ball if his life had depended on it, but all the opposing batters could think about was that he could see out of only one eye. They shook like cottonwoods in a breeze and stood as far from the plate as they could. Your father lobbed balls over the outside corner, and the opposition didn't even get a loud foul off him. The opposing pitcher, also in relief, was a fat old Dutchman who had pitched a couple of years for the Yankees back in the 1930s. His stock in trade

GEORGE HARBESON, *a member of the town baseball team in Towaco, New Jersey, poses in August 1946 in front of the 1935 International panel truck used for the Harbeson Brothers' short-lived farm business.*

was a big, slow, sweeping curve ball. He had Towaco's hitters flailing away in frustration. Your father kept yelling at his teammates, "Walk up on him. Hit it before it breaks." When he came to bat, he stepped up and smashed the ball into the corn.

PAPA HAD PLAYED baseball as a boy, in pick-up games in the Army on Saipan, and during college. In 1953 he took me to see a Yankees or Dodgers game, but I can't recall anything except the large stadium. He believed more in sandlot and backyard sports than organized venues, but when he brought us to Alaska, he must have known he was leaving baseball behind. One summer in Alaska after we had moved onto our homestead, he enrolled me in the Wasilla Little League. We local boys played on a field in front of the Wasilla VFW, where I pitched and played outfield. I liked baseball—we played it during recess, too—but basketball was more prevalent and my favorite.

Papa was discharged from the Army at Fort Monmouth in December of 1945, but he was late arriving due to car trouble—which caused his discharge to take eight days instead of one. He soon attended Montclair State Teachers College on the G.I. Bill, majored in English and stayed an extra year to get his master's degree. My Uncle Sterne and his friend Hal Post, and a friend of theirs named Don Slee, drove to Alaska in 1949 in a '34 Ford V-8 roadster named "Arabella," after Papa and Sterne had rebuilt its engine in my Aunt Dorothy's kitchen. Perhaps Uncle Sterne's Alcan and Alaskan tales stirred Papa's interest. In any event, Papa set out to fulfill his goals with our departure for Alaska in the summer of 1954. Our course was set for a journey that has lasted more than fifty years.

KATY HARBESON, *September 1951.*

Skinning a New Jersey Mink

Papa taught Mom to drive in our Willys station wagon, a vehicle she detested from the very first. He also gave our washer and dryer to my Uncle Sterne and Aunt Dennie during this time, when Mom was pregnant with me. She described that as "the maddest I ever got!" I was born while Papa was still attending college on the G.I. Bill, and as a newborn I was immediately put to work for a monthly salary of fifteen dollars—I raised the G.I. Bill expense allotment from ninety dollars a month to one hundred five. Shortly before Lee Anna was born two years later, Papa and I both caught the mumps while he was practice teaching. About those early years, Mom recalled, "We had very little money. Our relatives brought vegetables and delicatessen food for us on their visits, and we could hardly wait until they were gone so we could eat."

Papa finished his master's degree and began teaching at Rockaway High School in the fall of 1950, for $2,400 per year. There were up to sixty-five students in some of his classes, long examinations to grade, and an unending flood of papers to correct. We had free housing from September through July by being the caretakers of the State Camp for the Blind at Marcella. At the camp, Papa supplemented his teaching income by trapping for mink and muskrats, much as he had throughout his earlier life. One day he set out a line of sixty-five traps, only to find the following morning that sixty-three of them had been stolen during the night by a thief who had followed his footprints in the snow.

One day when he, Mom, and I stayed in veterans' housing at Montclair State Teachers College, he skinned a mink in the bathroom. This was no doubt an act little appreciated by Mom, but they needed money to pay for my Biolac formula. The mink smelled worse than all the skunks he had skinned. The musky stench pervaded every room, and despite the cold weather every window had to be opened. As Papa's notes relate, "I took the skin to the drugstore in Upper Montclair to trade for Biolac, but the owner told me to keep the skin, that he'd trust me for the money. Eventually, I got twenty-five dollars for the pelt from Sears."

This was more than the ten dollars he'd gotten once as a boy when his father had taken him to a warehouse in New York City. Gangsters were moving into the raw fur business then, and the place was heavily guarded, but that didn't bother my grandfather, who took Papa inside and helped him negotiate the sale.

My sister Lee Anna thinks that Mom handled larger hardships and adverse events better than smaller irritants. Homesteading provided plenty of both, but through it all her love for Papa and us children seemed to sustain her as she met and surmounted obstacles in her quiet manner. And so she faced the prospect of moving to Alaska. As the Sherlock Holmes character expressed in some of the mysteries she later enjoyed on PBS, the game was afoot.

"Bound for Alaska"

When Papa first applied for a teaching position in territorial Alaska he was offered one in the Pribilof Islands. He had taken weather reports from Adak while stationed at Saipan in World War II, so he had the presence of mind not to accept that offer—not with a croupy firstborn and an exhausted new mother. Instead he matriculated in the master's program. In the spring of 1954, he applied again to Alaska, saying he was setting forth regardless of the reported lack of available housing, and that he would show up in person with his wife and their three children (ages six, four, and twenty-one months), and pursue the matter further. Soon a reply came back. A position had opened up in Wasilla, a small community in the Matanuska Valley, fifty miles from Anchorage. The salary was $4,940 a year. So, on a foggy, rainy morning in early August of 1954, Papa, Mom, Papa's sister Louise, and Lee Anna, toddler Richard, and I left New Jersey for Alaska.

"BOUND FOR ALASKA" was stenciled on the back of our getaway vehicle, a dark green 1954 Chevy 3100 6-cylinder CarryAll, not a delivery van but suburban-style, with windows all around. It had a front, middle, and rear seat, and a tailgate. My memories of this trip are scant, and suffer confusion with our second trip up the Alcan Highway in 1958, but photos show us camping next to a cornfield in Illinois, and passing through the ghost town of Dover, Wisconsin, established in 1844 by the British Temperance Emigration Society of Liverpool, England. One of its residents, John Appleby, invented the knotter on a grain binder after watching his mother knitting. My mother became a prolific knitter on our homestead, but I never perceived such financial possibilities in her knitting—she knit so fast that I couldn't keep up!

On we went, through the Dakota Badlands and up into Alberta, Canada, stopping one noon for lunch near Grand Prairie. Diaper boy Richard was sick that day, contributing an olfactory element to our picnic and sightseeing itinerary. We visited an Alberta zoo, where I encountered my first moose. Papa carried me on his shoulders as he walked the path around the large fenced-in area, and I nervously hung onto his head and hair as we passed the huge animal. Continuing north from Mile 0 of the

Harbeson Family Looks Forward To Teaching, Adventure in Alaska

THE GEORGE HARBESON FAMILY—Mr. and Mrs. Harbeson are sitting on the steps. The baby is 19-month-old Richard. At the left is George, Jr., six and a half years old, and at the right is Lee Anna, five.

George Harbeson of Marcella, filled with the pioneer spirit of adventure, plans to leave his present ho... months stretched out until June. The teacher with his love of na- tur and... years old, who atended school at Hibernia; Lee Anna, five, and ... to enter school this fall, ... months.

THE LENGTHY STORY THAT ACCOMPANIED *this 1954 photo in a New Jersey newspaper said in part:*

"George Harbeson of Marcella, filled with the pioneer spirit of adventure, plans to leave his present home, toward the end of August, and with his family start off on a 5,000-mile trip by car to Wasilla, Alaska. He hopes to complete the trip in 17 days. . . .

"Wasilla is a town of about 90 people, so the teacher assumes the pupils are transport pupils. He learned six rooms are being added to the building but does not know how large it was before the addition was begun.

"The little town is about 50 miles from Anchorage, and he said, 'It gets pretty cold there.' . . .

"Harbeson finds the Alcan Highway has no special requirements except the necessary requirements to get in and out of Canada. Because he has a job to go to, the only requirement for him is that he has to have enough funds, in the eyes of the authorities, to get through to Fairbanks.

"His contract is for one year and he hopes if it works out well to renew it for a longer period. . . ."

Alcan at Dawson Creek, we camped under the impressive 647-meter Peace River suspension bridge, which collapsed three years later but was soon rebuilt. Battalions of mosquitoes on the river bank had us flailing and swatting throughout the night. The next morning we installed a bug and rock screen onto the front grill of the Chevy and set out across the bridge toward Fort Nelson. I remember, as we drove across the bridge, looking down from the dizzying height to the Peace River far below.

The "highway," famously punched through to Alaska in World War II, was a narrow two-lane gravel and dirt road that meandered for long empty miles through wild terrain. The little wooden mileposts that marked our location and progress were greeted like faithful companions, giving us a feeling of security and accomplishment. Even more than the mosquitoes, the predominant memory for all early Alcan travelers is the dust—a fine powder that coated everything, infiltrated every part of our vehicle inside and out, penetrated our belongings and supplies and noses. The Chevy billowed the dust around and behind us like a smoke screen. As we rolled along, the passing of the infrequent oncoming traffic swept it over us like a low-visibility beige-colored fog. Occasional rains provided relief but turned the dust to mud.

We stopped for rest, meal breaks, and overnight stays whenever, wherever, we wished. Some campground sites provided roofed-over picnic tables and wood-burning cook stoves. When we stopped at these, I toasted slices of store-bought bread right on top of the stove's hot iron surface, flipped them with a metal spatula, and spread margarine on the burnt and blackened glaze—a treat fit for a kid or a king! Mom diluted canned evaporated milk with water for a beverage. Canned milk kept well with no refrigeration, but I hated the cloying taste. Lee Anna liked it, however. On our '58 trip we supplemented it with powdered milk—a small but insignificant improvement for me, the former Biolac Kid.

Between Fort Nelson and Watson Lake we climbed over Steamboat Mountain, where Papa sweated the fully-laden Chevy around narrow curves and past steep drop-offs. We stopped to traipse the shore of Muncho Lake and got ice from a rusty, outdoor 50-gallon drum before pushing on to the Liard Hot Springs. The springs, a luxury for us, were set in the trees a quarter-mile from the road. A series of planks spliced end to end served as access across a swampy area. We observed a couple of

A BRIDGE AT ONE O FIVE CREEK, *Mile 395.2 on the Alcan Highway (distance from Mile 0 at Dawson Creek, British Columbia), August 1954.*

Katy and George Harbeson *with* Lee Anna *and* George Jr., *near Grande Prairie, Alberta, on the trip north in 1954. (Youngest traveler Richard was ill the day the picture was taken.)*

moose and a black bear along the trail, a sight that thrilled all of us. The mosquitoes were met with considerably less enthusiam, but the springs were a novel and much welcomed experience, and we luxuriated in washing away road dust and soaking weary muscles in the clear, steamy, sulphur-scented pools. I always stop at the springs when I travel the route, but with each visit I discover the heavy footprint of "Progress" spread wider and heavier on the site. The water has gotten hotter over the years, too, bringing visions of "long pig" to mind as I soak.

The "sign forest" at Watson Lake was fascinating, although I don't recall it being called that in those days. It was and is a collage of markers and signs denoting destinations and hometowns from all over the world. There are many more now, but even then it was an attention-getter and gave us a sense of a travelers' community.

When we arrived at the northeast shore of Teslin Lake, a large body of water several miles long, we pulled off into a small open area in the mid-afternoon sun to wash clothes in the lake, breathe dust-free air, cook a hot meal, and camp overnight. My burnt toast recipe had to settle for the open flame of a Coleman camp stove, but it was a satisfactory substitute. Open-range horses wandering in this and other areas piqued Mom's and Aunt Louise's interest, but these animals were tough-looking critters compared to the horses the two of them had ridden in New Jersey.

On we went past Whitehorse and into the Takini area. This first trip through the area proved uneventful, but on our second trip up in '58 I remember driving through the burning remnants of a forest fire and keeping a busy lookout through the side and rear windows of the Chevy as we drove the narrow dirt road through a smoke-hazed and fire-charred landscape. Charcoal sticks of standing and fallen trees were scattered everywhere, many still afire with dying flames licking their trunks—truly an eerie, alien world. Whether Papa had heard of the fire in Whitehorse and been told that the road was open, I don't know.

In 1954 we wound our way through the area and continued on to Haines Junction, Kluane Lake, and Destruction Bay. Kluane Lake is magnificent: vast and mountain-cradled, always a special stop for me on trips through the region. I have camped and hiked on its rocky slopes and shores many times. Grizzlies are common visitors to the peaceful camping there, with sheep and goats roaming the overlooking crags. The lake water is clear as new glass and the beaches are clean and covered with the pastels of northern gravel. On one trip in the '90s, I ran for an hour each day along the dirt road bordering the lake, giving passing truckers occasion to shake their heads and mutter about crazy tourists. And they're right, come to think of it—I really shouldn't be extolling the area!

But the open road beckoned. We left Kluane for the final leg of the Alcan, passed through Beaver Creek and Customs, across the border, and south and west to Wasilla, where the rest of our lives began and our family history resides to this day.

WASILLA, ALASKA, 1949. *Buildings along the right side of the street, front to rear, are Teeland's Shopping Center (later Teeland's Country Store), the Wasilla Road House, the Hilltop Café, the library (set back from the road, unseen), the post office (white building, dark roof). Of the unseen buildings beyond, one would be the Community Hall.*

Buildings on the left are the Wasilla Cocktail Bar (owned by Roy and Mary Virginia Morrison), the Cadwallader building; a house owned by Mrs. Wilmoth (white building), Mavis and Ernie Line's cabin, the Tharps' house (later the Woodwards'), Pat and May Carter's house (only the roof visible), and (unseen) a house owned by Bronwen Jones and rented by the Harbeson family the day after they arrived in Wasilla in 1954. Photo courtesy of Colleen Teeland Cottle.

2

The Territorial Years: 1954–56

IN LATE AUGUST OF 1954, WE BECAME PART OF WASILLA'S one hundred or so residents and spent our first night at Ernest Peck's cabin. The next day we moved into Mrs. Bronwen Jones' house in the middle of Wasilla. The house had an oil space heater and a wood kitchen stove, but wasn't insulated—common in those days. We drew water from a well with a hand pump mounted beside the kitchen sink, and Mom cooked our meals on our Coleman camp stove.

The hand pump was a step up from Papa's early days, when his family used an open hand-dug well with a pail on a rope much of the time. The stone-lined farm well, twenty feet deep, regularly went dry, and they frequently had to drop a ladder into it and clean out the dead toads, frogs, and mice. Papa said they could tell by the taste when such a clean-out was necessary, but his father also used a mirror to reflect light into the well to check for the intruders. I'm glad to say we didn't have rodent/amphibian-flavored water in the Wasilla house—or at least none I ever noticed.

Because of Papa's new job, the Chevy got a rest; he walked the short distance to the school, which was close enough for Mom to send Lee Anna occasionally to deliver a thermos of coffee and bag lunch to him, after checking for moose in the vicinity. Helen Carter Carney tells me that Papa took the position vacated by Miss Louise Potter, a published author who became a good friend during her annual visits, when she drove solo from Vermont to Wasilla and back. We were next door to the Pat and May Carter family, and across the street from the Community Hall (built in 1931), where Papa coached basketball a year later. Other neighbors were Ed Carney and his family, the Woodwards, and Clara Slumberger. Lee Anna became good friends with Ed's daughter, Roxanne

Axtell, and Ed helped us with some of our later homesteading tasks. Many years later he and his brother Doug were my teammates on a city league basketball team when we played in local area games and Anchorage Fur Rendezvous tournaments.

The people of Wasilla and surrounding area welcomed us as if we were newly discovered relatives. It was too late for us to have a garden that first year, so Papa's students brought vegetables from their gardens and farms to help us through the winter. As noted by Louise Potter, people in the area weren't as provincial as one might assume, since many of them, like Papa, had emigrated to Alaska with a broader world experience. As with people anywhere, local families and individuals had their occasional bumps in the road and skeletons in their closets to provide topics of conversation for those so inclined. But our neighbors made us feel at home.

We quickly acquired a brown puppy with a white blaze on its chest and named him Bruce, after our Irish setter that had died of distemper at the Marcella Camp for the Blind. Moose frequented the town and our yard, which added zest to local strolls about town. Lee Anna and I walked to school, a half-block over and one block down. I'd heard tales of the legendary George, a large bull moose with a broad rack in season, who'd made the town his home. He'd been such a common sight that he was considered one of the community. We arrived after George's time, but other moose claimed the town—irritable moose that didn't take kindly to the high school students who threw snowballs at them from rooftops—so I kept an eye out, dodging and detouring to my second grade class, taught by Sybil Woody.

Other entertainment included Hagen's Playland amusement park, an unusual enterprise for the town Wasilla was then. It featured a Ferris wheel, merry-go-round, restaurant, and an American LaFrance fire truck. The school leased Hagen's building a year or two for classes. He also ran the Palmer Theater for a time.

The post office was a tiny building a block from our house, with May Carter serving as postmaster and magistrate. It had two short walls of small mail boxes, each box fronted with a combination dial and a pointed clock-like hand. We used Box 87. I remember looking up at May sitting behind the barred window above the counter. I was just tall enough to rest my chin on its shelf. The Wasilla Public Library, which in later years became a favorite hangout of mine, was set back from the road on a lot bordering the post office. Some say it was Wasilla's first house.

The school was an old building containing all twelve grades, but an elementary addition was added in 1955 and opened that fall. Papa and other high school teachers each taught several classes, covering different subjects. He had come to Alaska to make a difference, and Wasilla was where, as car enthusiasts say, "the rubber met the road." He spent countless hours dedicated to students and education, taking on extra-curricular duties on a volunteer basis or for a pittance. During his years of service he reactivated the school newspaper, the *Wa Hi War Whoop*, using an old mimeograph machine donated by the Matanuska Electric Association. He sponsored and mentored the paper for seventeen years, spending many after-school hours on weekends and holidays instructing and supervising the students involved.

He also started and maintained a literary quarterly, the *Wonder*, for many years. In his early years he coached boys and/or girls basketball and track, previously having been an assistant track coach in New Jersey, where he ferried the team to meets in my Grandpa Bartholomay's '34 straight-six Buick 2-door sedan. (On June 1, 1955, a runner on the New Jersey team named Tom Skutka set a National High School record of 4.19.5 for the one-mile run at Morris Hills High School in Rockaway, New Jersey. I was impressed when Papa told me that at times Skutka's strides measured as long as fifteen feet each.)

In the 1954–56 years, Papa volunteered to be basketball coach. He enjoyed coaching and it gave him an opportunity to work with students outside the classroom environment. As a second-grader I watched their practices and chased basketballs in the old Community Hall, now the Wasilla museum. Sometimes Papa and other adults took part in the practice scrimmages to get enough for five-on-five. Skip Coghlan, a freshman in '54 and a member of the last Wasilla High School class to graduate under Alaska's territorial status, in May of 1958, remembers those times:

> In the spring of '55 they broke ground for the elementary school addition, which included remodeling the gym and adding the health center. The gym improvements included the dug-

Richard *and* Becky Harbeson *and* Roxanne Axtell *(standing on the swing) play in Pat and May Carter's yard in Wasilla, 1954. In the background is the Wasilla school.*

The Territorial Years: 1954–56

THE STAFF *of the* WA HI WAR WHOOP, *from the 1961-62 Wasilla High School yearbook. Back row, from left: Earl Erickson, Jerald Bouwens, Ray Shilber, Neil Browne, adviser George Harbeson; next row: Peg Woodward, Terry Roth, Jane Nunley, Judy Bergman, George Harbeson Jr., Georgia Starr; next row, seated: Karen Olsen, Helen Carter, Larry Teeland, Judy Garcia, Joan Nunley, Linda Carney; front, kneeling: Karen Andrews, Marilyn Gilbertson, Melody Toomey, Ida Hjellen.*

outs, balcony, and replacing the tile floor with a hardwood one. By fall, the grade school was ready for use, but the gym was not. I was a sophomore and your dad was the basketball coach, like he'd been the previous year. I was the tenth player on the squad —not because of my talent, but because of the small school numbers—there just weren't any more guys interested in being on the team.

We'd suit up for practice in the school, then jog over to the Community Hall for the actual practice. This went on for a month or two, until the gym was finished, in time for the first game.

Unlike Bill Lambert, hired to coach a few years later, I don't think your dad was "formally" hired to be coach. I had the impression that he did it on a volunteer basis. He worked hard at coaching and did a good job, although he didn't have much to work with. He had played ball when younger, and had a book on basketball that included plays, some of which your dad had us practice and use. We concentrated on basic fundamentals, setting picks, give-and-go stuff. The kind of things I see good players do mostly by instinct, but we struggled at times.

Team members I remember were freshmen Wally Teeland, Gilbert Hjellen, Jack Devlin, Donnie Carter, and myself. Frank Devlin, Bob Gershmel, and Jimmy Vickaryous were upperclassmen. Others possibly taking part were the Knutsen boys and the Johnson brothers. During a routine physical Frank was diagnosed with a heart murmur, not debilitating, so he had the choice of playing or not. He was a very good player, but he elected not to play. Jack was a very good, but short, player, too. The Gershmel family were colonists and lived five miles out of town, down on Trunk Road, above the Carsons. Every night after practice Bob had to run home for the evening milking of the family's cows!

PAPA ALSO STARTED a teen club, and he sponsored and helped with student fund-raising activities. Students remember his classroom creation of J. Chauncey Spivis and the "Yeah, But" Club, complete with membership cards that Papa handed out whenever a student, faced with an inquiry such as "Did you do the homework?" prefaced the answering excuse with "Yeah, but my Mom cleaned out my room and threw it away," or "Yeah, but I left it on the bus." He helped establish and supervise a regular organized cheerleading program at a student's suggestion, and held two annual art contests. He functioned for years as an officer in the PTA.

Papa and other local educators were instrumental in establishing the Wasilla and Matanuska-Susitna Borough education associations. He served for many years as an officer in both, and actively contributed much to the Alaska Education Association, later re-named N.E.A.-Alaska. He was active in the Alaska Democratic Party. His father had voted Republican for many years, had a Hoover sticker on his car and supported Hoover in the 1928 election before the Depression. But in 1932 Grandpa became a Democrat and stayed one for the rest of his life, and Papa followed that lead, as have I. Our ancestor, Benjamin Harbeson, served on the Committee of Safety in Boston with Benjamin Franklin, and was responsible for seeing that the boycott resulting from the passage of the Stamp Act was enforced. Papa had a high respect for Franklin, and our Benjamin also may have been something of a time-misted role model.

As noted, my grandfather Harbeson had a used book store on 23rd Street in New York City for a time and was a rare book dealer for many years. His avocation of translating the classics into several languages was certainly a source of Papa's high regard and devotion to reading and books. The small Wasilla Library held a special place in the hearts of all the Wasilla community, Papa's included. Enhanced by his program of regular student and class visitations, the library was one of the top five in circulation in territorial Alaska in the '50s, according to an article by Robert L. Tucker in *Alaska Ruralite* ("Making Do," November 1983, Vol. 30, No. 11). The library thrived over time. In later years, Papa, Mom, Bea Turner, Sue Goodwin, Bill Lorentzen, and others operated the Matanuska-Susitna Valley Bookmobile. His thirty-one-year involvement with the Library Association, including his last several years as its president, lasted right up to his passing in 1985.

By this time, Papa's love of books was shared by Mom. Besides helping with the Bookmobile, from our first days on the homestead she volunteered with Bea Turner and others in the library on Fridays. The reading fever in our and our friends' homes was contagious, and the library's books were a treasure trove for me.

Local history commanded an important part of Papa's interests, and he was active for many years in the Matanuska-Susitna Historical Preservation and Restoration Society and the Wasilla-Knik-Willow Historical Society. The Wasilla Community Hall, which became the Wasilla museum, is where he'd coached basketball in 1955, and it was where he suffered the heart attack that led to his death thirty years later. Heart disease is prevalent in the Harbeson family and he must have known something was wrong, but he didn't like hospitals and the medical scene, so he kept it to himself. He was doing volunteer work one day at the Museum in early January of 1985 when Opal Toomey, Ann Myers, and Esther West found him sitting at a table, in trouble. His efforts all came to an end when he died three weeks later.

Still, I know that if he had been alive during the 2008 presidential campaign he would have been dismayed to see the publicity the Library and Museum received as a result of Alaska Governor Sarah Palin's V.P. candidacy and her previous actions as Wasilla mayor.

Settling In

BUT THE END OF PAPA'S IDEALS WAS STILL many years in the future when Alaska began working its magic on us. We grew comfortable with the change from New Jersey, although adapting was harder for Mom, especially being so far from her relatives. We kids, of course, jumped right in and reveled in the new adventures surrounding us. We explored the town and discovered new friends. Shortly after we settled in, five-year-old Lee Anna brought home two little boys she had "found," possibly John and Pete Polis. A new toy for us kids was the long-handled pump at our kitchen sink, which had to be primed, and we clamored to "help" Mom with the priming. We acquired our new puppy, Bruce II, met classmates we would know for the rest of our lives, and grew to appreciate living with moose at our door.

During our first Alaska winter, in 1954, we enjoyed the holiday hospitality of the Jim Wilson family out on Fairview Loop. On Christmas Eve the temperature slid to minus thirty degrees, and it stayed cold for several days. We sent for a tow truck to start the Chevy so we could drive to the Wilson farm. In our Christmas Report to relatives on the far distant East Coast, Papa described the cold:

"Every time someone comes in from the outside, a ghost of condensation follows them into the room, forming a white cloud around them. One doesn't have to go outside for evidence of the cold. The windows are layered with a half-inch to an inch of ice at the bottom of the panes. The inside of the door is coated with white frost, as is the oil pipe leading to the oil heater—the hottest part of the house."

Living in such cold was a hardship then, but people were always ready with a quip. When I bought ice cream at Teeland's store, the clerk said, "If you'd like, I'll put it in a bag to protect it from the cold." One Christmas many years later, when I taught school in the Iñupiaq village of Selawik, east of Kotzebue. I purchased a soft ice cream cone from the school store managed by aide Roger Clark, and the ice cream froze harder as I walked home in the fifty-below temperature.

Cold as it was outside, hearts were warm at the Wilsons', and there was food for all. Eighteen people were in attendance to enjoy the roast pork that formerly had been Petunia. The menu included chicken, sweet and mashed potatoes, salad, Jell-O, apple sauce, olives, pickles, cherry and rhubarb and pumpkin pies, nuts, ice cream, and two fruitcakes that Mom had baked. Papa noted in the Christmas Report that two-year-old Richard "distinguished himself by eating half a deep-dish pumpkin pie." I don't recall that particular feat, but it must have included him wearing a portion of it.

Mom's contribution to the holiday letter relates, "Richard had a gay time grabbing at the lights, hanging bulbs, and the snow that George Jr. had made of Ivory soap flakes. Amid the confusion, I managed to make a huge stollen that I expected to last at least a week. It lasted for three days."

So our first Christmas was a joyful success despite the cold, and by January 13th the temperature had risen from thirty below to forty above.

During those first two years, Mom did have one relative to visit with, Papa's younger sister Louise, who had traveled up the Alcan with us to take a teaching job on Fort Richardson in Anchorage. Once in a while she would visit us in the Wasilla area. After one such visit, we drove her back to Anchorage. A few miles from Fort Rich we came upon someone with a flat tire and no jack. We stopped to help, as anyone would in those days. It turned out that we had a lug wrench but also had no jack. That was no problem for Papa. We constructed a ramp with wooden blocks and planks we had with us in the Chevy, scrounged a thick tree branch from the roadside, and drove their flat tire up the ramp. After stacking blocks precariously under the axle, Papa kicked the ramp from under the tire, leaving it high enough atop the blocks to change the tire. Then he pushed their car off the axle blocking with the branch, collected the planks and blocks, and delivered Aunt Louise to her home on the base.

Aunt Louise played the piano for us, and I was taken with the sea chanteys that she put forth, refrains such as "What do you do with a drunken sailor, ear-lye in the morning," and ". . . way-hay, blow the man down," and ". . . blow ye winds hi-ho, a-roving I will go" (Charles Edward Carryl's "Walloping Window Blind," a.k.a. "A Capital Ship," an adaption of "Ten Thousand Miles"). In 1934, when Papa's family picked black raspberries on their farm, singing "A Capital Ship" amid the rows as they worked, little Louise objected to the phrase ". . . in the teeth of the bloomin' gale." She thought that they were singing "girl" instead of "gale," and that they were teasing her. However, as an adult she played the chanteys, and the jaunty, lilting, irreverent music and lyrics struck a chord in me, reinforced years later with broader impact by Country Joe McDonald, and by Dr. Schultz' band in Alaska.

There we were, light years from the days of the bounding main. Nonetheless we sailed a tall ship on a voyage of our own, charting a course for the rest of our lives, sometimes into the "teeth of a bloomin' gale"!

Lee Anna *and* Richard Harbeson *practice barrel rolls at the Byers' in July 1955—preparation for Richard's later-in-life aerobatics.*

Country Living

AFTER THE 1954–55 SCHOOL YEAR WE MOVED out of town and rented Orlando and Margaret Byers' house on Fairview Loop, not far from the Knik-Goose Bay road. Surrounded by woods now, we cultivated a large garden space. We kids explored the woods and hunted spruce hens and rabbits. We had access to Cottonwood Creek for fishing via a trail through the woods in back of the house. We had a scare when Richard, late in his terrible-two stage, managed to open the basement door and tumbled down the steps to the floor below. To our relief, despite bruises and aches and a good cry, he was fine and recovered to go on to bigger and grander exploits.

In 1955, I was a third grader in Clara Slumberger's class in the new elementary wing, with the usual "I see England, I see France . . ." sort of humor. Once I ventured across the divide, into the wilds of the high school above the gym, and betook my Oliver Twist self into Papa's classroom to plead for milk money, much to his embarrassment and the high schoolers' delight. I, being the oldest and setting the example, paved the way for first-grader Richard in 1958. As Richard tells it: "I burst through the classroom door, ran up to Papa, and asked him if I could have eight cents for milk money. Papa had a loving, but slightly dismayed, look on his face while the high schoolers roared with laughter. . . ."

I joined the Cub Scouts and went to meetings and activities at the Levan residence, about a mile away, on the Knik Road. I was a member of Pack Number 319, with Cub Master Bob Lincoln running the show. The Lincolns owned and operated a family dairy farm named "Udder Confusion" four or five miles away. Roger Lincoln was in my class at school and was a good friend throughout our school years. The Cub Scouts provided an opportunity to socialize with other kids in the area and learn different skills, and I earned a Wolf badge in the process.

As a boy in the Montville area, Papa had attended Scout meetings held in a church community hall. One activity was a game called "Trench," presumably derived from WW I and played in the dark. The troop was divided into two teams, one spread along the wall at the far end and the other lined across the hall in the middle. A whistle blew out the lights and the team at the far end fought to break through the opposing middle line to gain the near end, resulting in considerable rough and tumble confusion. And people think dodgeball is tough!

My own Cub Scout times in Wasilla were days of the Scout Pledge —I, (name), promise to do my best, etc.—and the Law of the Pack, badges, uniforms, snacks, games in the front yard, and "grenade" wars employing socks filled with dust. At one meeting, I slashed my left knee on a rock while playing outside. It didn't cut my pants, but I suffered a two-inch gash on my knee cap that was, for whatever reason, never stitched. For a week I walked around home and school with its wrap constantly loosening and trailing out of my pant leg at the ankle. Embarrassing for a third grade grenadier! Fifty-some years later, I still have the scar and the memories—but not the embarrassment—and the thought that somewhere on the land behind the convenience store on Knik Road lies some of my long-ago blood integrated into somebody's yard.

Oddly enough, Papa suffered a similar experience as a boy, but his involved more mischief. Against explicit orders from his parents, he climbed a tent pole and gashed his left knee on a stub when he slid down. He told his mother that he had fallen on a rusty metal cot, causing her to worry about lockjaw, or tetanus. Like me, he received no stitches, sported a salve-treated wound wrapped in a clean rag, and wore the scar for the rest of his life.

MY FIRST SERIOUS LESSON IN LIFE, TAUGHT to me by a rabbit, took place in a chicken house. I was seven and kept a baby rabbit in Byers' unused chicken house. Faded straw lay strewn on the floor, dried remnants of droppings mixed with feathers smeared the roosts, and a musty odor clung to the sunlight that filtered in through smudged windows. I fed and watered the small white rabbit every day, and petted it from time to time.

The pet had full run of the building and its nooks and crannies, as opposed to the common cage environment of most pet rabbits, so it was harder to catch. One day, after I gave it feed and water, it jumped from my hands and proceeded to race through the straw on the floor, playing tag with me—or rather, me playing tag with it. The game was fun for a while, but the smaller and quicker rabbit was too quick for me. Young and impatient, I grew irritated. Spotting an old tennis ball near the door, I picked it up, and without really thinking or even trying to aim, I hurled it in frustration at the scurrying rabbit. In a split second the ball flew fifteen feet through the dusty sunlight and scored a direct hit.

As I stood in stunned disbelief, the rabbit jerked and kicked spasmodically in its death throes on the yellowed straw. I ventured over and crouched beside it. Shocked, I brushed at the dust and bits of straw streaked in its white fur. Its small frail body shuddered and stilled under my clumsy fingers, and I saw the shine in its eye go flat and dull. As I sat on the floor next to it in the thin light and breathed the stale air, the dawning realization of what I had done struck home.

It was merely the death of a rabbit, negligible on the grand scale of existence, but this was not hunting rabbits or killing chickens for food. This was careless, petty, destructive arrogance by an immature youth. For the first time I was brought face to face with a darkness in me I had not previously realized. I saw a responsibility for my actions and, above all, how fleeting and tenuous life could be. Decades later, Papa wrote in his memoirs of a sparrow he'd shot with a BB gun and the guilt he'd felt when he watched the trembling bird die in his hands. He also recalled the shock he'd felt when an opossum had moved while he was skinning it. As I grew older, I came to realize that life can also be resilient, adaptive, and stubborn, but killing that pet rabbit was my first step away from childhood, and it stayed with me.

As Papa noted in his memoirs, "There is a remorse that lasts for incidental cruelties."

GEORGE JR., RICHARD *and* LEE ANNA *pose on the stoop at Byers' in 1955 as Katy Harbeson watches from the front window.*

Growing Up Groton

AFTER TWO YEARS IN ALASKA, AND WITH Mom pregnant with my sister Becky on the trip down the Alcan, we moved back East where Papa taught in Groton, Vermont, and at White Meadow Lakes, New Jersey, for a year each. I assume we left Alaska because of Mom missing her family. We packed up our original "BOUND FOR ALASKA" Chevy, stuffed our ride-in-the-car-lovin' dog Bruce II into his half of the plywood-covered rear seat area, and the five of us took our places on the vehicle's brown vinyl seats, with me on the topside of the plywood over Bruce's nest. Papa provided me with a blanket to smuggle my measles-spotted face across the Alaska/Canada border, and I dutifully suffered and sweltered in eighty-degree weather—higher under the blanket—so that we would not be turned back.

Upon arriving on the East Coast, with a family and a large dog to feed, Papa took a teaching job as close to family as he could get, in Groton, possibly with the help of Louise Potter, the teacher and author he had replaced in Wasilla in 1954. Now that we weren't a continent away, we were able to see our many relatives.

I especially remember Groton, where I was a fourth-grader. For one thing, Becky was born there in October, three days short of my ninth birthday, across the border from Groton in the nearby New Hampshire town of Haverhill (pronounced *Hav'-rill*) where the nearest hospital was located. Years later in Wasilla, Papa bought Becky a high school ring, saying she had been the least expensive birth of us all: $40.00!

In Groton, Papa coached boys' and girls' basketball, baseball, and other activities. I became the boys' team mascot, sort of a subaltern position with the organization, complete with my own pint-sized team uniform #3, in the *Hoosiers* fashion of the day. It was heady stuff for a fourth-grader. I joined in the pre-game and half-time warm-ups with the 1956–57 Groton High Gremlins. The eight boys on the team were supportive and patient and the crowd liked it, but as the season dragged on without a win, they must have wondered if having me for a mascot was a good idea. It couldn't have been comforting that the girls' team, the Groton High Gremlinettes, also coached by Papa but without a mascot, was winning.

Groton was a small rural town with tree-lined streets, front lawns, friendly neighbors, and pleasant weather. There was a long open hill behind our house to explore in summer and sled in winter. A *Saturday Evening Post*, Norman Rockwell kind of place—but even better.

The neighborhood children gathered in the evenings and played kick-the-can, Red Rover, red light/green light, or hide-and-seek, until after dusk. During one such evening, two high school girls joined the hide-and-seek routine. They became the seekers and we became the hiders, but they added a twist of their own. They counted down to the "Ready or not, here I come!" and then, to our dawning dismay and disgust, while we peered from our hidden havens, they hunted us boys down, one by one, and planted a big, bright-red lipstick kiss on each of our young male faces. Oh, the horror! The horror! Embarrassed and not wanting Papa or Mom to see this red badge of shame, I sneaked into our house, tip-toed into the dimly lit kitchen, and vigorously scrubbed the lip-shaped scarlet letter "O" off my forehead.

In Groton, I also remember rising at sunrise and running down to fish the river or lake for rainbows, dollies, browns, and perch, using fat night crawlers the size of small snakes that I had "jacklighted" on our lawn the night before, and then hurrying back home and to school when the church bells rang eight o'clock, looking for the lazy afternoon to come faster so I could bike to a friend's place with cardboard strips flipping along the bike spokes, to trade his Moose Skowron and Whitey Ford bubblegum cards for my extra Mantle. On the lawn, we flipped the worn Barlow knife that Papa had given me through Mumbledy-Peg moves like Johnny-Jump-the-Fence and other knife flips and drops he had taught me. We laughed at my friend's name for his dog, "Uno" (or maybe "You Know"), and fished for suckers, or carp as some called them—fish with scavenging mouths and tough, plastic-like lips that never let go of a hook. I remember us shooting the breeze about chasing bats in Lyons' house-barn entryway with badminton rackets, and jumping off the loft into the hay below, and how I liked a girl in our class named Peggy, and how about that Buddy Holly singing about Peggy Sue. Then me telling him how Papa made me get a haircut at the town barbershop that cost him seventy-five cents! And the two of us promising how on Saturday, after we made the rounds collecting scrap metal to sell, we would go down to the dump

51 · · *The Territorial Years: 1954–56*

From the 1957 Groton High School yearbook: TEACHER GEORGE HARBESON *in his classroom in Groton, Vermont, January 1957.*

GEORGE HARBESON *with four-year-old* RICHARD, *on the porch of the family's rented house in Groton, Vermont, November 1956.*

and shoot rats big as cats with my new single-shot, bolt-action .22. And how I couldn't believe it when I gutted a ten-inch perch I had caught and found a whole trout fingerling squeezed up inside its stomach just like they say Jonah must have been.

I remember going to a 4th of July fishing derby with Papa and catching a six-inch dolly, with an old man hanging around on the dry-grass banks of the small slow-running derby stream who asked me if I was going to keep it and if he could have it and him lifting it with thumb and forefinger above his open mouth, then chewing and eating it whole and raw and still wiggling. And me not winning any prize for the fish but seeing a five-legged sheep and taking home a peacock feather that shimmied and sun-danced its coat of many colors in a New England afternoon sun.

And not knowing that when I searched through all the dust and years stored in an old Alaskan homestead basement a half-century later, I would come upon that rainbow feather and see the iridescent ghosts of another time, another place, purling in its faded colors.

White Meadow Lakes Interlude

Groton was a great place to grow up and I wonder what path my life would have taken if we had settled there instead of Alaska. But after a year we packed up our memories and moved to White Meadow Lakes in New Jersey, where Papa took a teaching job with Montville Township Schools for 1957–58. This area neighbored many of our relatives' residences, no doubt welcome to Mom, but I suspect that Papa still had his heart set on Alaska. This was the year that the Minneapolis Lakers signed me on as a player. I was merely a fifth grader, but they were happy to get me. I should say that the rest of the players on the team were fifth graders also, and that the team was in the Dennis B. O'Brien School in Rockaway Township, not *the* Minneapolis Lakers that eventually succumbed to some latter-day lure of Manifest Destiny and went west to become the L.A. Lakers. But it was exciting, and my team won some games.

Sunfish and crappie fishing was good in the nearby lakes. One day I caught a fish I didn't recognize and took it home to show Papa. It turned out to be an out-of-season bass, whether large- or small-mouth I don't recall. A rocky, hilly area lay behind our house—a great venue for kid games. Once, on the crest of the hill, friend Jay Wertz and I climbed to the top of sixty-foot-tall spruce trees, where we swayed in the wind and hollered a Manifest Destiny of our own. As Lewis and Clark might have done in the West, we gazed across the miles of grand and glorious landscape that was New Jersey then.

Jay and I were angry at another classmate one day for some slur on our ten-year-old honor and decided to hunt him down and pound on him in retribution. We searched the neighborhood with vengeful intent for two or three hours before finding him, but by then the problem had faded and the three of us went to a local outdoor basketball court and shot baskets and played "HORSE." I wonder how the years turned out for Jay and the unpummeled boy, whose name escapes my memory.

Eventually the school year came to a close. The sun was warm, the breezes were pleasant, the sunfish and crappies were biting. The rocky outcrops and boulders of the rough-and-tumble hillside behind our house sang alluringly of exploration, mystery, and adventure—but we were too busy packing up the trusty Chevy for a return trip north. We were minus only the future Peter the Great, since Becky's arrival in Vermont, but again Bruce was residing in his nest. Unfortunately Becky was carsick much of the way, adding her own unique contribution to the many sights, sounds, and smells of the trip.

This time our itinerary included the Painted Desert and the Grand Canyon where—too quick for Papa to stop *him,* but with enough time for Papa to stop *me*—Richard threw a rock into the Canyon from its rim, thereby claiming bragging rights eternal of having thrown a rock farther than I.

We continued to the West Coast to visit my Aunt Louise, who had met Ed Drumm while teaching on Fort Richardson and married him. They eventually provided me with ten additional cousins back in New Jersey.

So we returned to Alaska. Either Mom had changed her mind, or Papa's Alaska ambitions had prevailed. Friends of ours also followed this pattern of emigrating to Alaska, only to have second thoughts and leave—and then return. This time we were in Alaska to stay.

Second Time Around

BACK IN WASILLA BY THE FALL OF 1958, we moved into a house owned by Jim Wilson on Fairview Loop, a half mile from the Wilson residence and near the Carrs, Heavens, and Barnes—Victor Barnes a classmate of mine at the time. The Wilsons kept a cow and I often rode my bike there to get a gallon jar of fresh milk for our family. As usual, Papa put his early training to use. On the Montville farm, my Uncle Davis had shown him how to tap maple trees using an elderberry spout and a Mason jar, and Papa had observed maple syrup production in Vermont, at Crown's sugar house, so at the Wilson rental he made birch syrup. It wasn't bad, but even my inexperienced taste buds voted for maple syrup.

I explored the woods across the road. Once I traipsed through the area and stepped on an underground yellow-jacket nest. I flailed my arms, leaped over deadfall, and hightailed it back home without getting stung by any of the nest's annoyed inhabitants. In spite of such encounters, Alaska's insects have always been preferable to me over the scorpions, cone snails, rattlesnakes, and ominous-sounding "earwigs" found elsewhere.

Moose had regular hangouts around the house and driveway. Lee Anna remembers that we would reconnoiter the area and calculate the chances of making it to the school bus minus an encounter with the long-eared, long-legged escort service.

Like our earlier Jones rental in town, the Wilson house was not well insulated, but it was heated by a coal furnace. One wintry morning I discovered that the glass of water at my bedside had grown a frozen cap. During one snowstorm, snow sifted in through cracks in the black Celotex that covered the outside walls and created a small drift under Papa and Mom's bed.

"There's snow drifting in under our bed, Harb. Get up and fix it!" Mom exclaimed sometime during the night. Papa waited until the storm stopped and more suitable working conditions prevailed outside the next day—but it was Mom who cleaned up the drift inside. Again, the trials of everyday living fell heavier on her. Papa had his own challenges to face—making a living, keeping our vehicles operable, and other activities entailed in a traditional family household—but he, and we kids, went to school where warmth, light, social interaction, and entertainment filled the days.

Mom prevailed and we moved back to the Byers place that we had rented in 1955. It was a more finished building than the Wilson rental.

In April of 1960 Papa and six-year-old Richard contracted scarlet fever. Papa had evaded it as a child, but it sought him out all those years later. I remember wondering day to day when Mom and I and Lee Anna and Becky would get sick, but the fever's appetite must have been sated with Papa and Richard because we never came down with it. All of this came on top of Peter's premature birth in March and scary times for Mom. Her pregnancy included a couple of emergency trips to the hospital in Palmer. Peter weighed in at five pounds, so small that his cradle was a shoe box. But despite his early arrival and diminutive size, he eventually grew to six-feet-four and linebacker stature.

Papa and Mom yearned to settle down. With Papa's early farm life in New Jersey in his bones, he and Mom looked forward to us establishing a place of our own after all the years of moving. Homesteading may not have been exactly what she had in mind, but if she experienced inner doubt, I saw little, if any, of it. She loved "Harb," and we kids were the lights of her life, so she kept her trials and pain from us and put a positive face on our adventures. It was the last move we made; the homestead became Papa's and Mom's permanent residence, and it is still with us all these decades later.

PREPARING FOR SUBSISTENCE NETTING *on Harbeson homestead land along Cook Inlet, 1962: from left, Lee Turner, Peter and Lee Anna Harbeson, Bonnie Coghlan, Gene Coghlan, George Jr., Richard and George Harbeson Sr., with the Turners' Jeep in the background.*

3

Fellow Travelers

Friends and neighbors were important in the homestead era, in the small, thinly sketched skein of rural community life. Electronic companionship and diversion had not yet arrived. While independent-minded and to a large degree self-sufficient, people usually faced common problems and relied upon each other's friendship and generosity. The term "neighbor" was loosely defined then and might entail considerable distance of crude back-country roads through large tracts of unpopulated woodland. The human animal being what it is, there were conflicts and differences, but overall ties were strong, and they strengthened us.

The Coghlans

I have a vivid memory of a plaque made of a thin cross-section of willow or spruce cut on the bias, varnished, with bark retained around the edges, and stenciled words proclaiming, *"Ve Git Too Soon Oldt, and Too Late Schmardt."* This bit of homespun wisdom adorned a wall for many years in the home of one of the first families we became friends with, the Coghlans, Gene and Violet, and their children Gerald, Kathy, and Bonnie—Gerald nicknamed Skip after Percy Crosby's cartoon character Skippy, popular in the 1920s-40s. Gene had come to Alaska in 1941 with Pat Carter, whom he'd met in the military, and they did some trapping. Violet and Gene met in Chicago and soon ended up married and ensconced in Wasilla. For a short time they lived in the sorting room of the Wasilla Post Office; May Carter was the postmaster then. Like our family a few years later, they left Alaska in 1947 but couldn't escape the territory's siren call and returned in 1949. In 1958, after several other residences, they moved out to Jacobson Lake, a few miles west of Wasilla on Pittman Road—later known as the Nancy Lake Road, much later known as the Parks Highway. To muddy matters further, we knew it as the Big Lake Road, although that actually split off at the Big Lake "Y."

Gene and Violet were energetic and entertaining. Gene, a signing witness to our homestead application, had a jump-into-life attitude and an inventive curiosity. He was the school custodian then, and was on the staff of Alcantra Youth Camp with me after I graduated from the University of Alaska in Fairbanks (UAF). And he was a writer. He had a short story, "Backward Boy," published in the July 30, 1960, issue of the *Saturday Evening Post*, as well as one or two other writings, and had a trapping piece in *Alaska Sportsman* and a couple of squibs in *Harper's Magazine*. Intermittently, Gene printed a small local project of his own, the *Muskeg Journal*, an entertaining and irreverent commentary on local affairs, politics, and other topics that he deemed worthy of discussion or derision. He used pseudonyms such as "Bald Eagle" and "Garfield Scrog," especially when he worked for the state of Alaska, which frowned on employees printing politically oriented material. As a teen I was impressed with Gene's writing, and he had a positive influence on my own writing ambitions.

Gene was a pilot and interested in aviation. For years, he had a Benson auto-gyrocopter, which utilized two propellers: an unpowered horizontal prop that rotated due to forward motion and provided lift, and a powered pusher-prop. He kept it at home and at Philo's airport. He managed short hops but never got more than fifteen or twenty feet of altitude, and his efforts were harrowing. When he crashed, he mail-ordered for parts, giving the orders to Violet to mail. Unbeknownst to Gene, she sometimes refrained from mailing them, as she deemed his antics with the Benson to be a hazard to himself and others.

Gene belonged to the OX5 Club, an organization established in 1955 for those having experience with aviation and the OX5 engine. He flew an early Citabria and an Aeronca Champ, despite not having a license. He'd been diagnosed once as having had a stroke, and he fought the FAA for years, arguing that the diagnosis had never been confirmed. Dorothy Page, a local columnist, wrote about his occasionally taking family and friends for rides, and he called her to suggest that such articles might not be a good idea in that he had no license. My brother Richard also owned and flew a Champ years later, perhaps influenced by Gene.

Violet was an impressive force in her own right—had to be to keep up with Gene. Over the years, she worked as a bank teller, as the Matanuska Electric Association Board secretary, and for the Territory of Alaska in the Department of Agriculture. I remember her to be a take-charge, no-nonsense person who, like Gene, had a rich sense of humor. We knew a visit to or from the Coghlans would be interesting. She was a great cook and an entertaining host, and I think Vi's company lightened Mom's load and gave her a chance to enjoy time with a kindred soul.

During the year we spent in Vermont in 1956–57, Gene sent us a letter he'd typed on a recalcitrant rebuilt electric IBM from Montgomery Ward. He and Violet had taken up playing Scrabble. "Scrabble is the rage at the present. Violet and I caught the disease and have become so badly addicted that our chores have gone undone and we are out of wood and moose meat and there is dust and cobwebs all over the place and the kids are dirty as well as the clothes and our white cat. Oh, sir, don't ever play Scrabble."

Gene and Vi became notorious over the years for playing Scrabble together, often for money, on a daily basis. Gene usually won, but they were closely matched. The games, lively and on-going, with words contested and accusations of cheating flying about, sometimes ended with the dismayed loser chasing the winner around the house with mild mayhem in mind. The two eventually switched to chess.

Gene was the Wasilla school custodian at the time of the quirky typewriter, and he told in the same letter of a morning visit with Mr. Borden, husband of elementary teacher Anna Borden.

> This morning I hauled the school's ashes. I had two loads to haul but I foolishly accepted Mr. Borden's invitation to a chat and a cup of coffee. He no sooner had my coffee poured than he snatched up his fiddle and played a wild ditty of the type you'd expect to hear on a windy mountain top on a dark night with witches circling the peak on their brooms. He'd pause now and then long enough to look wildly around and exclaim "Ha!"

Then off he'd go again, rocking on his bony buttocks while both feet kept thunderous time upon the floor.

The music had such a startling quality that I shortly found myself plunging headlong through the door and heading for the Blue Goose. "Quick, Johnny, a Coke," I gasped as I burst into the bar.

Tell you the rest later.

THE LETTER ALSO reported other local news and commentary and ended with Gene's characteristic farewell, "Keep Smilin'!"

Mr. Borden was noted for driving slowly around town. I never saw him in a hurry. Skip Coghlan remembers him, too: "For years and years, Mr. Borden drove an old black touring car, maybe a 1929 model. It had wooden spoke wheels and many of us kids were fascinated by it. Word had it that he had another like it in his garage. Then, waaay out of the blue, the old Dodge was replaced in 1954 by a maroon Kaiser with really advanced rocket styling. A quantum jump in vehicles! The car could have done 120 mph, but he still drove it at twenty, just like he drove the old Dodge."

Lee Anna remembers her overnight visits with the Coghlans. They had a large black and white clock in the form of a cat, with eyes that rolled right and left and a tail that switched, both synchronized with the ticking seconds. Lee Anna remembers that on the rare occasions when visitors showed up and Gene and Vi weren't up for visiting, Vi would rush the kids under the beds and all would hide in silence until the visitors left—the presence of the family car in the drive notwithstanding. One get-together with the Coghlans, Vi was cooking up a storm and my little brother Peter thoughtfully gazed up at the cabinets full of food supplies and solemnly informed her, "I *like* food."

Vi made cookies called "sweet nothings"—thin, delicate wafers light as feathers and dusted with sugar. Richard liked them so much he says, "I could have eaten a wheelbarrow of them!" All these years later, I find Papa noting in his recollections that his mother had made similar "nothings" when he was a boy, for the family and for sale during the Depression.

Over time, Coghlans owned more than one old WWII Army surplus Dodge 6x6. These vehicles were common enough, but one of theirs had custom modifications. Gene had removed the sides on the truck's bed to accommodate hauling a D-4 Cat he had bought to go into business for himself. When Gene worked as school custodian, Skip helped him, using the 6x6 to haul furnace cinders from the school to a dumping area on the north side of the playground.

In the late '50s or early '60s, Papa, Richard, and I hauled firewood for the Coghlans. We drove the Dodge from their house onto the Big Lake Road for the short drive to another section of their wooded property. The engine was missing badly, coughing, backfiring, and sputtering like a teenager trying his first smoke or shot of whiskey. After a hundred yards it gasped and died, and we jolted to a halt. The 6x6 had a hood with an open space on each side, and we soon saw what the trouble might be: The distributer cap clamps were missing. Gene had tied the ends of a one-inch-wide strip of inner tube to the engine on either side of the distributor housing and stretched the rubber up and over the end of a piece of kindling mounted vertically atop the cap and plug wires. This Rube Goldberg affair, with the obvious need for occasional readjustment, enabled the 6x6 to bounce merrily along while spare parts were on order. We repositioned the kindling and the rubber strip, added string for good measure, and proceeded to the tree felling and wood hauling. The truck went on to provide several good years of service.

One incident in our history with the Coghlans is prominent above all others for me. It occurred in early 1963. Skip, a former student of Papa's and a 1962 graduate in engineering from the UAF, agreed to help locate corners and blaze the boundary lines of our homestead. The drive in to our place was sloppy with slushy snow and gouged with ruts by our Jeep, but Skip maneuvered it in his '48 Chevy sedan and joined Papa, young Richard, and me as we set to work in the woods. Things went well in the rolling terrain of birch, spruce, and cottonwood as we cut trees that blocked the line of sight. Then one cut birch fell and brushed against two or three neighboring trees on the way down, knocking a dead section loose from the top of one of them. We shouted a late alarm, but the snag plummeted and struck Skip, who stood near the transit. In a defensive reflex he had thrown up his hand, and the snag hit him on the hand and head, breaking the tip of his index finger and knocking him unconscious.

We rushed to help Skip where he lay in the snow. Richard and I watched as Skip's face turned a disturbing ashen shade of blue, but Papa turned him over on his side and cleared his airway, and Skip's normal color returned. We wrapped him in our coats to keep him warm, and Papa treated him for shock; then I ran for the house to drive Skip's car to the Redingtons or Gores on the Knik Road to phone for help. It was the first time I had driven anything other than our own vehicles, so I had some urgent on-the-job training in the muddy drive. In the meantime, Skip was drifting in and out of consciousness. He says his first memory of the accident is of being carried on a stretcher out to the ambulance on the Knik Road, where its driver, fearful of getting stuck, had opted to park.

Skip was unconsious for three hours. He spent the night under observation in the Palmer hospital, then rested at home for another day before he had the energy to get up and move around. The doctor said Skip's finger had taken enough of the hit to prevent more serious injury. He still had the splint on when he reported for Navy OCS later that spring. It is the only bone he has ever broken. Today, Skip says he felt "a funny, kind of spacey feeling, of being in limbo. It's the only time I was ever unconscious." However, he jokes, "beyond being mentally unbalanced ever since, I seem to have recovered."

Years after Skip's father, Gene, had died, my brother Peter visited Violet Coghlan, then in her seventies, plowed her driveway, and helped with other chores. During the Miller's Reach fire of 1996, he brought her to Richard and his wife Dotsy's house to be safe. The first evening there she started up the stairs to bed carrying her .44 caliber handgun. Richard, at the top of the stairs, nervously asked her, "You aren't going to have bad dreams and shoot us, are you?"

"You better take this, in case I sleepwalk," Violet answered, and with an exaggerated imitation of a gunslinger, she handed Richard the pistol and quipped, "I'm just a Pistol-Packin' Mama!"

Now the Bald Eagle and the Pistol-Packin' Mama have both passed away, but fond memories of them live on with our family, and their children Skip, Kathy, and Bonnie are as true friends as ever.

The Posts

HAL POST AND MY UNCLE STERNE HAVE known each other since the late 1930s, their friendship beginning in New Jersey. In 1948 Hal rode a bicycle to Alaska, and the next year Uncle Sterne and Hal, on a break from Drew University under the G.I. Bill, both cashed their month's check of fifty dollars and, with friend Don Slee, hopped into Sterne's '34 Ford "Arabella" and drove up the Alcan. The three of them rode in the front, with occasional naps in the rumble seat. They took a wrong turn at one point and ended up at Lesser Slave Lake, 70 miles off-course. On the back-track to the Alcan they came into mud that caked in the fenderwells enough to stop the wheels from turning. But a bayonet proved effective in dislodging the packed mud and on they continued. Upon arriving in Fairbanks, Sterne got a job as a mason, and Hal hired on as a warehouseman.

Don was hired to be a carpenter's helper for a man building a golf course, the one now known as the farthest north golf course, the Fairbanks Golf and Country Club, located near the university. Don worked on constructing a clubhouse. At that time the enterprise boasted one hole. The fairway was stubble oats and the "green" was oiled sand compacted by a roller. Golf balls were six or eight for a dollar. A thousand-dollar prize was offered for any hole-in-one, with no takers while Don was there. The clubhouse was set up with a bar, space for poker, and one-arm-bandit slots.

After a few months, Sterne's mother, my grandmother, passed away, and he returned to New Jersey, leaving Arabella for Hal to sell. Unloading a convertible in Fairbanks proved to be difficult. Hal practically gave the old girl away to a man planning to make an off-road hunting vehicle out of her. When Hal left to return to Drew University, his flight from Fairbanks to Seattle was on a DC-3 with an informal charter-style arrangement: "You bought the $50 ticket and hung around until the seats were full, and then the plane took off."

On Hal's bicycle trip to Alaska he was turned back at the Montana/Canada border—not enough money—so he proceeded west to the coast, where he managed to meander his way up into Canada and on to Alaska. He worked with the Anchorage School District over the years, and was a practicing psychologist. He and his wife, Joy, homesteaded in the Goose Bay area. During their homestead "proving-up" period, in spite of the distance and poor roads, he commuted to Anchorage, staying the week in town and rejoining Joy and their children Holly, Kim and Lee (Sue was born later) on the homestead for the weekends. He often turned up at our homestead, located along the route. Joy had agreed to the homestead deal—she'd stay on site with the kids until the residence requirements were fulfilled—but as with Mom this turned out to be considerably more hardship than she had expected. However, the Jameson and Claus families in the area were helpful and supportive.

The road names in the area were a clue to what one might expect: Goose Bay Road, Burma Road, Khyber Pass Road. Once when a seismic crew was working in the area and tearing up the already rough roads, a neighbor holding a rifle stood where the road was gated and made the crew promise to put gravel on the road. They kept the promise.

Over the years, Hal's exploits with motor vehicles frequently involved us. "Can I ride with Mr. Post?" was a common refrain among the more adventurous of us. In the summer of '61 our family went to visit the Posts. I wanted to ride with Hal. Papa agreed, so I rode "shotgun" in Hal's '59 VW bus, sitting on the edge of nowhere as one does in these vehicles. Somewhere on the Burma Road we topped a small rise doing thirty miles an hour and plunged down and through a broad mud puddle or a stream crossing—I couldn't tell which, since we were into it before I saw it.

The resulting sheet of water obscured the view through the windshield for four or five seconds. All the while, supremely confident from past experience and ever the optimist, Hal was pedal-to-the-metal to avoid getting stuck. The windshield cleared and we careened on toward the next Burma Road offering.

Gripping the hand-hold and the seat, I thought, "Whoooo! We don't need no four-wheel-drive!" and we didn't. We arrived at the Post cabin with Hal's faith in the VW's first gear synchro as unswerving as ever.

The second day at the cabin, in collusion with my father, Hal gave me an I.Q. test. I think I was told my score several years later, but I can't remember what it was. I must have failed, because I continued to ride with Hal.

One fall in the early 1960s, Hal took Papa, Richard, and me caribou hunting in the '59 VW bus. We traversed the 150 miles to the Lake Louise area of the Glenn Highway, where we turned off a side road and followed a faint winter trail for a few hundred yards before the VW bogged down in the swampy terrain. Taking advantage of our stationary status, we shot one of the inquisitive caribou traveling past our inadvertent rest stop, so we weren't skunked, but it took a fair bit of convincing by the four of us to get the VW to retrace its tracks back to the side road. On the way home, Hal informed us that we might be perilously short on gas. Or maybe not, the gauge being a little unpredictable. With the dressed-out caribou riding the roof, Hal coasted us down much of the return descent in neutral with the engine turned off, restarting the engine on the rises and level stretches, careening along at a strangely silent seventy miles per hour at times and creeping along at a walking pace at others. The area's magnificent scenery flew by in an unnerving blur, or leisurely crawled past us. We finally coaxed the VW into the nearest station, miles later, on the fumes of our imagination.

Because of Hal's long commute to Anchorage from their homestead, he sometimes carried a drum of gas in the VW. Once it slipped its moorings and flipped around in the bus and broke a window. And on one cold winter's journey when I rode with him in the heater-impaired VW—but with no gas drum in the back—my feet were kept company by a burning Coleman cook stove on the passenger-side floor. Once when the radiator of their tracked vehicle, a Weasel, needed repair, Hal belted the radiator inside a pair of pants, stretched the legs over his shoulders and tied them around his neck, and carried the radiator to where the VW had been parked. Intrepid as the VW was, sometimes road conditions prevented it from reaching the cabin. Food and supplies had to be packed in. Laundry had to be hauled both ways, including soiled cloth diapers out, clean ones in.

Hal had bought the Weasel and a '47 Ford stake bed truck for six hundred dollars. The Weasel was equipped with a Studebaker Champion engine. It had separate steering controls for each track: two sticks, two clutches, and two brakes. The previous owner provided a small tin tool box called a Weasel "rescue kit." The vehicle threw the track quite often, and the kit included two 30.06 armor piercing shells that were to be fired at the remaining connection when the track jammed half-off. Hal eventually sold the Weasel to Fred Burger of Point MacKensie.

One notable instance occurred when Hal had gotten the chained-up VW bus stuck in a stream bed in a dip on the Burma Road, bumpers jammed on opposite sides of the stream. The stream thawed during the day and froze at night, and the VW tires froze in place. Hal walked back to their cabin, and the next morning started hiking to our place (twenty some miles distant) for assistance. A few miles past the beleaguered VW he met a man driving a gray chained-up Jeep pickup. The two went back to the VW, chopped away the ice, jacked up the wheels with a hydraulic jack, and jammed cardboard boxes soaked in gasoline against the frozen brake drums to thaw them out. Then they hooked a tow chain from the Jeep to the VW.

The driver backed his Jeep up to the edge of the dip, as close as possible to the VW, then took off in a running start, much like a dog on a chain. When the Jeep hit the end of the chain, Hal gunned the VW and it came flying out of the dip like a crazed rabbit. Hal thanked the good samaritan and drove on to Claus's to pick up Joy and the kids. Tragically, some time later, the driver of the gray Jeep died when a dozer overturned on him.

Not all my Post memories are vehicular. The Post homestead, although difficult to get to, was an active place. Burt Lum and his family, Ray Haines, and others were frequent visitors—all great entertainment for us Harbesons. Hal provided one form of amusement. Their cabin had wood flooring with no insulation, and eventually the knots in the wood loosened and fell out. This left holes, of which mice took full advantage. The kids woke up mornings and covered their heads with their pillows while their father shot at the scurrying little invaders with a BB gun.

Then there was the time Hal brought several goats on the homestead. He thought the family could use the milk. Joy was not the least bit thrilled, however, especially with Hal at work in Anchorage most of the time, or walking, riding, hitchhiking somewhere on the road between. Joy hated the goats and they terrified her. They clattered up on the porch and blocked the door. They persisted in joining her on hikes to the spring for water, some distance away. She'd be carrying a baby and a water can, with son Lee toddling along and tripping over obstacles along the way. When she stopped to help him up, the goats bumped her and butted the water can—necessitating another trip to the spring.

Years later, Joy moved to Homer and with Lee purchased The Bookstore. Lee and Sue, with associate Jenny Stroyeck, have overseen and expanded the popular business, now officially Homer Bookstore, since their mother's untimely death in 1995. Hal, recently marking his eightieth birthday, continues to amaze me by snow machining to Eagle and canoeing on the Yukon.

My trips to Anchorage include lunch with Hal, when I can catch up and keep up with him—which is a little easier now that he has given up VW's and drives a Prius. With, as far as I can ascertain, no drum of gas in the back.

The Turners

IN 1958 LEE AND BEA TURNER, WITH their two young sons Jim and Lin, had left Indiana and were headed for the West Coast in their new FC-170 cab-over stake bed Willys Jeep when the trip took an unanticipated turn to the north. In Sand Point, Idaho, Lee heard of a man traveling through doing interviews for a teaching/coaching job in a place called Seldovia, Alaska.

"What do you think?" he asked Bea.

"Seldovia, Alaska," she repeated, willing but wondering "Are there trees there?"

Lee didn't know Seldovia from Secaucus, but in one of those life-altering coincidences a copy of *Alaska Sportsman* magazine caught their eye in a local store—with a cover story on Seldovia. That was that.

Two years later, in 1960, the Turners had acquired the Levan residence a few miles out on the Knik-Goose Bay Road, and Lee was teaching and coaching at Wasilla High School, where Papa also was teaching. Lee and Bea joined him and others working to improve education in the community and state, spending many long hours outside the classroom in the arduous effort, and thus began the friendship between our two families.

We had moved onto our homestead, and Mom's life at that point of our homesteading was a particularly strenuous one. While she attended to young Becky and infant Peter and the homemaking chores, the rest of us escaped to the bright lights, heat, and showers of school five days a week. Bea and Mom met on a visit to one of Peggy Betts' social gatherings and became friends. On Fridays, Bea was a librarian, and Fridays she would venture to our newly carved-out notch in the trees overlooking Cook Inlet to gather up Mom, Becky, and Peter for an afternoon at the Wasilla Public Library, where they assisted Edith Olson, the volunteer librarian. The Turners' small sedan was unable to navigate our difficult drive, so Bea drove their FC-170 Jeep, slip-sliding in the mud, snow, and ruts. When Edith left the library position Bea took over, with support from Peggy Behnke who also became a good friend of Mom's.

Those friendships meant a lot to Mom, and the library opened many worlds to her. In her youth she'd felt out of place in school. In the rural isolation of an Alaskan homestead, books provided entertainment, escape, information, and educational opportunities. She read art books on different painting mediums. She sought out historical novels of American frontier settlement, mysteries, and a variety of volumes on England—which she visited years later.

When Mom's mother, my Grandma Hazel, died in New Jersey, Mom needed a friend to talk with. Bea came in response to her call and took her for a drive, from Knik to Shrock Road, where they came upon some unusual white fireweed growing near a bridge and stream. Fireweed was a special flower to Mom—she unofficially named the drive into our homestead "Fireweed Lane." Seeing the white fireweed together on that sad occasion made a lasting impression on both of them, and Bea remembers it fondly yet today.

In 1981 Bea had been suffering with vertigo and fell one day while working in the Swanson School Library in Palmer. She wanted to go to the Virginia Mason Clinic in Seattle, where many Alaskans go for medical consultation and treatment, but Lee was unable to get away just then. Mom volunteered to go. The two of them made the trip Outside and spent a week there. Bea's problem was diagnosed as Ménière's Syndrome. Between her appointments, they walked around the vicinity of the clinic and visited a nearby art gallery. The director took them into a back room and showed them an Andrew Wyeth painting of pumpkins on a stump with a dark background (possibly his "Jack-Be-Nimble" one). Mom had been painting on her own for several years and always appreciated that opportunity to see Wyeth's art first-hand.

Bea was still experiencing residual effects of Ménière's when Papa died suddenly in early 1985 of heart trouble, and Mom had been diagnosed with multiple myeloma that spring. Mom was welcome at the Turners' and spent time visiting with Bea and the family. The Turners, as well as Peggy Behnke, Julie Ede, Charlotte Belden, Charlyn Martin, Vi Coghlan, Kathleen Smyth, Dorothy Page, and others were of considerable comfort to Mom as the cancer progressed over the next six years.

For a time in the '60s, I baby-sat the Turner kids—now joined by young daughter Dena—on Friday or Saturday nights, when Lee and Bea went visiting or to a movie in Palmer. Bedtime for the three kids came just in time for me to turn all the lights off—well, not *all* the lights—and settle into the easy chair for episodes of Rod Serling's *Twilight Zone* on the

After the death of George Harbeson Sr. in 1985, friends gathered with Katy Harbeson at her daughter Becky's home on Hollywood Road outside Wasilla; from left, JULIE EDE, ROBERTA ALWARD, CHARLOTTE BELDEN *and daughter* JOYCE, KATY HARBESON, BEA TURNER.

Turners' black-and-white television set. We didn't have electricity then, much less a TV, so it was a special treat for me. Their house was large and creaky and the dark Alaska winter night crouched outside and peered in through the windows. The nearest neighbor was some distance away. Nonetheless, I eagerly anticipated Serling's efforts to spook the heck out of me, with tales of aliens coming to Earth to serve man (in unexpected ways), of a little girl trapped in an empty world of space behind her bed's headboard, of pig-visaged doctors doing cosmetic surgery. Despite the black-and-white format and the use of simple, even crude sets and effects, the shows kept me on the edge of my seat. Occasionally I would tense and hold my breath, peering around the room in the flickering light from the screen and straining to hear evidence of an uninvited presence in the house—while the Turner kids slumbered in their beds, blissfully unaware of the ominous dimensions of alternate time and space that surround us all.

My babysitting was just one part of our friendship with the Turners. Jeeps were another. Lee's FC-170 Jeep adventures made an impression on his son Jim and me. Jim owned two or three of the smaller FC-150s over the years, and Jim and his Jeeps entertained us all. In the late '60s I acquired one. I found a better cab for it on a junker near Brewster's clothing store in the Mountain View neighborhood of Anchorage, and on a sunny hot summer day I went to remove it and bring it home. In the process, I disturbed a nest of yellow-jackets and one nailed me on the inside of my left wrist. The sting was annoying, but I remembered a home remedy and soon a slice of raw onion and some tape from a grocery store on Bragraw Street made an effective bandage. I wore the smelly "bracelet" until the following day. The pain soon subsided to an itch and the stinger puckered its way out. People wrinkled their noses at the onion smell, but I was amazed at how well it worked.

Lee, Papa, and I, and at times Dennis Calhoun and my brother Richard, went on hunting trips occasionally on the Denali Highway. The Turners, Coghlans, Gores, and Byers also joined us in setting out a subsistence net for salmon in our area of Cook Inlet. Once in a while Papa drove team members on basketball trips when Lee was my coach. Years later, when I was married, Lee would join our family and friends for nickel-dime-quarter poker sessions, bringing his inimitable style of play and commentary to the table.

Lee was active in the Ski Patrol in Hatcher Pass and took up dog mushing after retiring from teaching, but his hips gave him increasing trouble and eventually confined him in pain to a recliner. He finally had his hip joints replaced and became a young man again, reclaiming his dog mushing for several years before his death in 1994. My brother Peter, who assisted Violet Coghlan from time to time after her Gene died, helped Lee on a regular basis right up to the end.

I think most of us have special people outside the family who influence our lives. Bea, whose friendship was especially important to Mom, is one of those. Lee was such a person to Papa, and to me as a young boy and then an adult.

I first met Lee (*Mr.* Turner, then) when I was in junior high and he ordered me out of the bleacher balcony of the old Wasilla High School, where I was watching his players-only high school basketball practice. He had the intimidating appearance of the Brewmaster from old Rainier beer ads—short of stature, bald head, bushy black eyebrows—and a gruff manner that frightened small children and pets and made even adults nervous at times. I'd heard that as a coach in Indiana, he chased lazy players down the court with a wooden paddle.

As he stepped into my life, I came to know him as a forthright person with the unwavering and refreshing honesty that I saw in Papa. He had a propensity for doing unexpected things—which Papa didn't. In Wasilla one day he poured water from an envelope onto one of my U.S. History classmates who was dozing in class. Earl may remember that wake-up call. And when Roger wrote, mid-essay, on one of Lee's exams, "*Ha, ha. I bet you don't read this,*" he got his paper back with "*I bet I do.*" written in the margin and 2% taken off for his trouble. I grew to appreciate that directness and to seek to enjoy the things that add spice to our lives and to avoid the ruts.

He allowed us to play penny-ante poker on high school basketball trips. (I was told later that he'd owned a speakeasy when he was younger.) For me, poker wasn't about greed, or careless risk-taking. It was a challenge that included fair play, responsibility for one's behavior, and assessment of human nature. (As Mark Twain wrote, "There's a great deal of human nature in people.") I'm grateful for the many hours Lee Turner gave me in education, basketball, and poker; they help me to this day. I remember playing poker with him in later years, when he'd arch those black, bushy moustaches-for-eyebrows, rake in a pot, and exclaim in dry observation, "Well, the ol' blind sow found another acorn!"

With Lee's passing, the world lost a person it could ill-afford to lose. Lee was a kindred spirit of Papa's and remains an indelible part of my life. All things considered, the Old Blind Sow that finds each of us sooner or later has found one damn fine acorn!

A HOLIDAY GATHERING AT THE TURNERS', *December 1983; from left, Lee and Bea Turner, Jim and Julie Ede, Opal Toomey, Katy and George Harbeson.*

The Edes

JIM AND JULIE EDE BLEW INTO TOWN from teaching in Koyukuk and Naknek and joined the Wasilla School staff in the fall of 1963, my junior year. Jim taught eighth grade language arts and arithmetic, and Julie took on high school English, journalism, and speech. My father had been teaching journalism, and he oversaw production of the yearbook, *The Chieftain*, and sponsored the school newspaper, the *Wa Hi War Whoop*, beginning in 1954. The paper may have been the first regularly published monthly school newspaper in the territorial system. He spent innumerable hours on it with the students and it meant a great deal to him. He continued it after statehood, until the '63 school year assembly when the principal suddenly announced that Julie had been assigned the class and newspaper duties, an unpleasant surprise to Papa.

Julie says of those days:

> It was rumored that our hirings, especially mine, may have been a political move with reference to George. Regardless, George was generous and open with me, showed no hard feelings, and readily offered me valuable advice and assistance, which made the transition easier for me and helped retain the quality of the program for the students. If there had been such a political agenda, it certainly backfired. With the creation of the Mat-Su Borough, the three of us joined with Bea and Lee Turner, Betty Jo Riddle, Bill Lorentzen, Bill Butler, Bill McDonald, Jess Baker, Warren Jones, and others in establishing the Matanuska Susitna Education Association.

JIM AND JULIE became influential members of the staff and compadres of Papa. Jim was popular with his junior high students, along with Kathleen Smyth and Jerry Hendrickson. Julie was a hit with the high school girls, providing an exciting role model in her teaching—and with her owning and driving a red 1964 Ford Mustang. (Their son Stephen, a chemist with strict attention to detail, says it was a '63$^{1}/_{2}$ model.) The Edes, with their children Stephen, Diana, and Ella (Lori), became frequent companions. My mother's quiet and shy nature meshed with Julie's outgoing personality, and she and Mom became friends. When Stephen suffered a head injury in a motorcycle accident while working a set-net fishing site in Bristol Bay with his friend Larry Jallen, Lee Anna baby-sat the two young girls while Jim and Julie tended to Stephen. Stephen has commented that he didn't dream for many years after the accident. Becky also baby-sat for Jim and Julie, and Lee Anna modeled clothes for a time at the Beeline Fashion parties that Julie sponsored and was paid in merchandise, selecting clothes for herself.

Papa, Jim, and Julie were also active in Democratic Party activities. I didn't know it at the time, but in the spirit of "six degrees of separation," Julie had a bloodline connection to the Democratic Party: Her grandmother and Al Gore's grandmother were first cousins. On the 4th of July, 1970, state Senator Nick Begich Sr. and his administrative aide Gene Kennedy attended a picnic on our homestead. Begich was running for Alaska's at-large U.S. House seat, which he won by beating Frank Murkowski in the November election. Begich had worked in education and was supportive of the efforts of Papa, Jim, and Julie in that arena. Papa was the Wasilla area coordinator for Begich's campaign; Jim did set-net fishing in the Bristol Bay area, so he and Begich had fishing issues in common.

Once I went with Papa to the Wasilla VFW to hear Begich speak. In eighth grade I had won the VFW "Voice of Democracy" essay contest, and Begich's rapid-fire, articulate, knowledgeable, and to-the-point speaking style really impressed me—and gave me incentive as a college student at UAF to work as a volunteer for Earnest Gruening's 1968 general election write-in campaign for U.S. senator.

Of course, we had no idea then of the tragedy that was to befall us in Alaska, the loss of Congressman Begich on October 16, 1972, on a flight from Anchorage to Juneau. The plane was never found, and it was a loss that Jim and Julie agree changed the course of Alaska significantly. Years later I found a copy of the dedication volume for Senator Bob Bartlett's statue in the Capitol Rotunda. Inside the cover is a personal inscription of appreciation from Congressman Begich to my father. The book is accompanied by an official letter from Congressman Begich, dated a few days after the plane's disappearance, and unsigned. That small, blank signature space appears so vast and empty whenever I look at it.

Papa had a beneficial effect on the innumerable, often contentious, meetings and discussions he attended. He made sure everyone had their say, and he brought the steady, calming influence of reason to these events. He led by example and encouraged others to participate. My cousin John Wilde was a New Jersey Kennedy delegate to the 1980 Democratic Convention and at one point was seated next to an Alaskan woman delegate. He asked if she knew his uncle George Harbeson, and indeed she did, and credited Papa with getting her involved in politics and for her presence at the convention.

In 1974 we had some nonpartisan excitement during a 4th of July gathering at our home, with the Edes, Turners, and Vondolee and Dorothy Page, and others. The Coghlans would usually have been there, but they had "other plans"—which became clear when Gene's plane circled overhead. Jim Ede had been hinting to my brother Peter about Gene flying over the picnic and dropping a surprise package for our group, but Peter dismissed this as teasing. The area was a popular flyway, and Jim kept pointing at the planes flying high overhead and exclaiming to Peter, "There's Gene, Pete. You better go watch." Gene finally flew low and buzzed our house with his arm extended to drop a package in the field—a well-padded bottle of wine for the picnic, compliments of the "Bald Eagle," our home-grown precursor of Fed Ex/UPS.

Jim and Julie's son Stephen, his friend Larry Jallen, and I worked one summer for Ordeen Jallen, a family friend of the Edes and owner of Jallen Electric, setting up kitchen trailers for the schools in Anvik and Holy Cross on the Yukon River. His family's experience on the Yukon made it familar territory to Stephen, and my homesteading years gave me a good perspective. What we weren't expecting was the nighttime cacophony. We slept in a trailer with Ordeen and a couple of other men, one of whom was six foot six. Their snoring crescendos vibrated the thin aluminum walls. Larry may have been used to such nocturnal concerts, but they had Stephen and me staring at each other from our cots in bleary-

CONGRESSMAN NICK BEGICH
ALASKA
HOUSE OF REPRESENTATIVES
WASHINGTON, D.C. 20515

July 25, 1972

Mr. George Harbeson
Box 97
Wasilla, Alaska 99687

Dear George:

I want to thank you for agreeing to be my Wasilla Area Coordinator. As you know, it is only through the efforts of individuals such as yourself that I am able to represent the people of Alaska.

The official kick-off date for the campaign will be on August 1st. We plan to have much of our campaign material out by then so that the campaign can blossom all at once. You will be hearing from my office in the near future on this. If you have any questions call my Anchorage office. The phone number is 279-2410.

Again, thanks for agreeing to be an Area Coordinator in the campaign.

Sincerely,

Nick

NICK BEGICH

eyed consternation. Mosquitoes buzzed thickly outside, precluding that escape route. I discovered a stereo headset and clamped it over my ears —not as effective as I hoped, but we were young and survived the sleepless nights.

Survived, in fact, for me to be hired in 1973 by Jim Ede and Selawik City Schools. This established me in a career of bush teaching and provided me with many years of rich, multicultural experiences—a roller-coaster ride if there ever was one.

The Pages arrive *at the* Harbeson homestead *for a picnic in 1984; from left, George Harbeson, Vondolee and Dorothy Page.*

The Beldens

"Ahhh, yes, I feel a whole lot more like I do now than I did before." (Or was it the other way around—I never have figured that out.) Announced with a satisfied stretch and a dash of southern drawl, Melvin Belden's words topped off the many sit-down feasts our family had with the Beldens during our homestead years. Melvin and Charlotte Belden first lived in a Quonset hut during the early '60s on Vine Road, located before the "Hollywood and Vine" intersection off the Knik-Goose Bay Road, seven miles out of Wasilla. They later moved to a site on West Hollywood Road, where Goose Bay and Knik Elementary schools stand today.

Melvin did finish carpentry and cabinetry work, along with other jobs as he could get them. Charlotte kept the home fires in order. For me and my sibs, being friends over the years with the Beldens meant an increasing number of kids' faces to see when we visited: Melvin (Gene), David, Dennis, twins Ronnie and Connie, Floyd, Joyce, Cheryl, Kathy (named after Mom), and Christy. A recent reunion in Anchorage proved the Beldens were thriving after a half-century, with the family tree still spreading.

The first Belden memory I have is of visiting their Quonset hut home for Thanksgiving, in 1961 or '62. They had a cow and gave us fresh milk, which Lee Anna didn't like because she was so accustomed to the powdered stuff we drank. I remember marveling how the pale butter appeared from nowhere when I shook a gallon jar of milk that Charlotte had handed me with the smiling admonition, "Here—make yourself useful for a change." They also had a hand churn in the back entryway. We produced homemade ice cream in a hand-cranked mixer, or made "snow" ice cream. When they left the Quonset for their new site, I admired an apparatus they devised to circulate water heated by their woodstove through a car radiator and fan, as a means to distribute heat.

For several years we got together with the Beldens to play pinochle. And Melvin and some of his boys, David in particular, helped raise the top log beam on our house. Son Gene (first name Melvin) was my classmate all the way through high school graduation. In sixth grade a book entitled *Melvin, the Moose Child*, inspired teasing from the rest of the class, albeit with some degree of risk. I had to grin-and-bear the usual Georgie Porgie stuff, so for me it was "misery loves company." Gene later became an Alaska State Trooper, as did his brother Ron, and I imagine no mention of the "moose child" arose then.

The Beldens owned a dog that was officially "barkless"—a Basenji, I believe—although with practice it developed a respectable rasp. We never had occasion to learn if its bite was better than its rasp. They kept a horse that Lee Anna and Connie rode double. They also owned a goose that, much like the goose that chased Papa in Montville thirty-five years before, seemed to have a grudge against my brother Peter.

The first time Lee Anna stayed at Beldens on an overnight visit with Connie was another experience in cacophony. She says, "I slept on the top bunk. Everyone had gone to bed and I was sleeping when I was awakened by a thunderous noise filling the darkness. It scared the heck out of me, until I realized it was Mr. Belden snoring! Papa snored some, but Mr. Belden really could raise the roof!"

David Belden and I worked one summer on a rock crusher for Fritz Kalmbach in the Kenny Lake area on the Edgerton Highway, on the way to Chitina. One day my left index finger got between a six-by-six timber and its hinge pin target on a dump truck. The Copper Center clinic splinted it, and I returned to work, but the splint was inadequate. I drove my LeMans to the Palmer hospital for a lower arm cast that held my hand in a "stick-em up" position. That raised some eyebrows on visits to the bank. Then it was back to Kenny Lake, and cleaning roots and debris out of the rock that flowed by me on the crusher conveyor belt.

Dave may also have been on the Kalmbach crew with other local Wasilla guys and me, jack-hammering the holes for the footings for the Hurricane Gulch bridge during the beginning stages of the Parks Highway construction.

I enjoyed the Belden sense of humor. Dennis and Ron chased Becky with a jar of spiders, and held roughhouse wrestling matches with Richard. When Richard bragged about his height Charlotte dryly commented, "Gee, Richard, I didn't know they stacked it that high." Dennis, on a hospital stay once, surreptitiously pumped up the blood pressure while the nurse took his pulse. Tragically, Dennis later perished with members of the Reverend Wykoff family in a boating accident on Skilak Lake.

I look back and am grateful for the Belden family, as I am for the Coghlans, Turners, Posts, Edes, and others. People in the Mat-Su area came from a diversity of backgrounds, each with unique experiences, which, when shared in our everyday lives and in times of need or crisis, kept us from becoming too provincial in our outlook on life.

And after all the years that have passed, I can finally say that I do, indeed, "feel a whole lot more like I do now than I did before."

Or is it the other way around?

GEORGE HARBESON *and daughter* BECKY *at the homestead's first living quarters, summer 1959.*

4

We Become Homesteaders

After years of renting, in 1959 Papa decided we needed a place of our own. His salary at the time—master's degree with experience—was $6,250 a year, with an additional housing allowance of $300. We were a family with four kids and a baby. The Homestead Act was still in effect, and he decided homesteading was the way to go. From May Carter he learned of a small parcel near the old town of Knik and applied for it, with George Gore and Gene Coghlan as witnesses. Small for a homestead allotment, it was a 32-acre piece overlooking Cook Inlet, about seventy percent of it in Cook Inlet tidal flats that included the mouth of O'Brien Creek. Access began at the Redington place on the Knik Road, twelve miles from Wasilla. The Redingtons, our nearest neighbors, became the famous dog-mushing family. Joe Sr., backed by his wife Vi and in conjunction with Dorothy Page's efforts, became known as the "Father of the Iditarod Race."

From Redingtons', our "driveway" followed a $^3/_4$-mile dirt trail through the trees along the bluff and ended at a magnificent view from a tree-covered bluff, a beautiful spot for a home. We literally started from scratch, setting up a tent in the woods and racing to construct a basement during that first summer, before winter and a new school year descended upon us.

This was the late spring of 1960. The trees were budding, misted green with new foliage, the current school year was almost over, the scenery was stunning, and prospects looked bright in "Sunny Knik." Walking the property and the surrounding area turned up one half of an old abandoned military squad tent, which we combined with another civilian tent and a homemade camper shell to form our shelter. We immediately had the excavation done and started raising a block basement. Papa had worked for Mom's father, a stone mason by trade, before coming to Alaska, so he was knowledgeable about the work to be done.

We borrowed a gasoline-powered cement mixer but also mixed cement by hand in a plywood box, screening the sand and gravel from the excavated pile. We poured the footing, laid the blocks using rebar and wire, poured and tamped bond beams, troweled the joints, poured, screed, and floated the floor. Papa led the way, with Mom and me serving as apprentices. Lee Anna, Richard, and Becky ran go-fer errands and watched toddler Peter.

Through the months of that first summer, the basement took shape. We installed a flat roof and spread tar on it with mops, using tar melted in a metal bucket over a rock-encircled fire. A flat roof looks good on paper, but in real life water is not to be denied and tends to find its way through to the dwelling beneath. Leaks were many and persistent, despite periodic re-tarring. The music of the numerous drips and their respective tin-can containers lulled us to sleep on rainy nights, and on melting-snow days joined in our conversation. Mom must have yearned for the days of renting.

On a subsequent re-tarring of the roof, toddler Peter saw Papa extinguish his cigarette and toss the butt onto the gravel. Peter decided to emulate the boss. He clambered across the gravel pile to the butt, picked it up and put it to his lips, but one of us older kids took it away. He must not have liked even that brief experience because he never smoked in later life—in fact, none of us did, despite or maybe because of Papa's lifelong habit. Mom hated it, as did I, because of the second-hand smoke, the odor, and the ashes. When I was in junior high and high school, Papa helped me with a Latin correspondence course and algebra and had me help with grading papers, and I still vividly remember my eyes and lungs burning from the smoke. He had smoked for as long as I could remember, possibly starting the habit in the Army. He tried to quit in later years but never beat the addiction, and it most certainly contributed to his death by heart attack at the age of sixty-four.

89 ·· *We Become Homesteaders*

The whole family pitched in *as the "basement house" took shape. Here Katy Harbeson works at pouring the cement floor.*

Prometheus' Gift

WE HAD CLOSED IN OUR BASEMENT BY August and used a barrel stove for heating and an upright wood cook stove for cooking and heating. We kept sharp eyes peeled for chimney fires, since our use of birch firewood lent itself to creosote formation. We occasionally had a stack fire in the stovepipe, but in all our years of burning wood we managed to extinguish them. Papa's family on the farm hadn't been as fortunate. In May of 1933 their farmhouse burned to the ground, probably started by a chimney fire. Papa wrote:

> **I was an eighth grader in Montville school** and saw it burning from the school window. My teacher Monica Murphy was going to drive me home, but couldn't, so the old-time teacher/Principal Mrs. Decker did. There was a freight train on the tracks across our lane blocking the crossing, but I crawled between the freight cars and ran to the already flame-engulfed house. The fire engine arrived but was held up, delayed by the train stopped on the tracks.
>
> We and the firemen saved a few things from the house. Papa had owned the 23rd Street Book Store in New York from 1905 to 1919 and we had hundreds of books stored in the attic—the entire stock, including bound copies of the St. Nicholas magazine that I had read. The books were thrown out of the windows but promptly burned. Billy Baldwin carried out a piano by himself. The heirloom gold watch that I was to receive when I reached twenty years of age melted and I found it later in the ashes we put on the muskmelon hills. We also found the melted remains of a shotgun that earlier occupants had hidden in a wall. Some talk circulated of sparks from the train causing the fire—which happened sometimes—but apparently the cause had been a chimney fire. There must have been some insurance, because we built a new home on the old foundation for three thousand dollars.
>
> Ironically, the new house had a stone-faced fireplace with a heatilator unit, and soot collected behind the damper. One dark

night, Sterne and I were playing ping-pong on the oval kitchen table. We looked out the window to a scene bright as day. We ran outside and discovered flames shooting from the chimney. Someone ran to the garage on the main road to call the fire department, but my father climbed an extension ladder to the roof and put a piece of tin over the chimney opening, putting out the fire. Afterward, the front room took considerable scrubbing to cleanse it of the smoke stains.

WE ALSO MADE use of a Coleman lantern, as had Papa's family. We had no problem with our lantern, but in the 1930s New Jersey replacement house, then less than a year old, Papa's older sister Dorothy's husband Ed Wilde was working with a Coleman pressure gas lantern on the lower landing of the stairs when it sprayed burning gasoline on the landing, steps, banister, and a drop-leaf cherry table with its fringed cloth. Ed tried to put out the fire, but Papa's father, my grandfather, took charge. He grabbed the lantern by the handle, ran through the kitchen and on outdoors, where he flung it down the hill into the snow. The flames in the house were extinguished and things calmed down, but soon my grandmother saw smoke coming from a dresser in the kitchen, which held silverware, towels, dish rags, and other such items. The drawers were pulled out and the fire was squelched. Dorothy gave Papa and each of his siblings an orange to reassure them that matters were well in hand.

Chimney fires weren't the only danger. Once, on the New Jersey farm, six-year-old Papa talked his three-year-old younger brother Sterne into sneaking hot dogs from the family ice box, which in those days literally was an ice box, and the two set out on a wienie roast. Papa's notes relate the ensuing event.

> *We went down by the woods next to the* farm's barn and tried to start a cook fire, but it was too windy, so we found a sheltered spot between the chicken coop and a high pile of buckwheat that my father and brothers had cut with a scythe and laboriously stacked. We got a fire going and were roasting the hot dogs on sticks over it, when I glanced up to see the buck-

wheat pile ablaze. We ran up to the house and I fled upstairs and hid under the bed. My father and brothers ran to fight the fire. The Montville Volunteer Fire Department arrived on the scene, but merely sat around watching, because the fire district line ran between the house and the barn and the fire was in Towaco, out of their jurisdiction. Gentile, the fire warden from Towaco, then arrived with a spray tank carried on his back. In the end, the fire burned a few acres, but was contained by my family, Gentile, and neighbors. After a bit, Gentile came after me, dragged me from under the bed, and told me I was going to jail.

YEARS AFTER BOTH Papa and Mom had passed away, Mom's sister, my Aunt Mary, told me that the engineer of a train passing by the hot dog-buckwheat fire had blown the whistle to alert people of Montville and Towaco to the blaze, adding to the excitement.

Everyday Homesteading

Our first summer quickly rolled by as we made a life on the bluff overlooking Cook Inlet. Our wood cook stove, the old type with removable round lids over the fire box, had an oven with a simple thermometer in the middle of its door and a shelf mounted at the top of the back sheeting. Mom was the first up in the morning, to roust the rest of us out of bed—not always an easy chore. We preferred to wait until she fired up the stove for breakfast and the basement warmed up a bit. For a few years she heated an old-style iron on the stove to press our dress clothes and Papa's suit, but cooking and baking were the stove's primary purpose. Keeping the temperature even and steady in the oven was tricky, but Mom made absolutely the best homemade bread, taking tips from Vi Coghlan, who made absolutely the best homemade bread.

Mom baked tall loaves, sweeter and lighter in texture, whereas Vi's bread was more compact and had a headier flavor. Mom usually baked three or four loaves at a time, twice a week—or more when the rest of us persuaded her to sacrifice a loaf or two hot off the rack. We reveled in the delicious aroma and slathered thick sawed-off slabs with margarine and homemade raspberry jam or high-bush cranberry/rose hip jelly, or honey. To her dismay, after the laborious work of hand-mixing, kneading, and baking, the loaves would disappear almost instantaneously, and she had to put her foot down in defense of the next few days' supply. Cookies, cake, and doughnuts shared a similar fate.

Berry-picking was a common seasonal activity for us, and Mom spent many hours turning the berries into jams and jellies. Papa paid us 10 cents a gallon for low- and high-bush cranberries, which were abundant and easy to pick, and sometimes he sold them to the Alaska Wild Berry Products people when they visited Wasilla on buying trips for their store located in Homer. We rambled the homestead area for raspberries, rose hips, and rare red and black currants. Salmon berries and watermelon berries were less prevalent but still to be found. No wild strawberries grew anywhere near us, so Papa planted a large patch of them in our field, along with rows of domestic raspberries.

In his Montville youth, Papa once picked eighty-four quarts of strawberries at three cents a quart for a neighbor, Sam Ford. Turtles frequented

Four-year-old Becky *takes her turn at bathing in the homestead tub, January 1961.*

their strawberry plots and would take berries from his hand. One of the turtles had the date "1914" carved into its shell. On the homestead we had no turtles on which to carve dates, and frogs were poor substitutes.

Mom experimented with different combinations of berries for her jams and jellies for our meals and brown bag school lunches. I still envision her standing by the cook stove, straining berry juice for jelly. She filled flour sacking with the hot pulp and suspended it over a pot, her hands and the plump, steaming bag stained a rich crimson.

Papa pickled assorted vegetables, and he particularly liked sliced green tomatoes from our greenhouse. He coated them in flour seasoned with salt and pepper and pan-fried them in oil. Zucchini, of course, overflowed. We stored potatoes and cabbages in burlap sacks. Carrots, beets, turnips, onions, and rutabagas kept well in boxes filed with sand. We also canned food—vegetables from the garden, occasionally moose meat, and in particular salmon garnered from our subsistence nets and rod-and-reel efforts. At first, we smoked salmon in an old refrigerator, but then Papa and we kids constructed a small birch pole structure for that purpose, burning alder for fuel. We liked the salmon strips, with our recipe being drier, glazed, and less oily than some, but very tasty. Mom used the canned salmon in several ways, and we looked forward to her salmon loaf: a cookie-pan-sized "biscuit" filled with vegetables, salmon, and spices, topped with a white sauce or cream-of-mushroom soup—sort of a homesteader calzone.

Mom didn't actually enjoy cooking, especially with the crude stove, our lack of running water and electricity, and the amount of food the other six of us consumed. For the first several years, until we got power, we stored perishables outside in below-freezing temperatures. Our refrigerator in the winter was a box up against an area of basement wall away from our stoves—a workable method, considering that Lee Anna remembers scraping a quarter-inch of frost off the block wall by her bunk. In the summer we dug a hole in the ground, installed the tub part of a wringer washer in it and used the lid to cover it. It worked well enough to keep things passably cool. Shelf dates didn't exist then and wouldn't have mattered anyway because leftovers were unheard of in our family. We also used the bottom half of an oil drum set in the ground for a cooler. It wasn't until the late '60s when we built our log home that we got electricity, a freezer, and a well, and life became easier, especially for Mom.

Becky and Richard *are the sit-down crew as* George Sr. *and* Jr. *work at cutting wood in the homestead driveway, June 1959. The log structure in the background is the outhouse known as the "Fortress."*

For a long time we used Boontonware, one of the first melamine dinnerware products to be marketed, produced in a factory on Myrtle Avenue in Boonton, New Jersey. Made of molded plastic, it came in solid colors and was considered unbreakable, although it could be chipped and also cracked with age and use. Perhaps it served as an unconscious connection to our relatives back in the Boonton area. We also used Tupperware products.

Mom's recipes came from the Betty Crocker cookbook, which was her faithful guide and served her well. Over the years I've taken a stab or two at cooking and I stand in awe of what she endured. Our menus were simple, but we always had plenty to eat, and we really should have expressed our gratitude more often.

Barrel Stove Adventures

SEVERAL CORDS OF WOOD FOR THE barrel stove were needed each winter. We began by using swede (or bow) saws, an art in itself, but soon acquired a Homelite C-51 power saw, which did many years of duty. Long woodpiles around our house rose, lengthened, and dwindled over the years, as if in a time-lapse movie. We cut wood from the surrounding forest, seeking dry or dead trees—mostly birch, with some spruce, cottonwood, and occasionally alder. Four-wheeling through the woods to the source reduced the labor of carrying the heavy lengths on our shoulders over the rough-and-tumble ground to the vehicles. We constructed rough cradles from birch poles to saw up longer lengths. What we split, we split by hand with an axe, or a maul and wedge. I well remember trying to split wet birch rounds when the temperature was above freezing. The axe bounced off the wood like it was chopping rubber—yet in lower temperatures, the frozen wood split clean and easy.

The wood was often damp, or green, and didn't burn that well, so Papa rigged up a used motor oil drip arrangement to help it burn better. Creosote production was considerable. A watery blackened mess drained from the stovepipes and stuck to the chimney in a shiny black glaze. Luckily, we never had a major stack fire, but the tarry odor was ever-present. Richard lamented that he sometimes went on a date with his clothes smelling like smoked salami.

Worse yet was the tar paper incident, for which no one has stepped forward to 'fess up. According to Lee Anna, in the early '60s we'd set out our subsistence net up the inlet from our house with a tent and camp so we could pick the net at night. She says, "When we returned home and opened the door to our basement, we were astonished and dismayed to find everything covered with black soot. And it smelled bad—terrible! Someone had tried to burn a piece of tar paper in the barrel stove and the door had popped open. The resulting smoke and soot had settled everywhere. Nobody would admit to the deed. Our clothes, blankets, furniture, food supplies, walls, floor, and ceiling were blackened and the smell lasted almost a year. We had no well and hauled our water at that time, but everything had to be scrubbed or washed. Some things had to be tossed out because of the black tar. In particular, it made Mom's life more difficult because she was the one that did most of the clean-up. Thank goodness it happened in the summer! How it happened is a mystery to this day."

We weren't the only ones. Vince and Larry Rhea, schoolmates of ours who lived in Willow, left a pot on their cook stove that boiled away its contents and tried to incinerate itself. The resulting odor on their clothes at school garnered them commiseration from us.

Mom kept the barrel stove going during the day when the rest of us, except for little Peter, were off in school. Once she dropped a heavy three-foot length of birch on her foot and broke three toes. I can't remember her going to the doctor for it, either.

On another occasion, with a good fire already blazing, we stuffed in more spruce logs when suddenly someone hollered, "ANTS!" A horde of huge black carpenter ants was fleeing the fiery furnace, spilling through the slots of the draft door in a spreading flood across the basement floor. We rushed around stomping and sweeping and smacking at the invaders and eventually eliminated most of them. From then on, whenever we added spruce to the stove we kept one eye cocked for signs of insect infestation.

I think of insect pests as Nature's little practical jokes. I never saw any ticks in Alaska, although they ran me to ground years later in Oregon. In Alaska, yellow-jackets were an occasional source of pain, and horse flies another. The flies were large, with a one-track, not-to-be-denied determination and a goodly bite, but they flew slowly enough that we could usually ward them off. For people residing in the woods as we did, the most ubiquitous insect was the mosquito, prevalent much of the spring, summer, and fall months. Breezes blowing off the inlet could mitigate their harassment, but they held sway over the woods and calm areas. They bred in melt-water on the flats and in puddles in the driveway, in the two ponds nearby, and in marshy areas. The first ones, the males, arrived in the springtime and took over the flats. They were fewer in number, lumbering and almost amiable, a light chocolate brown in color, but large, big as locusts, and they had *fur*! They flew straight in to land on your face or arm individually or in twos or threes, and gave you time to notice them, even converse with them, before they began feasting. Their size and slower speed allowed for the fine satisfaction of squeezing or smacking them almost at our leisure, unlike the smaller, sneaky females that came later in the season.

We used OFF! and 6-12 repellents outdoors to some effect, but inside our basement abode we burned Buhach, a beige-colored pyrethrum powder that came in a distinctive bright yellow container and is still available today. A small amount of Buhach on a jar lid or saucer burned like a tiny smudge fire and sent its smoke slowly wafting through the air. The effects of our breathing the fumes may not have been beneficial, but it took care of the mosquitoes indoors.

We built an outhouse out of birch poles twenty-five yards from the basement—two holes, no door, with a low—uh, squat—appearance. It faced the trees but had a partial view of the inlet and Pioneer Peak. We didn't have blue-board insulation for the seats in those days, so it was just a layer of roofing felt to sit on, which could chill one's intentions during the winter. Mom called it the "Fortress." We used it for several years. She planted flowers in the dirt against the outside back wall, but it still was an outhouse. Flies loved it, despite the lime we sprinkled, and mosquitoes besieged us when we used it. We kept an enameled "honey pot" inside the basement, but only Mom and the "little ones" were allowed to use it. Fortress though the outhouse may have been, I never became accustomed to the idea of insects gaining undue familiarity with the nether regions of my dignity, and I was glad when we installed indoor plumbing in our later log home.

Mosquitoes have a strong affinity for me. On the flats, in the woods, in the fields, in the house, awake or asleep. Only one mosquito around? It's after me in a flash. During our homestead years and later, I spent many sweating, swearing nights at the mercy of one or two of the indefatigable fiends. Their high-pitched keening attacks sent me diving head under the covers or had me lying rigid and listening and waiting for that tiniest brush of air from their wings on my face. Sometimes in the dark I offered my arms as bait and waited to smack them. But I was rarely victorious, and red itchy welts arose on the cutaneous platter that was my skin.

Papa seemed impervious to their presence. On our hunting and fishing hikes and our forays for firewood, I would be slapping, scratching, coughing them from my throat while he moved through the day unconcerned. I noticed him spritzing with repellent and/or lighting up a cigarette at times, but no way was I going down that KOOLS road.

Once, in high school, I visited Sharon Reeder and we hiked through the woods to a small swampy pond in back of their house. Bad mistake. We were beset by the singing hordes, and a half-mile arm-swinging flight through the trees back to safety ensued. On a caribou hunting trip to the Tangle Lakes area on the Denali Highway, Lee Turner, Papa, and I blissfully hiked in with the wind at our faces, intent on caribou detection, but found the wind favoring the aggressively swarming mosquitoes on the return. And later in life, while teaching in Selawik, my wife-to-be Kathy Schwartz went out on the tundra to pick blueberries, accompanied by the wind's false charm, and ended up in a cool water bath to reduce the swellings from the multitude of bites inflicted on her return trip.

So mosquitoes were our common companions. Relief came with the fall frosts, but by then other pests filled the vacuum. We faced black flies or white-sox, gnats, and those tiny bits of nasty nothing, the no-see-ums, also known as midges or pinkies. The white-sox and the nearly invisible no-see-ums swarmed over our faces, crept in our ears, noses, and mouths. They possessed more discriminating tastes than mosquitoes and searched for the delectable areas. They settled on eyelids, crawled under eyeglass temples and hat brims, wormed under collars and cuffs, and infiltrated any mosquito netting we wore. Their bite was a hundred times their size. Truly impressive critters.

The Law of the Firstborn

Gradually, we adapted to life on the bluff. We concocted some adventures ourselves. Young Becky decided to sample a root-beer-flavored Fizzie without following the accompanying instruction to dissolve it in water. Fizzies were small candy disks meant to be plopped into glasses of water to effervesce in a cold boiling action that spit bubbles like a later Alka-Seltzer commercial. A stale, flat-tasting, fruit-flavored drink similar to Kool-Aid resulted. Fizzies were not high-class refreshment, but we rarely had soda pop. Much of their appeal was the fizzing. Becky swallowed her disk straight from its foil package. This immediately led to consternation or amusement for the rest of us. She ran outside crying, gasping, burping, coughing. Mom ran to her with a glass of water that was speedily drained. Papa brought another.

We kids stood and watched in wonder, amazed at the excitement that such a drab little item could produce. Becky recovered, slightly the worse for wear, and Papa quickly warned Richard not to follow his sister's example. All in all, a lesson well learned, for years later when Pop Rocks appeared on the scene, none of us fell for that temptation. Except for Richard. And possibly Peter, who had been very young at the time of the Fizzie incident. I became intrigued with alternate uses for Fizzies—replacing throat lozenges with them, or integrating them into the Catholic communion, for instance—but my upbringing and fear of bodily harm and/or divine retribution prevailed.

For me, other pests surfaced from time to time, as when Papa and Mom took time off to go to the movies in the old Palmer theater, or to visit friends for an evening *sans* offspring. They presented themselves as soon as Papa and Mom disappeared down the driveway. According to the Law of the Firstborn, I was "in charge." We dwelt alone in the woods and we had no phone, save old military portable ones that Richard had taken over, so I was on my own. These leprechauns got where they weren't supposed to get, messed with things not to be messed with, jumped, bounced, and generally conspired against me.

Responsibility hung heavy in my heart as Richard, the instigator, led the charge, invariably inciting and teasing the others. I focused on his burr-haircut head with pleas, demands, and fist-smacking-into-palm

IN THE HOMESTEAD BASEMENT, *April 1966, Richard, Becky and Peter look as if they might still have some plans for "the firstborn," their babysitter and older brother, George Jr.*

suggestions. His impish grin would widen, the chase would begin, to end in a clout on his shoulder or a push. Down he'd collapse on the cement floor, wounded to the quick, to lie immobile, silent, feigning injury. I knew his game, but after several minutes of his lying inert and my getting no response from poking him, demon doubt crept into my soul, despite our having gone through the routine before—the Law of the Firstborn is truly a weighty burden to bear. Finally, he would leap up laughing and run gleefully for cover in another one of his "Gotcha's!"

One duty of my reluctantly assumed command involved toddler Peter and his Jekyll and Hyde appurtenances—cloth diapers. Clean-smelling squares of white cloth stacked neatly in a Blazo gas box cabinet—innocent enough, but each one held a history. Pushed up the chain of command by the instance of my birth, I grew far too familiar with the word "soiled," certain speculative expressions on young Peter's face, and the uneasy relationship between skin (mine included) and safety pins. Pampers were not in the vernacular. Smells are powerful memory stimulants, and the thought of rinsing those tiny quilts of human hygiene in an enameled pot back then evokes olfactory visions in me to this day. Fittingly, in later years a washer and dryer occupied the same spot as that vessel.

But the imps were merely my brothers and sisters and things eventually quieted down. As midnight drew near, the headlights of my relief cast dancing rays into the basement corners through the ground-level windows, signaling the release of my command. Once again I returned to the lower ranks: eldest son, brother, fellow traveler, sleepy-head.

"Oh, you're back?" I'd comment, yawning. "So soon? Did you have a good time? What? Oh, no trouble. Fine, just fine."

Emanations from the diaper pot drifted along beside me as I stumbled off to the top bunk bed. The weight of the world faded as I nestled under the weight of the covers—only to bounce upward with Richard's foot-shove from below.

Laundromat Lowdown

WE DIDN'T HAVE A WASHING MACHINE, a wringer one, until we got power and indoor plumbing in the late '60s. Still, it was considered an act of courtesy to others to wash your clothes from time to time. So on Saturdays we loaded up our week's laundry and made for the self-service laundry located behind Lovejoy's Garage in Wasilla, in sight of the Hulke residence. Frieda Hulke was one of my esteemed classmates, and she had a job as the local newspaper "boy," or "carrier" as we say today. She was far ahead of her time, a pioneer in the news industry. I think she made a nickel a paper, and I thought it was a cool job to have.

But my job was to heed the Law of the Firstborn—however demeaning and uncomfortable that might be. In this case, it was to do our laundry and free Mom to shop and socialize around town with my father and the rest of the family. This assignment included second encounters with Peter's little hygenic quilts.

Actually, it wasn't that bad. The laundry had some of the aspects of a scientific laboratory—white walls and ceiling, white-painted machines, white work tables, linoleum floor, lots of windows. It was, with apologies to Hemingway, a clean and well-lighted place. The tumbling thrum and beat of the machines—a muted *nada nada nada nada*—mixed with the intermittent gushing of water, was pleasant, almost hypnotic. But Hemingway committed suicide, did he not?

I was nervous my first time or two doing laundry, deciphering the instructions: how many quarters (or tokens) to use, discovering when to add detergent and that three cups was way too much—the sorts of things alien to a washboard veteran diaper-changer like myself. And what's with that bleach business with clothes of many colors? Couldn't I just stuff the machines, dump in the soap, feed it money, and let the splash and dash begin?

But alas, no. Clarion signs glared at me from the walls. People bigger than me—like, women—were there to see that proper protocol was observed. People's mothers and grandmothers and godmothers and grown-up daughters and nieces and aunts. And, for all I knew, mistresses. Friendly and polite, most of them knew me by sight and by name, knew my family, knew where I lived. It quickly dawned on me that there were no other men there. Oh, one slunk in the front door once in a while and dumped his armful of clothes and a handful of quarters in a machine, but then he quickly slouched back outside to sit on the step and pass the time smoking, or step over to the garage to discuss horsepower and pistons, head gaskets and O-rings, helper springs and grease guns. Try out the new Creeper. Dirt and grime time. Man talk. But there was no escape for me, except for brief visits to the restroom.

"George, honey, why don't you run and tell Shorty his load is done," and, "George, be a dear and let Jim know his dryer's stopped." Bertha was the red-haired overseer who ran the operation, but others chipped in with various bits of laundronomic advice. And that's the way it was; the Law of the Firstborn—no waivers, no exceptions. Delegation of duty was frowned upon, even when facing the sympathetic smirks and tobacco-knotted lower lips of Shorty and Jim when I relayed the message. So I brought a *MAD Magazine*, or checked out books from the Wasilla Library to read while the clothes and sheets tumbled and gurgled in the machines. But it didn't take long for me to pick up on other more interesting stories gossiping through the detergent-scented air around me. One tale in particular had me gaping in amazement.

The washer women said that someone or something was sneaking around at night and drawing blood from local horses. Mason jars partially filled with blood had been found in the Schrock Road area. People were uneasy, and presumably the horses weren't too happy, either. This went on for a Saturday or two, and I got to asking Papa to drop me off with the laundry before going to the library. Finally, one Saturday, the tale took a turn from the eerie to the bizarre. While I was out of earshot at school during the week the Laundromat itself had become a part of the drama.

When my machines finished their cycles and buzzed loudly, I didn't notice. I hung on every word that weighed anchor from those women's lips. Rumor had it that a patient at a mental institution in Anchorage had escaped and bled the horses. Perhaps a fan of Mary Shelley, or a reverse Dracula, he then had taken the jars of blood to the cemetery at the edge of town on Fishhook Road, dug up a previously interred buddy of his, and injected the corpse with the equine blood, struggling to bring his pal back to life. After his attempts to raise the dead, the man had found his way to the Laundromat, walked in, taken a shower with his clothes on, and then set to rinsing the blood-stained jars. He and the Mason jars were soon whisked into custody and hauled away, leaving behind enough excitement for years to come.

It might have been a collective practical joke, or an "Urban Legend," as they say these days, but there was no "Urban" in Wasilla then. As far as I know, it is a true story. As for the "Legend" part, it grew into that. My brother Richard recalls hearing it, too, when he tagged along with Mom when she did our laundry.

Fact or fiction, I began keeping my eyes peeled whenever I took a shower in the Laundromat, and the old stand-by sponge bath in the washtub at home didn't seem so bad after all.

5

The 1964 "Good Friday" Earthquake

I WAS A HIGH SCHOOL JUNIOR IN THE SPRING OF '64 and looking forward to the summer and its outdoor activity. Yes, even getting firewood—a much more desirable task in summer than in winter. Shooting baskets at our outside basketball hoop at home was also more desirable in the summer than in the winter. The March blahs were dissolving into the freshness of April when the ground beneath our feet began to shake violently.

And shake it did. On March 27th—Good Friday—at 5:36 pm, I was in the elementary school waiting for Papa to finish up his school business for the day so we could head for home and the weekend. Lee Anna, Richard, and Becky had already taken the bus. Suddenly things started to rock and roll, and then to roll and rock. Within thirty seconds the few people still in the building that afternoon scrambled for the exits. Papa and I ran outside and stumbled down the front steps into the street. Like drunken sailors we struggled to maintain our footing. Parked cars near us bucked and rocked with the quake, and tree tops whipped through the air like brooms frantically collecting invisible cobwebs. People talk of hearing a roar, a rumble from the ground, but I don't recall hearing any such sounds.

Lurching about in the middle of the street I watched the chimney in the older section of the school bash back and forth, enlarging its roof opening. Unbeknownst to us, a part of the elementary roof out of our line of sight collapsed. As the quaking continued, I pulled out my trusty Sears, Roebuck pocket-sized transistor radio (Silverstone 6, MODEL 1205) and tuned it through the dial—nothing but hiss! No stations on the air. Not a good sign. Finally, the interminable four-minute shaking stopped. We collected ourselves and scouted for casualties. Fortunately, the few people in the area were uninjured. With our senses attuned to the potential of more ground action, and our knees still jelly, Papa and I headed for Wilbur Atkins' garage two blocks away, where Wilbur had finished repairs on our Chevy CarryAll early that afternoon.

Very worried about the rest of the family, we sped home, swerving and slipping in our muddy driveway. No damage was apparent when we pulled into the front yard, and everyone ran to greet us. No one was hurt. They'd been sitting at the kitchen table when the quake struck, Lee Anna and Becky recall.

> Mama kept glass jars in which she stored flour, beans, rice, pasta—some empty—along with other canned food on the shelves. They all started rattling. We looked around at each other, wondering what the heck was going on. We jumped up and ran outside, including Richard who had by then recovered sufficiently from his major broken-leg accident with a pickup truck. It's amazing what little kids think their parents can do. Peter was yelling, "Mama, make it stop! Make it stop!"

The glass jars all tumbled off the shelves and shattered on the floor as we ran out and hung onto the old Jeep—the trees were swaying, almost hitting the earth, swinging back and forth. We thought we were on some kind of roller coaster, or a boat where the waves come up and knock it around.

ON THE WAY to our homestead from Wasilla was the Turner place, where Lee and Bea and their young sons Jim and Lin experienced the quake. Lee and Jim were unloading drums of bulk gasoline off the bed of their stake-bed Jeep onto a rack in the yard. While they struggled to stay on their feet and keep the drums from crashing to the ground or onto themselves, Lin was caught in the top of a tree he had climbed next to the rack. He clung desperately to the tree as it swayed back and forth, catching glimpses of his father and brother wrestling with the drums. He says he thought of jumping off when the tree hesitated in transition near the ground, but Lee shouted at him, "Lin! Hang on tight!" So Lin did exactly that and survived the quake in the ride of his young life. The three of them managed occasional glimpses of Bea through an upstairs window that overlooked the yard. She was struggling to remain upright, disappearing and reappearing as they watched. Again, no one was injured, and despite the quake's prolonged and violent motion, damage was minimal.

Hal Post remembers that he was in the woods on their Goose Bay homestead, loading logs onto a truck, when the quake hit. The trees were whipping violently around, threatening to up-root, so he dove under the truck for protection. Spruce needles were raining down by the millions in a weird green snowstorm. He could feel the waves of ground motion pass through him as he lay on the ground under the truck. Desperate to get back to Joy and the kids after the quake stopped, he borrowed a truck and headed back to Anchorage. When he got to the Knik River bridge, it was still standing but had a one foot break in it, with the two sections at different heights, blocking the pickup's path. On the other side was a snow slide covering the road where the bridge met the bottom slope of the mountain. He climbed across the gap and caught a ride in a police car to Anchorage and his family.

Joy was in Anchorage with the kids, including two-week-old Suzie, when the quake started. She scooped the baby into her arms and everyone, mother and children, scrambled to stand in a doorway, holding tight to the door frame. In the aftermath of the quake, she gathered the kids and they all went to stay with a neighbor, which was where Hal found them, and the family was safely reunited.

In earthquakes, as in homesteading and Yogi Berra, it ain't over till it's over. The main quake didn't bother me that much. I saw little damage, and no one seemed to be injured, so I found it kind of interesting, except for my initial worry for the rest of the family and the dark unknown of what was happening to the rest of the state. The aftershocks, and the anticipation of them, were the real attention-getters for me. Eleven major aftershocks occurred in the twenty-four hours after the main quake. We sat around listening to the hiss of our Coleman lantern and reliving the event until after midnight. I was on the couch waiting for any new seismic activity. I soon felt a tremor and noticed a pen in my left shirt pocket shuddering. "Uh-oh," I thought, "here we go again." I tensed, ready to run, watched the pen, and searched the darkness of the basement with my eyes and ears before I realized it was my heartbeat shaking the pen. But my nervousness didn't go unrewarded. We had a serious aftershock that sent us fleeing into the night. We had a toy, a tiny monkey on a stiff upright ten-inch wire, that functioned from then on as our family seismic monitor. The monkey sat at the top of the wire until a quake shook it loose. It then toggled its way down the pole. We were long gone out the door before the monkey hit the bottom of the wire.

The high school at the time was a block building. It sustained minor damage and a few cracks in the wall, one right next to my hall locker, but I think classes were held the Monday following the quake, when another major aftershock emptied the school for several minutes. The elementary school suffered more damage. Richard went to his elementary classroom during the next week and saw his desk covered with rubble from the roof.

Lee Anna remembers, in the days after the quake, "When we sat at the dinner table eating, we kids would jig our legs under the table to make it shake until Mom glanced around with a look of fright in her eyes before realizing that it was a joke. We'd start to laugh, and she'd get madder than heck at us."

The subduction (or mega-thrust) earthquake registered 8.4 on the Richter Scale (9.2 magnitude), the most powerful ever recorded for North America. Other areas suffered much greater damage from the quake and from the resulting tsunami actions. Coastal communities such as Chenega, Afognak, Kodiak, Seward, Valdez, Girdwood and Portage were seriously damaged or destroyed. The Fourth Avenue, Government Hill, Turnagain, and other areas of Anchorage sustained spectacular destruction, much of it from soil liquefaction. The quake and its wave action were recorded or felt around the world, in Oregon and Hawaii, and notably in Crescent City, California, where a major part of the tsunami hit.

The death toll from the quake and tsunami was 131, with 16 of those outside Alaska. The state's sparse population was the main reason the toll wasn't much higher, and the Easter weekend holiday and time of day also helped. We live on the northern edge of the "Ring of Fire," so lesser quakes, as well as volcanic eruptions, have been common over the years. During one eruption of Mount Augustine on the Alaska Peninsula south of Anchorage, Mom collected the fine gray ash that fell on our homestead.

In the fall of 2005, I visited John and Brigitte Cooper on the slopes of the Big Island in Hawaii and danced with them in a 5.7 quake epicentered off-shore of Kailua-Kona. That was a wake-up call, too: quakes are part of life in the Pacific, and they may occur at any time.

Work and Play and a House, Oh My

BESIDES EARTHQUAKES AND ERUPTIONS, nature provided us with assorted entertainment opportunities on the homestead. We explored the woods and inlet, raced up and down the bluff and on the flats, rode old one-gear bikes with fat tires, made string-and-can telephones, played chase tag and hide-'n'-seek. We built forts of birch poles, floated homemade toy boats in the inlet and O'Brien Creek, and collected frogs and other small critters. I, too, was a Robert Frost swinger of birches.

In the winter, we ice-skated on the flats and the pond, built snowmen, and erected snowball forts for King-of-the-Hill. Sledding was popular. Besides sleds and saucers, we used cardboard boxes, old pieces of carpet, auto body remnants, and scrap pieces of plastic. The tall pile of our basement's excavated gravel made an excellent beginner's slope. The proficient or foolhardy among us sledded a course that ran from the top of the pile down to the drive, downhill for another three hundred feet, and onto the flats. Hovering over it all was the distinct possibility of being unable to stop or veer off on the flats at the bottom, to end up sliding into the deep cut of O'Brien Creek, with its icy water at various stages of tide, frozen mud, and ice sheets mixed with reedy grass.

Papa enjoyed watching us and recalling his sledding as a boy on the farm down Peach Hill. His ride started at the Conways' house, turned right down the road in front of the Quints', dropped into the valley and then went up over the next hill and finally down across the railroad and onto the highway. Older boys built a high mound of snow on the way that threw sleds high in the air. Missing the road meant landing amid the peach trees that lined the sides.

Our agenda for a summer day on the homestead might include hauling water, cutting wood, tarring roof leaks, enduring earthquakes, working on the Jeep/Chevy/Corvair, walking on the flats, setting out subsistence nets, weeding gardens, working on our house. Summers were busy, since school took up our time in the fall and winter. My first jobs in the paid labor force, not counting berry-picking sales, included local roto-tilling, picking potatoes for Barbara Kelton's father, Claude, on the Kelton farm on Wasilla-Fishhook Road, and helping Papa put in footings, block walls, and cement floors when he took on occasional summer concrete work to augment his teaching salary. Again, it was family expertise being passed down: My grandfather Frank Bartholomay and his son, my Uncle Frankie, were masons in New Jersey, and Papa had worked with them before coming to Alaska. I had mason training when we built our own basement, and we had worked on a basement for Henry and Ester Hansen, who lived on Fairview Loop near Dinkels' farm, and put up a block building in town near Ed and Bev Gurtler's place in Wasilla.

However, during the summer of 1964 we were too busy at home to take on outside jobs, as we began construction of a 36-by-32-foot two-story log home atop our basement. We hauled cottonwood logs from a mill located on the hill out of Palmer, on the Wasilla-Palmer highway. Why cottonwood and not spruce, I have no idea, except that it must have been cheaper. We used Hal Post's '47 Ford flatbed, which we now owned, for the job. In raising the logs, we used a brace and bit to sink holes into each one, and drove ten-inch spikes down through the holes into the log below to help steady the wall. Papa and I did the work, sometimes assisted by Dave Belden, a friend and long-time classmate of mine. I had attended a summer science program at the University of Alaska in Fairbanks for a few weeks the previous summer and had missed the field clearing, but not this time! Mom helped out, but less than she had with the cement work in 1959, since the younger children had become a greater handful, and the housekeeping chores had increased.

We cut spruce log rafters and beams for the ceilings and roof, and incongruously hauled them atop the Scout's thin metal roof, despite some of them being twice the Scout's length. I had carried the blocks and "mud" for Papa's work on our basement, and he'd had me lay some of the blocks—log work was definitely easier! One nasty job Mom took on was to strip the bark off the raw logs with a draw knife and chisel, and she scrubbed the mildew off them after they had sat for a time awaiting installation. She used rubber gloves, Clorox bleach, and brushes, and I imagine the bleach wasn't healthy for her skin or lungs. Friends helped in raising the rafters and beams into place. We used ropes to slide a heavy forty-foot

Katy Harbeson enjoyed her eventual studio on the homestead, whether with her own art projects or with friends invited for tea and conversation; in this photo from 1975 the visitors are (from left) PEGGY BEHNKE, KATHLEEN SMYTH, *and* MRS. SPENCER, *who was probably a teacher.*

log to the roof peak, which was twenty-five feet above ground level. We built the house on a $10,000 V.A. loan, which took Papa many years to pay off.

With the log structure in place on top of the basement, all of us, especially Mom, were ready to move up to a real house. It was an extra relief for Papa to have the better living conditions for his family. No more piles of wood stacked in our kitchen and curtained-off rooms. No more leaky flat roof, frosty block walls, and cold dim interiors. And the view from the higher, larger windows of the house was spectacular.

After moving up, we met a family named Oswald that lived on the other side of Fish Creek, and the two young Oswald boys stayed with us for a couple of months one summer. We also acquired a small shed-style cabin from their area, which Papa, Richard, and I chain-sawed vertically in half and towed back to our place on a trailer with the Scout. Beyond our house, halfway down the driveway to the flats and creek, we poured concrete pilings and stitched the cabin back together atop them. It rested in the trees on the edge of the bluff but sat closer to the level of the flats than our house. This was Mom's "retreat," and it became a summer studio for her painting and other art, and a place to host tea parties for her women friends.

Mom loved her cabin. It was a simple structure, where the serenity was accompanied by the peaceful sounds of nature and the easy drone of an occasional high-flying plane. The view of the flats, the mouth of O'Brien Creek, Cook Inlet, and the Chugach Mountains rising on the southeast side was inspiring. It was an ideal setting for her to savor her "sun tea," made in huge glass pickle jars that we cooled in O'Brien Creek just three hundred feet away. We had picnics there to take advantage of the magnificent scenery and warm summer weather. Becky in particular still enjoys iced tea and the memories of those days. Mom had sacrificed much in our Alaska years up to then, and she was more than deserving of the tranquility and joy she found there. As her friends Bea Turner, Vi Coghlan, Charlyn Martin, Peggy Behnke, Charlotte Belden, and Julie Ede agreed, "Well, it's about *time*!"

ON THE HOMESTEAD, AUGUST 1963: *apprentice mechanic George Harbeson Jr. at work on the 1954 Chevy Carryall that carried the family to Alaska, twice.*

6

Lug Nut Theater

OUR HOMESTEAD YEARS WERE FRAUGHT WITH mechanical adversity compounded by weather and road conditions. Vehicles were called upon to perform beyond the limits of their designed purposes, abused by necessity. Raised on the Montville farm in the '20s and the Great Depression, Papa was not unfamiliar with such challenges, as his written recollections of the Montville years indicate, beginning with a pre-vehicular fixture on the farm.

Our horse was "Old John," and he was huge and gray. He originally had pulled garbage cars in a dump in Brooklyn. He had been a dray horse in the Fulton Fish Market, a favorite hangout of my grandfather, and may have been a brewery horse at one time. His legs carried many scars, and his hooves were huge and he often stepped on our feet. He pulled the wagon we used on the farm and for produce sales in Boonton. At noon in town, he would take off for the feed and hay place run by a man named Ford. One time he fell while pulling our wagon down the steep hill in back of our barn, but remained still, holding the wagon until my father had blocked the wheels and released him.

Old John was tremendously strong and usually went where he wanted to go. My father—we called him Papa—plowed and cultivated with Old John, and sometimes I led the horse through the crop rows. We rode on his huge back, but he didn't like that and reached around and pulled us off by grabbing our pants. He also brushed us off by going under low-hanging tree branches. We were lucky to get a fast walk out of him. Once he got into our garden and when Mama, a substantial woman, grabbed his bridle, he merely lifted her off the ground and refused to budge. Papa grabbed a hoe and broke its handle over his back, but Old John didn't seem to feel it. Sometimes Old John got the colic and Papa gave him huge doses of bicarbonate of soda. I vividly remember his dying in the stall below the wagon house. My older brothers Davis and Bill dug a large hole out past the Bott place and dragged him there, where he rests today in the tree-overgrown field near the meager remains of our two Maxwell autos.

After Old John died, we used a Fordson tractor. We spent hours and hours cranking that tractor. It had magneto boxes for the spark, and a spark retard-advance lever to the commutator. If you left that advanced, the crank kicked and did injury to you if your thumb wasn't placed correctly. In colder weather, we put rags and corn cobs soaked in gasoline in the spaces between the exhaust manifold and lighted them to warm the engine. We also used alcohol for antifreeze.

The Fordson had steel cleats on the wheels and iron wheels all around, and if you weren't careful, it could pull the front end up and back over on top of the driver, especially if the back wheels were weighted with concrete.

- -

MY COUSIN JOHN says he learned to drive on the Fordson. Grandpa and our Uncle Davis told him that if a front wheel rose up off the ground even an inch, he was to jam the clutch down. Sure enough a wheel started to rise once and John scrambled to push in the clutch—he was too short to depress the pedal fully while sitting. The Fordson "came out of its act," but John never told anyone about it; he was scared he'd get a scolding. We didn't have horses or a tractor on our Alaska homestead, but Papa's assessment of his early years was true for us as well.

In those days on the farm, if something broke, we rarely had the money for parts or repair, so we made do and fixed things the best we could. We had a long, black, 1925 straight-6 Touring Studebaker. Its clutch went out pulling a disc through our peach orchard. We also had two Maxwells over the years. My older brother Bill was given a 1918 King V-8 touring car with an aluminum head and wire wheels, which we started on gasoline and ran on kerosene.

For a long time we had a 1930 Chevy 4-cylinder, which broke axles so often we carried a spare, and my brother Davis had a 1930 Pontiac that taught me about reverse thread lug nuts.

I took my first driving test with a police officer in Morristown, New Jersey, in my older brother Bill's '30 Plymouth Roadster. The Plymouth had a defective starter, so I kept it running during the test. The car stalled a block into the test when I approached a stop sign, but I shifted into second gear while it was still moving and started it again. I remember the officer looking at me, and then saying, "Okay, turn around. You can drive. You passed the test."

My cousin John says that Bill told him a story about the 1918 King touring car mentioned above. "Bill drove it to work in Boonton. When the tires wore out, he drove along the railroad. The metal rims sparked when they ran over the embankment's limestone ballast. Bill said it was quite a show after dark. One night he heard thrashing in the underbrush. He stopped and spotted a bunch of hobos running for dear life through a gravel pit. (There were rumors of a hobo camp in the area.) Bill assumed they had seen the sparking King coming at them and thought that the devil himself was approaching."

Papa continues:

> *After the war Sterne and I started to farm our* place again. We bought a 1935 International panel for marketing and general use. We planted tomatoes, but they got the blight and we picked no tomatoes. Eugene Vreeland tried to sell us a tomato field. We found out it had the blight and passed on the deal. Next, we bought nine hundred chickens. Unfortunately, about seven hundred died or were killed so both Sterne and I started college in the fall.

I still drove the International then, but it wouldn't start with the starter and I had to park it on a hill. I'd leave early for class and park it in the last space before the "No Parking" sign. Several times someone parked ahead of me, giving me no room to turn out into the road. I carried two pieces of 2x4 and would put one under the front wheel, take the panel out of gear, set my back to the bumper, push it back, throw the other 2x4 under the wheel, and do this enough times to get enough room to turn out into the street and roll-start the car. I carried two spare tires and usually had to fix at least one flat to be ready for the next morning.

The panel's windshield was made of a type of safety glass that turned amber on the inside with age, and visibility was poor, but it was our only vehicle. There was a mandatory inspection for cars in New Jersey, which the panel could never pass, so I would turn right in Caldwell and travel the residential section until I got past Verona, where police were always stopping cars. Then I'd turn left and continue to the college. I picked up a warning ticket to get the inspection and had to transfer the registration to Katy for the next year. The following year it came back to me, and the next year I transferred it again to Katy.

IT SEEMS THAT others in the Harbeson clan also employed the registration ploy occasionally. But when Papa got a teaching job in Rockaway and purchased the Willys, such tactics became a thing of the past for him—I remember seeing an inspection sticker on the Willys' windshield. Then in the '54 CarryAll—duly sporting its sticker—we migrated to Wasilla where there were no such inspections.

Once Papa and his brothers drove to New York City and had to fix and patch eight flats along the way. A few of the early cars they owned, like a Chevy station wagon they got in 1925, used clincher rims and had wooden spokes. The tubes in these tires constantly got pinched, and the drive home would be on the metal rims. In the late 1930s, when he was seventeen and worked as a law office runner, the rear tire came off the 1930 Ford Model A he'd bought for twenty-five dollars from his older brother Davis' father-in-law. The tire rolled up on the sidewalk ahead, sending pedestrians scrambling.

Another vehicle Papa had was a '34 Buick that Mom's father gave him. It was a fine car but hard on tires and got poor gas mileage, despite its six-cylinder engine.

> *I used the Buick to cart the Rockaway High School* track team to the Camden, Newark, Elizabeth, and Long Branch relays. My sister-in-law Mary had been learning to drive with it and had run off the road, struck a stone wall, glanced off a pole, and run into the shrubbery, crumpling the right front fender. I tried to knock the dent out with an eight-pound sledgehammer, but the metal was too strong. It was probably the strongest made car I've ever seen. When I left it at the Willys sales lot it was running beautifully, but it had three flats, even after I'd fixed two tires that morning. They gave me sixty-five dollars off on a new $1,700 Willys station wagon.

ANOTHER OF PAPA'S early training exercises was a trip to Florida from the family farm in the Model A with his younger brother Sterne and older sister Ella, when he was nineteen.

> *The Ford had a front wheel out of alignment,* so on the way we replaced the worn tire with one purchased from Sears in Miami, which wore out in a few hundred miles. The car also had a bald tire on the back with a split in it that I'd bought from a woman in Boonton for a quarter. You could see the tube through the cut in its sidewall, but it made it all the way home and then some. The Ford got twenty miles to the gallon, so we had enough gas money for the return trip, but only sixty-five cents to spare for other expenses. We bought soda pop and five-cent hamburgers at a White Castle stand when we got hungry.

PAPA'S PREVIOUS PRACTICAL experience guided us through our homestead years and encouraged the rest of us to adopt his grin-and-bear-it philosophy, although there were times when I failed to muster the "grin" part.

The '54 Chevy

W<small>E DROVE TO</small> A<small>LASKA TWICE IN OUR</small> '54 Chevy CarryAll, which Papa bought new for $2,000 with a loan from the County Bank and Trust Company on Market Street of Paterson, New Jersey, co-signed by my Uncle Davis and Aunt Louise. It had rear-wheel drive with a standard 3-speed shift hung on the steering column. The dimmer switch and starter "pedal" lived on the floor. Access to the middle and rear seats was through the front passenger door.

The Chevy was a large part of my life. It lulled me to sleep as a small child on rainy night dash-glow drives in New Jersey, smuggled my measles-stricken hide across the Alaska/Canada border, and gave me motor-purring assurance in its dark night homestead scrambles up the "Big Hill," as well as providing glare-ice skids, height-assisting basketball "half court" shots and slam dunks in our yard, and innumerable moose-counting trips to school. The CarryAll lived up to its name during its span of use. It carried all of our increasing family on our first trip up from New Jersey to Wasilla, via the Alcan Highway in the summer of 1954; back down to New Jersey and up to Groton, Vermont, in '56; to White Meadow Lakes, New Jersey, in '57; and back to Wasilla in '58. Two years later we and it embarked on the homestead era.

From the time of our first entry to the parcel and throughout the years to come, one dominating feature of our lives was "the driveway," an innocuous sounding term that belied its fickle persona. A narrow, winding, hilly, dirt lane close to a mile in length, it had multiple personalities, defined by the season, the weather, the time of day or night, and the volume of traffic traversing it.

Mud of many textures, bone-jarring ruts, and significant "puddles" of water ruled spring break-up and fall freeze-up. Its summer surface was more benign after we had drained, shoveled, and scraped the ruts into a facsimile of level, but then fine powdery dust accumulated in spots and enshrouded visitors and residents alike. Fall entailed aspects similar to spring. Winter held a special set of conditions: snowfall, sleet, rain, and ice.

Wind, fog, and darkness had their way on both our vehicles and us. Heavy snowfall or ice lengthened "the driveway" considerably, while in our minds sunshine magically shortened it. Wind blew trees across it.

123 · · *Lug Nut Theater*

RICHARD, BECKY, *and the Chevy Carryall wait while* GEORGE HARBESON *gets ice at Muncho Lake for the next leg of the trip up the Alcan in 1958.*

Shoveling fifty feet of snowdrift felt like a near eternity. Once I turned into the drive from the old Knik Road and had to drive up into the brush to maneuver around a cow carcass that one of the Redingtons or another local musher had dragged and temporarily left there on the way to feeding it to his dogs.

The type and condition of the vehicle we happened to be utilizing—and as noted elsewhere we had many over the years—determined the degree of success or failure. Low clearance and worn tires had a definite say, as did disgruntled batteries, lazy clutches and brakes, worn-out shocks, weary trannies, recalcitrant carburetors, and pitted points.

The drive itself was composed of a series of segments, each having its own personality and obstacles. There was "The Big Hill," "The Hill After the Big Hill," "The Fork," "The Curve," "The Big Puddle," "The Other Big Puddle," the stretch along "The Field," "The First (and Second) Turnaround," and assorted "Dips." "The Drop Off" or "The Edge" applied to any section where the drive paralleled the bluff. The lay-out of each of these types of terrain determined the techniques of attack.

Ruts in the drive were sometimes gouged deep enough to high-center the '54 Chevy and later vehicles like the little '47 military-style Jeep and the '66 International Scout. There's a device called a "Handyman," or wagon jack, and blessed be the person or divinity that invented that treasure. It was a four-foot-tall bar of steel with notches closely spaced down its length, and it had a spring-loaded apparatus with a flat lifting prong and a slot where a three-foot wooden or metal pipe handle resided. The handle was removable for convenience in transporting and, if all else failed, for bashing the obdurate vehicle. The whole thing was heavy, close to thirty pounds.

We dragged the jack from the rear of the Chevy and struggled to get the lift prong under whichever bumper we thought the strongest. We had to jam pieces of boards or logs under the jack's small foot, otherwise the jack drove itself down into the ground without budging the Chevy upward. But with a good base, we placed the jack in the middle of the bumper and ratcheted the Chevy as high as we dared, and hoped the bumper braces held. Then we shoved tree limbs, boards, rocks, small children or animals, whatever was available, under the wheels while the whole affair teetered precariously in the breeze.

A finger-crushing latch on the jack had to be set securely, or the spring mechanism could send the vehicle suddenly downward, with the jack handle snapping upright or violently ratcheting up and down against the length of the jack and any of our body parts that might be in close proximity. Finally, we nervously removed the handle, which had a mean roundhouse swing as well as an uppercut, gave the jack a shove sideways, and the Chevy's rear wheel was tossed over onto the ridges of the rut. Or not. In the latter event, the jack with a couple of lengths of chain became a cumbersome mechanical winch. In those days, if it worked we didn't complain.

Well, we still complained, but less vociferously.

Imposters

Sometimes in the '50s as we drove the Chevy along local roads in the Wasilla and Palmer area, gravel rattling in the wheel wells, we'd come upon vehicles parked on the shoulder of the road near streams where the salmon were running. It was amazing how quickly car hoods were raised, and how interest in the mechanical workings therein suddenly developed. We'd stop to offer assistance, automatic in those times.

"Car trouble? Need some help?"

"Oh, just a carburetor problem, maybe water in the gas. We can handle it."

Or, "Just checking the radiator hoses, but we got it covered."

Or, "Spark plug wire came loose but, hey, thanks anyways. Appreciate the offer."

All the while their eyes would surreptitiously inspect us and the Chevy for Fish and Game insignia, since the Chevy was the exact color and make of some of the Department's vehicles.

"Good luck," we'd grin then, and trundle on. Behind us, the hoods would clang down, no doubt accompanied by heartfelt sighs of relief and maybe a few vulgar improprieties.

A Battery for Any Occasion

We always knew that we rode on the edge of automotive mischief, that some recipe for mechanical misfortune was being cooked up by our otherwise faithful steeds. We just never knew when it would be served. Common ingredients included malfunctioning or breakage-prone spark plugs, distributors, radiators, starter solenoids, thermostats, brake lines, transmissions, clutches, shock absorbers, axles, tires, wipers, vacuum lines, ignition and wiring, generator brushes, steering assembly, batteries —and the menu was not limited to the parts manuals.

Batteries were like family, and they, like us, would get drained, tired, suffer a lack of energy. As with most families, when one member had a problem the others would pitch in to help. Early on, most batteries were 6-volt, followed later by 12-volt. Having to jump-start vehicles was normal, and jumper cables (themselves in various states of wear) were mandatory equipment.

Since our spare batteries were often not up to snuff, we sometimes needed not just one, but two, even three batteries. Six or 12-volt, we hooked them together in series or in parallel. Once we had the use of a 24-volt Cat battery. Of course, as in family matters, sparks sometimes flew. Jumper cable clamps possessed the unnerving capability of sticking, indeed welding themselves, to the battery's lead anode. This caused great consternation, resulting in improvised forms of dance and cries of "Holy Cow!" or "Whoa! Whoa!" or "Son of a Biscuit Eater!" Jerking the offending clamp loose in the acrid smoke that roiled up from the depths usually remedied the situation.

Often, the network of batteries produced the stomach-sinking "RR . . . Rrr . . . rr . . . r" followed by a disappointing silence. This led to our carrying chock rocks with us in the vehicle, and to the practice of desperately searching wherever we went for downgrades on which to park. Many years later, when I saw the film *The Gods Must Be Crazy*, the antics at the gate with the hill and the rock and the Rover were a trip down memory lane. And I must say I admire the equanimity of the guy in the movie.

Cold-Weather Options

Because we had no electricity or block heater, cold weather presented a regular problem in starting the Chevy. When the temperature dropped to 20, 30, or 40 below we poured boiling water over the outside propane tank, and on the pipe feeding our overhead kitchen light and propane cook stove, to keep the gas flowing. That was not a practical strategy for the Chevy.

When it was really cold, in order to get to school the next day we had two options: 1. Papa or I, usually Papa, could get up every few hours, start the Chevy and let it warm up; or, 2. We'd drape blankets over the hood down to the ground and place a catalytic heater under the oil pan for the night. This heater, a forerunner of later Kero-Sun devices, looked like an oversize Coleman lantern body with a broad flat dome on top. The dome had a cloth-like wick spread over it, with a protective screen over that, and it burned kerosene.

We also placed cardboard in front of the radiator and took the battery inside until needed. Sometimes we drained the crankcase oil and kept it warm in the house during the night, before pouring it back in the morning. Spraying starter fluid or Blazo (white gas) in the carburetor helped. Pushing the car down the hill past our house sometimes worked when the temperature wasn't too low, but with the tranny and axle grease so stiff from the cold, it was difficult to get the car moving. If it still didn't start, we were then stuck with the car halfway down the hill to the flats.

Can We Do That Again, Papa?

The Chevy wasn't the greatest vehicle for Alaskan homesteads because it had two-wheel drive with no posi-traction or limited slip. Tire chains definitely helped—we could ignore their clattering and banging, the volume commensurate with the speed—and we kept five-gallon buckets of chains in various states of repair scattered around the homestead for decades. But sometimes we were caught with our chains down. The area on the edge of Wasilla Lake near Hagen's Playland amusement park, where the city park is today, was open to the lake and a prime spot for snowdrifts. One night we came home from Palmer with the wind swirling snow across the ice-shadowed road most of the way, which limited visibility and headlight range, but no major drifts had piled up, so we weren't running chains.

We reached the spot by the lake and suddenly, in the blowing snow and headlight glare, loomed glimpses of a drift, not too deep, but fifty to seventy-five feet long. Papa saw it, shifted into second gear, gunned it, and we roared into the drift. Snow exploded over the hood and assaulted the windshield in clouds. We were a self-contained bubble in a disoriented world. Second gear kept us moving for a bit, but when the engine lugged down, Papa shifted down into first gear and we surged forward. When the drift had dragged us almost to a halt, we broke free, back onto bare road. Cheers went up for The Mighty Chevy That Could, and we promised it a nice drink of HEET. As we continued on toward home, I heard Richard's excited voice call out from the rear seat:

"Can we do that again, Papa?"

Cousin Billy

One of my New Jersey cousins, Billy, a few years older than I, stayed with us for the school year when we rented Orlando and Margaret Byers' place. During the summer, he, Papa, Mr. Byers, and I set out on a fishing trip to the Willow side of Hatcher Pass, with dreams of rainbows, dollies, and grayling dancing in our heads.

I remember one mystical place on that excursion, one that I couldn't find many years later. We walked a short distance off the road and came upon a small sand and mud beach. It bordered a good-sized pool sporting a large smooth boulder where the stream came down out of a gully. I immediately noticed a set of grizzly tracks imprinted in the beach. It seemed to me, an eight-year-old, that each track was big enough to fit my head into, so this kept me alert while we fished there.

After filling our creels, we walked back to the road and started home, only to discover that the Chevy had a problem holding onto one of its wheels. Billy had changed the tire before our departure from home but apparently hadn't tightened its lug nuts sufficiently. I can't remember if the wheel required five or six nuts, but we managed to get two or three tight enough for the drive home. This may account for my later and still current propensity to over-tighten lug nuts, to the detriment and dismay of others—and myself—in getting them off. For this, of course, I accredit Bill, although I haven't seen him for many years. He might protest, *à la* the NBA's Charles Barkley, that he was not a role model, but to no avail.

The lug-nut incident was forgiven, however, because Bill taught my six-year-old sister Lee Anna a vital element of every child's education, how to blow bubbles with Bazooka bubble gum.

Ditch-Diving and Other Dances

Another Chevy episode occurred on a late December winter night after a Warriors' basketball game that I had played in, with Lee Anna as a cheerleader. The Chevy was carrying us home when a steering knuckle broke. We were traveling the long downhill straight on Fairview Loop, just up from the 180-degree curve at the bottom of the grade. (Lee Anna thinks it was farther along, near the bottom of the hill past Dinkel's farm, but that was another incident.) Suddenly Papa found himself steering a renegade Chevy that swerved and followed its front bumper into a snowbank.

We reconnoitered the scene in the glow of the snow-covered headlights, then traipsed up the road to the Knutson place and presented our sorry selves on their doorstep on the short side of midnight. They were most accommodating as we explained the situation, all of us then commenting on the game. Somehow we got home, and the Chevy was later extracted from the ditch and returned to service.

One winter morning I drove the Chevy to school after it had rained and turned colder. Wet ice covered the gravel roads, so I chained up. For some reason I took the roundabout route of Hyer Road. I drove slowly and the chains chewed along on the ice, loose ends clanking in the fender wells. (The clanking reminded me of my bicycle in Vermont, with cardboard strips that were clamped to the frame and flapped against the spokes. The faster I rode the bike, the faster they flapped.) Eventually I came to the steep hill with the curve at the top where the road led past the Yadon and Reeder places before merging with the Palmer-Wasilla road.

I eased the Chevy around a curve and the hill came into view. I gingerly picked up speed, gained momentum for the climb, and applied minimum accelerator in the ascent, so as not to power out on the grade. Suddenly I saw that a school bus had preceded me, parked on the right shoulder three-quarters of the way up, with no lights flashing and no one in sight. I had a split second to decide: skid to a stop in the ditch, or go for the gold and try to crawl past the bus on the left.

But gold turned to silver, and then to lead—and my feet to clay. I ran out of momentum a little short of the bus. The Chevy slowed to a precarious halt. I tried to hold it in place by braking, but the hill was too steep and the road too icy; I had to try to back down. With the chained wheels locked, I twisted around to see the road behind me as the car and I began a slow slide backward, chains desperately clawing at the ice. A couple of experimental pumps of the brakes proved inadvisable. The car slid down the hill, pirouetting around counter-clockwise. By the time I had ridden it back down the hill, the front end had completed the rotation to face back the way I'd just come, and miracle of miracles, I was still on the road!

So it was a farewell honk of the horn to the school bus, and like the yet-to-come Starship Enterprise, I chugged off on another route to school, to seek out new roads, where few had slid before.

Life Was Good!

A Chevy episode in my senior year occurred on a dark, below-zero winter afternoon. I had planned to drive over to Reeders' to visit Sharon, my girlfriend at the time. It was a forty-mile round trip, but the Chevy had other priorities and refused to start. No amount of battery networking, starter fluid injections, or whacks upside the fenders placated it. Somehow we got word to Cottle's Garage, and they sent a tow truck to start it.

By then evening was overpowering the season's minimal daylight, but I was determined to spend time with Sharon and her folks, so I followed the wrecker into Wasilla. It must be realized that the heater in the Chevy was a barely adequate device for the large interior. I held out for a few miles, but still cold from the efforts to start it I flashed the headlights at the tow truck driver, who obligingly stopped and allowed me and the Chevy to warm up—me in the heater-roaring truck cab with him, and the Chevy idling behind us. After five minutes of blessed warmth, I returned to the helm of the Chevy to proceed once again.

I managed a couple hours' visit with the Reeders before following the Chevy's headlights back home. I was young and in love, and it was a clear, crisp night, fifteen below zero. Speckles of frost sparkled and floated in the roadway ahead of me, the heater did its valiant best, and the engine thrummed reassuringly in the dash-lit interior. Overhead a great array of stars spread their ancient light across the roof of my world like the sheet music on a player piano, each star a crescendo note in a primeval scrolling melody.

Life was good.

Out to Pasture

The years and miles rolled beneath the Chevy, and its many bouts with the homestead drive took their toll. We used it to haul the heavy loads of birch, spruce, and cottonwood logs that our ravenous barrel stove demanded. Papa once jacked it up and contrived a system to drive the portable Sears generator we had at the time, after the generator's motor had conked out. This looked strange but worked after a fashion. It turned out that Papa was drawing on his boyhood experiences. His family had rigged up a similar arrangement with one of their cars to power a woodcutting saw.

We'd been a year on our homestead when the Chevy's motor went *kaput* in '61. I repaired it a couple of summers later and used the Chevy during high school. I conducted self-taught lessons with its inner workings, immersed in details like head gasket, tappets, push rods, rocker arms, manifolds, distributor and points and condenser. This experience served as a prerequisite for years later when I owned a series of two '57 Fords, the first of which I purchased for a hefty $175.00.

The Chevy's tutelage came in handy; for instance, a big cloud of white smoke meant head gasket replacement. At the time, I envied my classmate Dave Bryant's '56 Chevy with a high-performance oil pump. He was taller than I and liked to cruise the streets of Palmer sitting in the driver's seat—absent the seat. A few years later, Pete Polis showed me his '57 Ford retractable hardtop, and I thought, "Now *that's* a cool car!" But during high school, I had to make do with our Chevy.

Dreams of Flying

At one point, while patiently sitting in our front yard on one of its sabbaticals, our Chevy entered the aviation arena. In New Jersey Richard had observed Uncle Frankie flying a model airplane on a clothesline tether, and it had sparked an interest. When he was still young on the homestead, Richard would sit in the Chevy by himself and imagine it was an airplane, pretending he was practicing touch-and-go landings down on the flats below our house. He later earned his private pilot's license, getting part of his training in a Tomahawk with Vern Air at Merrill Field in Anchorage, where Jeff German provided flight instruction. When Richard ran the patterns on his first solo, June 27, 1984, he liked it so

Richard and Peter *on the Harbeson homestead flats where Richard landed his Aeronca Champ, about 1980.*

much he flew five or six patterns instead of the three suggested by Jeff. He took me for a flight in the Tomahawk once and let me taxi on the landing, instructing me to sit on my hands and steer with my feet. And for a few years, he worked at his part-time hobby of building a Christavia Mark IV from blueprints.

Sometimes we heard explosions out on the inlet's broad expanse, which we thought were from shelling practice at Fort Richardson. This caused us to keep an eye on the sky. Once, in April 1961, a wounded "bird"—an Army banana helicopter from Fort Rich, probably a Piasecki H-21—descended into our world.

As it flew across the inlet, the helicopter developed engine trouble and auto-rotated down onto the flats at the edge of the inlet, not far from Frank Smith's small cabin and the old landmark wreck of a boat that may still be there today. We were allowed to crawl through the 'copter, check it out, look at the instruments and cabling. The soldiers set up a tent, and the next day they slung a new engine under another chopper and transported it to the site. They spent two days switching the damaged one out, fired the replacement up, and off they flew into the wild blue yonder.

Richard tells another "bird" story from the early '60s. A fighter jet, possibly a "Six" or F-106 Delta Dart from Elmendorf, performed an illicit tail-stand over the flats and inlet in front of our house. It roared in at a high angle of attack, a hundred feet off the ground, nose up, tail down, waggling and employing its thrust to keep it stable as its speed dropped. It came uncomfortably close to stall speed before it lowered its nose and screamed away up the inlet. "Spectacular!" Richard says. This was front-row entertainment for any homesteader but was especially thrilling for Richard.

Grownup Richard owned a 1946 Aeronca Champ for years and flew family members and others on sightseeing trips. Even Mom, nervous before succumbing to her aviator son's silver tongue, admitted after a flight with him that it had been "kind of fun." Once he met Patty Wagstaff at the Birchwood airport. Patty, before she became the first woman to win the title of U.S. National Aerobatics Champion, an Olympic medalist, and recipient of many other distinguished awards, went up with Richard in his Champ and they did a couple of touch-and-go's. Patty told Richard of the time a set of keys fell into the controls of her plane and she had to fly and land using the rudder and elevator trim tab. Richard later practiced landings using the rudder and trim tab (without dropping his keys)—in case the need arose in his flying. Sometimes Richard treated people to the thrill of "humpty-dumps," a simple maneuver creating brief periods of weightlessness—with prior passenger permission, of course.

Richard used the Champ on many hunting expeditions and flew his son Dooner to Kotzebue in the Champ to visit Richard's wife Dotsy's relatives. He navigated through smoke from forest fires and stopped in villages to buy gas. He had no VOR but flew by checking landmarks on sectional maps, using five-minute tic marks. Some of the lakes on the maps didn't exist anymore, and he had to look for their old depressions on the terrain. The actual flying time up was thirteen hours, and the return was ten, but with the stops it took two days each way. While in Kotzebue, he flew the short hop across Kotzebue Sound to Sheshalik, landing on the spit of land where Dotsy's family has long maintained a camp. He also stopped in Selawik, where I had taught several years earlier, and was welcomed as the long-lost brother of George.

He flew his stepson Brian on hunting trips, and gave rides to Lee Anna's and Jim Barlow's son Bryan, who later got his own private pilot's license. Richard let Lee Anna take the controls on one calm flight, which she said "wore her out." I flew with him to Birchwood, to the Knik Glacier/River area, Palmer and Wasilla, over our homestead, and to the 99's airstrip area to go fishing. This was a gentle introduction to the hundreds of passenger hours I later racked up in small planes during my years of teaching and coaching in rural Alaska villages.

Years after his flights of imagination in the Chevy, Richard landed on the flats below our house in his Champ in the 1980s and 1990s to visit the family and pay his respects to the old car, which had a long dusty-road contrail of its own strung across the United States and Canada and territorial Alaska. Its tires were worn and its paint faded, and we finally parked it out to pasture in our field overlooking Cook Inlet, where it remains to this day. But like the rest of our family, it must have been proud to share in a young homestead boy's coming of age and the fulfillment of his dreams of flight.

The '47 Jeep

IN 1960, WE'D BEEN ON THE HOMESTEAD a few months when Papa rounded up a little buddy for the '54 Chevy—a '47 Jeep. It was originally owned and brought to Anchorage by a Henry Holliday of Rolla, Missouri, who sold it to Joe and Sallie Hyde, who had a home in what is now Settlers Bay. We purchased it from the Hydes. It is said that misery loves company, and the Jeep provided both misery and company. It was a WWII-style Jeep CJ2A with flathead-four engine, high- and low-range 4-wheel drive, and 6-volt electrical system, similar to the Jeeps that General Patton might have stood in when he surveyed the field of battle and reviewed the troops.

The Jeep had two metal pipe-frame "bucket" seats in the front. Behind these, opposing benches ran front to rear, formed by the wheel wells, with a removable rear seat stretched between them. It had two small vacuum-powered wipers that never seemed to master the concept of coordinated rhythm. Usually requiring hand assistance, they performed in fits and starts, stopping altogether at times. The Jeep had acquired a rattletrap homebuilt wooden cab somewhere along the way, and the whole affair was painted robin's-egg blue. It was the worse for wear, but serviceable.

Its toughness and four-by-four talents were much welcomed, but it was a tight fit for a family of seven, which now included our new addition, baby Peter. At the time I thought that Peter had come with the Jeep, that it was a four-wheeled mechanical stork. It wasn't until a few years later that I began to realize that there were other tried and true methods of delivery.

Like all matters homestead the Jeep acquired its own personality. At one point in its tour of duty, I remember running behind it as Papa coaxed it up off the end of our driveway onto the Knik Road. While James Wesley Redington, Joe and Ray Redington's father, watched from his small cabin on the slope above us, I observed the tail pipe spewing unsettling streams of acrid black smoke lit with intermittent flurries of good-sized sparks visible even in the sunlight. This may have been the reason for our using sixty-weight oil in the engine during the summer months. Occasionally I would add a quart from a five-gallon can, and I can still see that thick goo, more mucilaginous than oleaginous, ooze into the filler opening like stale Karo syrup.

Homesteaders in the Headlights

"No matter where you go, there you are." That old saying was true of our family. And getting to where you're going generally involves vehicles, and in those days our homestead vehicles often took us where we *didn't* want to go; yet just the same, there we were. One such story involves our Jeep.

It was Christmas vacation in 1961, and I was a Wasilla High freshman. Ike had given his Farewell Address warning of the military-industrial complex, JFK was the 35th president, the Beatles and Bob Dylan were stirring, and a chimp named Ham had been launched into space. The Peace Corps was a reality, the Bay of Pigs had gone down, Hemingway had killed himself, the Civil Rights Movement was gathering steam, and Roger Maris had hit a record sixty-one home runs. The year itself was a rare upside-down year. We rotated the number 180 degrees and it still read the same: 1961.

Papa had ordered a turkey for the holiday through Teeland's store, so the day before Christmas Eve we prepared to go to Wasilla to collect the bird. Our original Bound-For-Alaska Chevy was awaiting my overhaul efforts, so we looked to the Jeep—and to the outside thermometer. It read an inch below zero.

"C'mon, George," Papa said to me. "It's eight o'clock, starting to get light outside. We better get moving if we're to get the turkey before tomorrow." To my mind, his phrase "starting to get light . . ." spoke of optimism more than reality. But upward and onward, I groaned to myself.

The usual procedure of starting the Jeep, Plan A, was observed. The Jeep resembled a bundled-up Charlie Brown planted in the snowy yard, but we pulled away the blankets and canvas tarp that covered its faded blue hood and cab, removed the catalytic heater from beneath the oil pan, retrieved the battery from our basement warmth and re-installed it, and treated the carburetor with a liberal bracer of starter fluid.

It would be nice to say it cranked right up and we were off, but no, it didn't, and we weren't. On our first attempts, the starter turned the engine over well enough, but it wearied of its task. A dead cell, water in the gas, or plain orneriness—who knows. Plan B: we added HEET, cleaned the points, checked the plugs, assembled a squad of jumper batteries, connected them in a mélange of hookups, kicked the fenders, smacked the hood, promised it high octane, expounded on its ancestry and its future—nothing worked. Alas, Papa's boyhood days of putting corn cobs soaked in gasoline against the block of their old Fordson tractor and lighting them to warm its engine were long past.

By this time it was nearer noon and only a half-inch below zero, and time for Plan C: Go inside for soup and to warm up, and to ponder why we had acquired this turkey of a vehicle.

But if at first you don't succeed. . . . Inlet tides flooded the flats along the base of the bluff at times, and froze into a smooth highway, enabling us to go the back way and avoid most of our driveway's ups and downs. Years later Papa borrowed my '57 Ford and tried to drive the flats highway —against Mom's advice, I might add. The Ford sank in a foot of freezing water, and Papa had to get a wrecker to pull it out before it froze in place. Happily, that was not the case this day, and we proceeded to Plan D: Put the Jeep in gear and push it downhill to the flats in the hope of starting it by popping the clutch. With me at the back and Papa at the driver's door, we both pushed, strained, and slipped until it began rolling. Papa jumped in to do the honors. Miracle of miracles, it started! He kept the Jeep running at the bottom of the hill, waiting for me to skid, tumble, and roll down to join him. My downhill antics were exacerbated by the bunny boots I wore in those days. They were not the inflatable rubber ones of today but were made of felt with smooth, hard soles. They laced partway up the front, and had an attached flap with two buckles that wrapped around the shin. Lightweight, they were by their nature two sizes too big, and slippery to walk in, but I made it to the bottom, clambered into the Jeep, and away we went, careening along our ice highway at a madcap thirty miles per hour, the delicious aroma of roasting turkey already wafting past our noses.

When we approached the curve opposite Frank Smith's cabin in the trees on the far end of the flats, the Jeep slid to a silent halt. Papa and I sat there for a few minutes looking at each other, and meditated on the turn of events. It was one o'clock in an afternoon suffused in vibrant golden sunlight. The day rested clear and cold under a brilliant blue sky, and a heavy hoarfrost coated the birches crowding the bluff. The broad expanse of Cook Inlet stretched before us like a vast azure-domed amphitheater. We sat there, two bit players in a diminutive motor carriage, knowing that darkness would be settling in all too soon. Finally Papa decided on Plan E.

"Let's walk back up to the house, get the generator, and lug it back down to the Jeep," Papa mused. "We can hook up our battery charger and boost the battery."

Our generator was a Sears 3000-watt portable that we used for an hour or two most nights and that had a two-handled carry bar on top. We had purchased it to provide light at night and to help us get our vehicles going, especially since there were no personal days for teachers then and Papa didn't get paid if he didn't make it to school. Lugging the heavy generator three-quarters of a mile through the snow and across the ice and patches of slushy overflow seemed a bit much, but so be it.

Back up to the house we went, back down to the Jeep we returned. We toted the generator awkwardly between us and tried to avoid places where the Jeep had broken through the ice into an inch or two of slush and water. (The bunny boots were not waterproof.) To cut part of a long story short, Plan E failed. By now I was tired of this alphabet stuff, but it was time for Plan F.

"You stay with the Jeep," Papa directed. "I'll short-cut across the flats to the road and hike to the Knik Bar, see if I can round up Bill to give us a tow." (Bill J. owned a store near the bar.) The flats between us and the road formed a quarter-mile-wide bay with a wet marshy area near the road. It was then another quarter-mile along the shore of Knik Lake to the bar.

"Okay," I agreed. "But hurry. I think I'm losing my toes. . . ." The cold didn't seem to affect Papa as much as it did me. Maybe it was his stocky build, or simply because he was more stubborn about it than I. He'd waded in icy water to set traps in New Jersey, but my feet felt as if they were *caught* in traps.

For forty-five minutes I kept the Jeep company and stamped my clod-hopper bunny boots up and down to keep my feet from freezing, tap-dancing and soft-shoeing a path around the Jeep. Finally, Bill's old rig—a dilapidated once-upon-a-time pickup—barreled out of the woods at The Fork and around the point, to halt in front of the Jeep, with Bill and Papa enclosed in its weathered two-by-four and slat-patched frameworks. The cavalry had arrived! Plan F was looking good.

Bill greeted me cheerily with hearty assurances of success. "Hey, there, kid!" he exclaimed. "We'll have this here li'l lady up and runnin' in no time flat!"

Papa and I took Bill's chain and tied it to the Jeep's front bumper while Bill meandered his truck around so we could tie the other end of the chain to its rear. I say meandered because it quickly became apparent to me that Bill had started celebrating ahead of the Magi's arrival. But he was in high neighborly spirits and bringing his own gift to us, so we were appreciative of his help. Soon all was set to go.

"George, you ride with Bill. You watch me and tell him if the Jeep starts, so we can unhook." Papa climbed into the Jeep, adding, "If it won't start, I'll signal and he can drag us back to the house."

It sounded like a plan to me, so I clumped over to Bill's truck and hopped up onto the passenger seat, which wasn't difficult, as there were no doors. Bill reached over and clapped me on the shoulder. "Welcome aboard, kid!" he barked. He slammed the truck into gear, and we bolted down the ice road, dragging the Jeep along behind us like a tin can at the end of a honeymoon string.

I twisted around to watch Papa maneuvering inside the Jeep, and I could see the Jeep's wheels skid and slide several times as he engaged the clutch. As we entered The Fork where the road led into the trees to merge with our drive, he signaled that it was of no use. I hollered at Bill over the truck's engine.

"Bill, the Jeep won't start! We need to stop! Bill? *Bil*..."

But Bill, feeling no pain, was headed for the barn. I scrambled around on the seat as we bounced up the last part of the drive toward the Knik Road. The way I saw it, I could hang on, maybe get thrown out and run over by a fishtailing Jeep, or I could bail before we got rolling too fast.

So I bailed.

I shoved off out of the seat, sailing through the gap where once there'd been a door, narrowly missing the oncoming slats of the truck's sides. The Jeep flew by, and I caught a glimpse of the pale blur that was Papa's face through the frosty windshield. I rolled into the snow and brush, scrambled to my feet as I hit, and brushed the snow from my face. In the meantime, Bill, thinking I had fallen out, jerked the truck to a stop and staggered back to see what had transpired.

"Damn, boy!" he exclaimed. "You was there, and then you wasn't! You okay?"

When he ascertained that I hadn't been run over, and was in fact standing, he sternly lectured me on automotive safety, then ambled, reassured, back to the truck cab and set out again. As the Jeep began to move past me, I wrenched the door open and dived into the front passenger seat. We bounced on up the drive while our generator excitedly hopped around in the back on its little spring feet. As for me, I figured if we were going to die, it might as well be a father-and-son thing.

However, Bill came through in the clutch, so to speak, and we slid to a halt in the bar's parking lot in front of his little store. Bill got out of his truck, said he'd be back in a minute, and went inside. Papa and I waited outside for several minutes, then went in and found Bill draped on a cot, snoring like there was no tomorrow. Plan F? Scuttled. It was true that our outlook had improved; we were now on the Knik Road, but we had gone a mile in the wrong direction. We unhooked the chain and went inside the bar to warm up. Papa and I stood at the window and peered into the deepening dusk at the Jeep sitting morosely in the parking lot, its headlight-and-chrome visage coldly indifferent to our glares.

To emulate Walter Cronkite, the most trusted man in America, I might say, "And that's the way it was . . ." and we trudged on home to warmth and family and supper and left matters for another day. Except that wasn't the way it was. Not yet. Like all homestead sagas, it never ends until it ends, and this one was still a work in progress.

We sat there in the rainbow glow of the bar's neon lights, soaked up the warmth of the room, and watched the red slide lower in the thermometer outside the window. Papa rarely drank, but that day he may have contemplated the array of liquor bottles behind the bar a time or two. Presently the door opened and in walked Phil, a man Papa had worked with on the Alaska Railroad in the summer of 1955. Phil hadn't been celebrating early, and he drove a pickup with doors, and we went to Plan G. We borrowed Bill's chain and towed the Jeep once again until it started. We unhooked, showered Phil with thanks, gave him money for a beer, hopped in the Jeep, and roared off. We took a chance and side-tracked home to drop off the generator and to tell Mom and my brothers and sisters what was up. Then we headed for town again, still hoping to make it before Teeland's store closed.

We zipped along in the Jeep, the welcome sound of road gravel cavorting in the wheel wells. Three or four miles on, halfway up a small rise in the road, the motor coughed and died. Quickly Papa shifted into reverse and popped the clutch as we rolled backward. The wheels stuttered and skidded on the frozen gravel and the flathead-four engine gagged a couple of times, then caught, fired up again, and on we continued, Plan G still holding steady.

A mile or two farther down the Knik Road, on the Wasilla side of the current Settlers Bay, we growled up another rise and the Jeep stalled again. This time the reverse-gear-roll and clutch-pop didn't work and we slid to a stop at the bottom. Papa looked at me, I looked at Papa, and we both cogitated for a while. Papa was well-versed in cogitating, having a master's degree in Advanced Cogitation from Montclair State, and I, a relative neophyte, was learning fast. A very weak Plan H emerged: Maybe if we just sat there for a bit, the Jeep would reconsider and cooperate. Once in a while, it did just that . . .

But it didn't. And that "there you are" thing? Well, ". . . there we were." At least for the moment. And many moments after that.

Without much choice, we watched Plan I lockstep into place. It was six or seven miles of walking in either direction; it was on the late side of five o'clock; it was dark. It was twenty below. By default, we'd wait for somebody to come along—the *deus ex machina* gambit. The gods were bound to notice us sooner or later, so we chopped branches with a hatchet we carried under the seat, gathered dead wood, and built a fire in the ditch near the Jeep. The warmth was welcome, but the snow-dampened wood didn't burn easily, so we coaxed it along from time to time by adding the quarts of motor oil we kept stored in the Jeep. The hours passed: eight o'clock, nine o'clock. The night was clear with only a breath of wind. The burning wood popped and crackled in the cold air, sparks from the fire drifted upward. Firelight flickered on the side of the Jeep. Stars filled the night in their slow rotation in the sky over us, the Jeep, and the nearby treetops.

Papa didn't complain; he never did. At my age, he'd sat under those stars with my grandfather on the family's hard-scrabble farm during the Depression. In his World War II service in the Army Air Communications Squadron in 1945, he'd gazed up at their southern counterparts while bivouacked near airstrips on the beaches of Eniwetok, Saipan and Iwo. Then, years later, he stood with me as the two of us looked up at the Alaskan sky. He was a taciturn man, and spoke little of his boyhood and military service, but that night he pointed out the mythic figures in the sky over our heads and we revisited their strange and wondrous names. Orion the Hunter was a prominent one who has proved to be a constant companion throughout my life, striding across the tundra and wading the Chukchi Sea when I taught in Selawik, Noorvik, and Kivalina, towering over me on the frozen Yukon River between Emmonak and Alakanuk, and even today stepping across Cook Inlet onto the shoulders of Mount Iliamna. That night Papa and I located the Big and Little Dipper, located the North Star Polaris, Orion's Betelgeuse and Rigel, Cassiopeia, the Pleiades or Seven Sisters, Mars, and Venus, as our hours at the side of the road advanced.

Ten o'clock. Papa discussed possible solutions to the Jeep's problems. He also offered a comment or two on improving my basketball skills—he'd been a coach. Keep your head up on your dribble. Expand your court vision. That sort of thing. We stamped our feet, flapped our arms against our sides, performed clumsy jumping jacks in our bulky clothing, gathered additional wood, poured oil, hugged the fire. It had been a long day.

Eleven o'clock.

Suddenly light danced in the treetops toward town. The sound of a motor vehicle grew louder, and a truck loomed over the top of the rise. *Deus* and the *machina* had arrived! Papa and I ran into the road and waved our flashlights at the oncoming rush of lights.

As it drew near, we kept signaling and squinted into the glare. Our shadows dodged on the road behind us, and there we were, standing near the middle of the road: homesteaders in the headlights.

"Will they stop?" I yelled to Papa.

"Of course they will," he replied. And they did.

They were soldiers returning to the Nike Site, the military installation located past Knik, in the Goose Bay area.

"Need help?" they asked.

We explained the situation. A bustle of activity broke out. Plan J took the stage; a retreat, actually. We kicked snow on the fire; they pulled the Jeep; it started, but stalled whenever Papa turned on the headlights. We ruefully informed the soldiers of this.

"Hey, no problem. Use ours," they offered, and we agreed. They drove on the wrong side of the road behind us—or maybe it was us on the wrong side of the road. Barreling along in their bow wave of light, we drove the Jeep in the zigzagging glow of their headlights. They chased the dim red eyes of our taillights while currents of night eddied behind theirs. The stars streaked by overhead. We rounded curves, sped up and down hills and along the straights, until there it was: the entrance to our driveway. On the final stretch before home, we slowed and waved farewell from the darkness that flowed in to surround us as they passed. The snow reflected the starlight and I held a flashlight on the drive in front of the Jeep. Its beam pitched about as we wound our way through the trees, took The Fork onto the flats and its ice highway, growled around the point, and zipped along the base of the bluff. I glanced over my right shoulder and saw the soft nimbus of light in the distant sky over Anchorage. We made our way around the 180-degree curve before O'Brien Creek and powered up the hill to our yard.

When we pulled up, our propane kitchen light cast a soft carpet of welcome through the basement window onto the snow. The door opened and Mom stood back-lit in the doorway, Lee Anna, Richard, Becky, and little Peter the Great gathered together and peering out from behind her. Papa shut the Jeep's engine off.

"Well, tomorrow's another day. Who knows, maybe it'll warm up. We can try again, get the turkey tomorrow," he said. Plan K. Fortunately, Hal Post came by the next day from his homestead in Goose Bay, offered his plan of "I'm Here to Save the Day," and took us to town to pick up the turkey.

But finally arriving back home that night, we climbed out of the Jeep, made our way to Mom and into the basement, into the heat from our

"Peter the Great," *age 15 months, with the Jeep-of-many-jobs on the homestead in 1961.*

barrel stove, and into the warmth of hearts, hearth, and home. In the end, no matter where we'd gone that day, there we were.

A little older, a little wiser.

Homesteaders in the headlights.

Mowing Daze

We used the Jeep when the aging Chevy wasn't up to homestead tasks. Its four-wheel drive and heavier suspension were obvious assets but also trade-offs for its small cargo capacity. In spite of getting on in years, the Jeep was often our little engine that could. The short wheel base was good for use off-driveway, saving us from carrying firewood on our shoulders. We called upon it for more creative tasks, too—for instance, pulling an old single-beam horse-drawn sickle mower. In our explorations we'd found the abandoned mower. It had a five-foot blade assembly that rose from a horizontal cutting position to a vertical angle for traveling. It was old and rusted, with frozen parts and rotted wood, but we restored it to working order. It had a metal seat with openings, mounted on a large, arcing flat spring. Its large metal wheels were devoid of even the remotest suggestion of things pneumatic. But it worked.

It had to be pulled, however, because it was also devoid of things involving combustion. We had no horse or tractor, and Papa may have thought of hitching us to it, but after considering the certain cacophony of complaint, he discarded that notion. We had no other options at hand (except for Bruce the Second and our assorted cats, but Papa had had enough experience with cats—his family's nasty, black-and-white, notch-eared, battle-scarred-and-bitten Sidney in particular). So it fell to the Chevy and the Jeep, and later a '66 Scout, to pull the mower.

Using the Chevy, we mowed the grass and brush along the driveway bordering our field, but its higher gears yanked us in an alarming Keystone Kops manner. The Jeep in four-wheel low was better adapted to the cutting jobs at hand, although perhaps less entertaining to mower operator, car driver, and any spectators drawn by the loud clatter that the mower's oscillating teeth made. The Jeep could idle along at a walking pace or less, oblivious of the lightweight connected to its rear bumper. The mower was impressive when operating; its sickle blades reciprocated from a leisurely pace to an alarmingly rapid staccato almost instantly in its low gear (it did have gears). The chatter and flash of its shark-like teeth made your toes curl. If the blades were sharp, it took down birch saplings.

We mowed the oats planted in our field, the grass and tidal vegetation on the flats, and occasionally the small strip of lawn in front of our house. Locomotion responsibility for these tasks was later handed down to the 1966 International Scout when it arrived.

Beats Shoveling

The Jeep, tastefully accented in rust, performed winter duties as well. It had a Rube Goldberg-type "V" shaped snowplow, almost as wide as the Jeep itself, constructed of heavy metal with strong cross-bracing, which hung on the front bumper courtesy of a couple of heavy-duty brackets and positive thinking. Hydraulics and electric winches would have been effete (and expensive), so it was basically a one-note Charlie when it came to raising and lowering or angling the V-blade. Once in a while, after spring break-up, we endeavored to level the dried-out ruts using the plow-equipped Jeep. Winter snow plowing was easier but took at least two passes to clear a minimum width. When the snowfall wasn't too deep, we chained up, plowed around the house, and pushed a path out to the Knik Road. Some may have mocked the crude set-up, but believe me, faced with hand-to-hand shovel combat with drifts, I'd say mock all you want, because I'd dance with our rusty, trusty blue angel any day.

Later we contrived a drag constructed of a cabled-together lumber/metal plate contraption, not as tall but broader than the plow, with a half-sheet of plywood cut to fit horizontally between the "blades." We tied an old engine block onto this plywood floor for weight and dragged it with the Jeep, and later the Scout, to level the ruts. Rudimentary as it was, it worked well enough for us to keep repairing it.

Waterhole #1

The Jeep also provided a means to haul water, but that too could have unexpected results. We used the universally accepted array of containers for this purpose: two 10-gallon milk cans with plug and umbrella lids, a 30-gallon barrel, and a flock of plastic one-gallon Clorox jugs that numbered anywhere between five and fifteen—depending on how many we had and who was counting. We loaded the lot into the back of the Jeep, sometimes in our laps when the flock propagated, and headed for a spring on the Knik Road, across from where Raymie Redington's place is now.

It was good water, clean and sweet-tasting, and it flowed year-round from a three-inch pipe at several gallons a minute. It may have contained arsenic, often found in water these days, but we drank deeply of it, sometimes straight from the pipe. We plopped the milk cans and barrel under the flow, and filled the plastic jugs one by one. Since we had no insulated rubber gloves, in winter this meant putting your bare hands in the cold water when air temperatures could dip to minus-forty degrees. Somebody, somewhere, had them, but they were not for the likes of us. Besides, Papa chided me for wearing gloves when working on jobs in the cold.

"Take those gloves off. You can't work with gloves on," he'd snort in exasperation. "The water's warmer than the air!" His hands were broad and thick; mine were narrower, with longer fingers. Years later I read that the poet Robert Frost had huge hands. Papa's weren't *that* large, but I thought he was in pretty good company. I didn't mind Papa's philosophy on gloves though, because he didn't insist, expecting that I would learn one day from his example and suggestion. I never did.

At any rate, one late afternoon after school we arrived home in our red Corvair, with the driveway and countryside covered in a sheet of ice from a recent rain and freeze. We failed to make it up the Big Hill and slid down backward. The car jolted to a stop, causing the spare battery on the rear deck to hit the framework. Sparks flew everywhere, acid splashed on the deck (adding to our baking soda costs), and the battery was destroyed. Papa fell twice on the ice as we slithered and crawled the rest of the way to our basement. When we arrived, Mom informed us that our water supply was low, that we had to go to the spring. We loaded the jamboree of empty containers into the chained-up Jeep, and since the main drive was now blocked by the ice-stranded Corvair, we set off down the hill to the flats, which had flooded and frozen into our alternate driveway.

Reaching the spring, we carried the containers to the outlet pipe for filling. I fell on the ice, and Papa fell, too, flat on his back, banging his head. (We had ancient strap-on cleats that we tried wearing, but using them was like skating on nails.) Finally, the Jeep was filled with containers of water, and we headed home. We neared O'Brien Creek, turned the corner, and powered up the hill toward the house. Just short of the top the Jeep's motor quit. Papa noted later that he should have left things well enough alone at that point, but he figured he could start the Jeep by rolling backward. He released the clutch, and the Jeep started, but it continued backward down the hill, quickly gathering speed for thirty feet as Papa pumped the lazy brakes. It abruptly cut a hard ninety-degree turn bass-ackward up over the berm into a stand of small birches and crashed to a halt in the icy snow.

In the back of the Jeep, the entire Clorox family had leaped up to see what was happening. But they were too late. The show was all over, save for the shouting and the sloshing. We exited the Jeep and dragged the surviving containers up the hill through the woods on our hands and knees, grabbing at trees and bushes along the way for assistance.

Finally, in the latter '60s, we had a well drilled near our house and installed new-fangled indoor plumbing. However, we discovered years later that the well water had a high hardness and salinity content and may have contributed to Papa's eventual heart attack. And ye olde spring? Alas, when the Knik Road was straightened and widened, the spring fell victim to the march of progress.

As do we all, sooner or later.

Night Caucus

Amassing firewood to feed our barrel and cook stoves during the winter was a vital but often tedious chore. We hauled and stacked most of it in the summer but supplemented the supply in the winter with a few hours' labor on Saturdays and Sundays as needed. Many a winter afternoon I warmed up for an evening basketball game by cutting and hauling firewood. We waded through the snow, cut down trees, and bucked up deadfall. We carried the lengths of birch, cottonwood, and less frequently spruce on our shoulders—around roots and devil's club, and through the deep snow to the Chevy, Jeep, or Scout parked in the drive.

One serene, below-zero, star-snapping moonlit midnight Papa and I went foraging for wood. It was a spectacularly beautiful night, with Cook Inlet's broad expanse glowing all the way across to the Chugach Mountains. We drove the Jeep to a deadfall halfway out the drive, waded through sixteen inches of powdery snow into the trees and moonshadow, and set to sawing, using the swede saw.

It was one of those special father-and-son slices of life. The two of us didn't talk much; we knelt in the snow and sawed back and forth with the small thin-framed metal saw. Papa had cut wood in his youth with his brothers, a chore rife with accusations of bending the saw or pushing it on the return stroke. If ever there is a way to teach or learn cooperation, it is when two people use a swede saw. Each person must anticipate the other's pull and push and the tenuous slide of the ribbon-like blade's teeth through the wood. The rhythm develops a choreography of its own, similar to that found in sports and dance, and in this case there was the deep-seated psychology of working together for the welfare of our family.

So, hey! All you politicians out there—forget your ad-hocs and photo-ops and grab a swede saw. Get off your fat caucuses and into the woods. It might teach you a thing or two, and we'd all be better off for it.

Mud-Hole Escapade

In the Jeep's time with us, it saw action on roads in the Goose Bay area near the Post homestead. Once or twice we drove to Big Lake via the Burma Road, as people sometimes did, but mostly we traveled the Khyber Pass route just to get to Hal and Joy Post's homestead. Hal's being a good friend of my Uncle Sterne had led to our families gravitating together in Alaska. We often ventured out to their cabin in the woods, as did the Burt Lum family, Ray Haines, and others. On some trips we squeezed a hundred-pound tank of propane into the back of the Jeep and hauled it to the Post cabin, which sounds deceptively more mundane than it was.

One long mud hole in a section of the road near the Jameson or Claus place had dried to form a surface crust. Suspicious of the innocent-looking expanse, we stopped and surveyed the scene. I walked onto the crust and jumped up and down. I sensed a shiver or two and it felt reasonably solid, but I did notice a surface undulation.

"Let's give it a shot," Papa said, and we piled back into the Jeep amid our food and gear. Two options presented themselves. We could ease across slow and sneaky, or we could go hell-bent for leather and be across and gone before any mishap could occur. We chose the second option. The assumption was that proceeding slowly would allow the weight of the Jeep to break through, and that if we went fast enough, we would tread lightly, so to speak. This line of "reasoning" sprang from the belief that if you run fast enough, you can cross a span of water without sinking.

Further on this theory: Years later in the late '80s or early '90s, Roger Bliss and I went to a strange neo-Druid gathering of a couple of hundred people at Big Lake on a hot 4th of July, where we observed go fast/don't sink principle in practice. People—I think they were people, they looked somewhat like people—were driving snow machines on top of the water. From a point on the beach they zoomed to a small islet a hundred yards distant, horsed the machines around, and zoomed back. A raft-like contraption with tripod and hoist floated in the general area to retrieve the riders ending up in the drink. (I suspected some of them had ended up "in the drink" before they got to the water.) Some riders wore helmets, a mystery to me. It may have provided something of a breathing bubble, or a PFD effect—"Personal Flotation Device," that is, not the "Permanent Fund Dividend" so dear to our Alaskan hearts. The general area reeked of oil and exhaust fumes and other more exotic scents, and the crowd was noisily supportive. Each machine exploded in a running start off the beach, screamed out across the water and, if successful, regrouped on the island and headed back, directly at the wildly cheering audience watching from the starting point. Amazingly, most were successful. I figured the attrition rate of the riders and machines to be about twenty percent, so the raft people generally had an easy time of it.

Alaskans. What can I say. And they weren't even homesteaders. Well, maybe a few were. After an hour we departed that planet and went on about our business.

However, all that was yet to come when Papa and I backed up and sped onto that 1960s mud hole. The Jeep gradually slowed as we progressed. Two-thirds of the way across, the left rear began to sink noticeably and the Jeep abruptly halted. We climbed out and saw that the wheel had broken through, with the axle now sitting on the crust. After sounding the depth, we determined that the soup under the crust was approximately ten inches deep. Out came Mr. Handyman, down went its base to firmer ground, up rose the wheel, under went corduroyed logs and branches, down ratcheted the jack, and away we went, the crust rolling up and down in our wake as it settled to await our return.

Push-Start Miracle

Some time after the mud-hole incident, the family again set out in the Jeep to the Post homestead. It was summer, but road conditions still could change almost daily, and secondary roads became increasingly primitive the farther from the main road one traveled. By the time we pulled up in front of the Post cabin, the "road" was down to a narrow bushwhacked trail through the trees. Scattered stumps sawed off at ground level were numerous, and the route retained most of the natural ground cover, but we made it.

When we got ready to leave, the Jeep wouldn't start, despite our jumper-cable pleading. The trail was soft and root-riddled—not the easiest surface for pushing a vehicle—and ended in the trees a mere thirty feet ahead of the front bumper. Having little choice, we decided to push-start it. This usually worked—if we managed the right choke setting and could get up enough speed to turn the engine over. Several of us chased the underfoot goats out of the way and gathered at the rear and sides of the Jeep, with Papa at the driver's side, ready to jump in and perform the starting honors.

It was one-two-three, and *Heave Ho*! The Jeep rocked but didn't budge. Investigation revealed a root blocking a front tire. An axe appeared and the root was dispatched. Again, a mighty *Heave*! Slowly, reluctantly, the Jeep began to roll. A couple of us pushers slipped and fell but scrambled up to push again. The wall of trees in front of the Jeep was now alarmingly close. Papa leaped into the driver's seat, jammed the gear-box into first, and popped the clutch, with barely enough speed to turn the engine over once or twice. But the goddess of Push Starts smiled on us, or just wanted rid of us, because the Jeep sputtered to life.

Papa nursed the engine into a tenuous fast idle and we piled in amid a chorus of "Farewell!" and "So long!" and "Good luck!" and "See ya sittin' alongside the road!" Papa worked the Jeep around to face in the direction of home, and we waved to the Posts as the goats bleated their cloven-footed prayers for our safe journey.

The Little Jeep That Could and Did

Toward the end of the Jeep's tenure with us, five-year-old Peter and big brother Richard rode with Papa as he drove it along the Knik Road. They happened upon some soldiers and an Army six-by-six. This was not unusual, for military travel to and from the Goose Bay Nike Site was a common occurrence. In this instance the big vehicle had stalled and the G.I.'s hadn't been able to get it started again. Papa stopped to see if he could be of assistance, which anyone would have done in those days, especially since soldiers from the site had come to our rescue on the previously related ill-fated Christmas turkey run.

It was probably an M35 series 2.5-ton truck, weighing six or seven tons empty. I imagine it had a 24-volt system, so jump-starting it with our Jeep's 6-volt battery was, well, overly ambitious. It was time to gear down the Jeep and pull-start its giant cousin. Richard says that is just what they did. He says the old Jeep slewed around, tires scrambling desperately for traction on the gravel road, its flathead-four screaming in the mighty effort to get the 6-by up to speed.

"I was really impressed," says Richard. "It amazed me what that little Jeep did. The soldiers were also amazed and glad to be on their way again."

So I guess that goes to show that while there may be rust on the body, there can still be fire in the cylinders.

Maybe there's hope for all of us.

The '61 Corvair

SOON AFTER THE CHRISTMAS TURKEY UNDERTAKING, probably because of it, Papa ventured into the carnival world of automobile dealers—specifically, Hartley Motors in Palmer—and returned home with a 1961 red Corvair Lakewood 700 4-door station wagon—bright red to please Mom, who loved red and had painted our basement door and trim red. The car had an air-cooled, rear-mounted, six-cylinder engine. It came with a Powerglide 2-speed transmission and the ground clearance of a Zamboni. The trunk was in front, so in a collision our groceries would cushion the impact.

It was an odd choice for a homestead vehicle, but perhaps it was a result of too much mud on our brains, and some escapist desires. Regardless, while it was a well-advertised new car, and provided a modicum of comparative comfort and ease, it fell readily into the company in the Harbeson used car lot, and brought its own brand of mischief to the game.

It is true that the rear-mounted engine provided greater traction, but a 4-by-4 it was not. The low ground clearance served up a bone-jarring, high-centering menu of delights. Years later I revisited the low-clearance world when I owned a '65 Sunbeam Tiger sports car with clearance so low that it would scrape bottom on a beer bottle but could top 130 mph on smooth roads. In the Corvair, we tried desperately to ride the driveway's ridges, but it slid into the ruts with a butt-jarring *Wham!* that resonated throughout the engine, the vehicle, and any passengers incarcerated therein. Many anxiety-ridden moments and tête-à-tête's with Mr. Handyman occurred. On one rut-slithering run in our drive, infant Peter slept on the back seat with his head toward the left side of the car, but was flipped around to lie in the opposite direction—all without waking.

Driving through heavier snowfalls sent snow flying up over the low front, creating one-vehicle white-outs, even on clear days—much the same as Charles Schulz's *Peanuts* character Pigpen with dirt and dust. Over its years of service and homestead abuse, the Corvair became something of a "road oiler." Being air-cooled was not helpful either. Fluid leaks vaporized within the catacombs of the engine compartment and the olfactory results were transferred throughout the vehicle via the heater ducts. Its automatic transmission ensured less control over the car's maneuvering in the driveway gauntlet, but its bright red paint glowed cheerily through layers of spattered mud to alert other traffic of our presence when resting on the shoulder of the Knik Road.

Corvair Potpourri

In January of 1962, a year after buying the Corvair, Papa wanted to drive it to a teachers conference in Fairbanks. He asked Clint Thomas' son, Neil, the school bus driver on the Knik Road route the year before, if he wanted to go along for the ride because it was better to have two on such a trip in case of mishap. The temperatures were very low, but it was a chance to get out of Wasilla for a while, so Neil agreed to accompany Papa. Neil says it was a trip that he vividly remembers today.

> We drove the Glenn and Richardson highway route—the Parks highway being built much later. It was cold and snow berms rose above us on the roadsides. We soon encountered an irritated moose blocking the roadway. We played the car and moose game for 30 minutes—backing up, going forward, before getting past the animal, which attacked the car at one point.
>
> The Corvair engine was air-cooled and its heater proved inadequate for the temperatures on the trip so it was cold inside the car, but we made it to Fairbanks. After the conference the two of us headed home. We discovered that weather had closed the road in the Black Rapids area south of Delta, so we took the alternate route to Tok. We stopped at the lodge to eat and warm up, but George left the Corvair running—it was 72 degrees below zero!
>
> When we left Tok and headed for Glennallen it was so cold I knew we were going to freeze to death. The Corvair wouldn't go any faster than thirty miles an hour and George had to continuously scrape ice from the windshield as he drove. I thought the end had come. But the temperature warmed a bit as we traveled south. The car slowly picked up speed, its heater began to make a cautious effort at warming us, and eventually we arrived in Wasilla, glad to be home.

THE CORVAIR SOMETIMES served as a front row seat to street theater. We drove into Cottle's service station in Wasilla for gas one summer day and heard the sound of an engine laboring in an atonal duet with metal screeching on pavement. We watched a beater station wagon approach from Big Lake direction, traveling very slowly. It gradually turned off the highway and limped into the station area, where the driver sat gunning the motor. We strolled to the vehicle to see what was what. The driver shut down his engine, staggered from the car, and regaled us with his breath and a tale of having a flat somewhere to the north—near the Big Lake "Y," he claimed—and driving all the way to Wasilla on it.

The station wagon had a definite lean to the right rear, so we checked it out. No tire was in evidence, and the metal rim had been ground down considerably. It was then we noticed a groove in the pavement that trailed from the unfortunate wheel in a long "S" curve out onto the highway and north toward Big Lake.

This no doubt brought a sense of late '20s childhood nostalgia to Papa, of his family's first car in New Jersey: a Chevy station wagon with a wood body, isinglass curtains, and clincher tires. Flat tires were common in the 1920s, and driving for miles on the rims occasionally a necessity, but usually on unpaved roads. Papa and his brothers once drove wooden wedges between an oversize tire and its clincher rim on a truck they owned and managed to drive home. At any rate, we thanked the Man From Big Lake for the show, pumped our gas, and scurried away, contemplating once again the wondrous relationships of man and machine.

Often, when men and machines interact in Alaska, there are moose roaming the roads. The Corvair had a low profile, so hitting a moose head-on would have provided a front-row seat to some serious nasty. One snow-falling-on-birches night, Richard and I rode with Papa to a school activity. A mile on the Knik side of the future Settlers Bay, a cow and calf burst out of a bank of trees and plunged across the road. The Corvair went skidding between them. Their dark bulk loomed over us on both sides as we passed, and a headlight rim clipped the cow's hind leg, bending a piece of chrome trim. We stopped and searched briefly, but the two animals had disappeared into the night and falling snow. We reported the incident and found out later that the cow's leg had been broken and the animal had been put down.

Another close call came one dim winter afternoon when we were headed up the hill below the Girl Scout Camp road, on the way to playing basketball. I was driving the Corvair when a moose leaped into the road in front of us. I slammed on the brakes and the Corvair alley-ooped a complete 360 and ended up on the right shoulder of the road, facing in the same direction that we'd been traveling: no contact, no moose to be seen.

The Corvair's Powerglide transmission was controlled on the dash by push buttons (or maybe a small lever) and it was hard to tell if it was in gear when the engine was idling with the parking brake applied. We stopped by Coghlans one day and went inside—"just for five or ten minutes." We ended up staying longer, which is not surprising, considering it was the Coghlans, but Papa had left the engine idling with the transmission in gear. Our visit lengthened before we discovered this. Richard and I agree that the Corvair never was quite the same after that.

In the years the Corvair put up with us, we took it to Hartley Motors in Palmer a time or two when it ailed. When its engine sputtered and missed and complained of a power deficit, we would drive to Hartley's, park along the side of their building, and proceed inside to regale their mechanics with our tale of woe. They offered their sympathy and took the car for a ride to get a first-hand impression of the trouble. Of course, when a mechanic started the car and drove it around town, the Corvair donned its Sunday-Go-To-Meetin' behavior and ran as contritely as could be. Confounded, we expressed our puzzlement, offered our apologies for wasting their time, and piled back into the car and headed for home. The Corvair ran fine for a few miles, then resumed its cantankerous ways. On one such occasion we immediately turned around and drove back to Hartley's, only to have the same scene replayed.

Corvair Icecapades
We often rode to school in the Corvair with Papa, instead of taking the long bus ride. One frosty below-zero morning the Corvair sailed along, its heater keeping us relatively warm and smoky, and we hadn't hit any moose. Things were going well. When we reached the site where in later years the Knik Knack Mud Shack drive joined the road, we came upon a large puddle, a small pond actually, thirty feet across, that had covered the

road and then frozen. No problem: We'd drive across and continue on our merry moose-counting way. Something looked amiss, however.

We stopped at the edge and reconnoitered the scene. The surface of the puddle had been broken into large, floating cakes of ice, either by the school bus on its outbound run or by a Nike Site vehicle.

"What do you think, Pop?" I asked anxiously. "We can make it, right?" I wanted to get to school for basketball practice and the before-school/lunch-time shooting around.

"I think so," Papa answered, taking measure of the puddle's depth. Chunks of ice two inches thick lay strewn in a broken watery path down the center of the expanse.

"Oh, boy!" exclaimed young Richard, always one for thrills and chills. Lee Anna sensed impending doom but said little. Young Peter at home with Mom may have felt a cold draft.

"But we better get a run at it," Papa decided, and that's what we did.

We sat on the edge of our seats, hung on to whatever came to hand, and entered the ice-tossed sea at thirty miles an hour, a crimson four-wheeled miniature Titanic pushing a bow wave before it. Things went well in the first second or two, except for some loss of momentum and an odd floating sensation, but our speed dropped alarmingly. The engine revved and the tires spun, but the right rear one developed a thumping noise, and we came to a dead halt halfway across.

"This can't be good," someone stated.

"What the heck happened?" asked someone else. I looked at Papa. He looked at me. Lee Anna and Richard looked at us. We all looked out the windows at the water surrounding us, then rolled down our windows and peered down to where the water and ice bumped against the bottom of the doors.

"That's odd," Papa mused. "If I didn't know better, I'd say we have a flat."

"What do we do now?" we asked our captain.

After a moment, Papa commanded, "Don't open the doors. Roll down your windows. We'll have to wade ashore."

And that is what we did.

Papa put on a pair of calf-high galoshes (yes, galoshes—big buckles and all) that we had with us and Richard and Lee Anna climbed through their windows onto his back and shoulders to be toted ashore, while I climbed out and carefully waded ashore in my water-resistant Sorel-style boots, the tops barely above the water level.

We stomped our feet to stay warm, and stared at the red island in the middle of the puddle for ten minutes before a truck came along. Papa waded back out, reached down into the frigid water (yes, without gloves) and tied a rope to the Corvair's back bumper bracket. Out the red lady came, dripping icy defiance. The truck pulled it to the side of the road as the school bus drove up. The driver, my classmate Barbara Kelton's father, Claude, swung the bus door open and looked down at us.

"Can we help?" he asked, and we piled into the bus's warmth and everyone's questions to ride the rest of the way to school. After school we took the bus home and walked our driveway. The next day Papa and I took an ancient blowtorch, which burned gasoline or Blazo, and drove the Jeep to the Corvair. We changed the flat, thawed the wheel bearings, and met Cottle's tow truck. The Corvair was towed to their service station, dried out and checked over, and we picked it up a day later, no apparent damage done.

To this day some forty-five years later, even though the road upgrade has bypassed and obliterated the actual layout, whenever I drive by that area I envision those two days and shake my head, marveling that such events of my youth and I still meet like old friends passing along the way.

The Missing Mouse

Richard, when in junior high, captured a house mouse or a small vole on one of his exploratory patrols. Surprisingly, Mom would have none of his keeping it in a box in our basement. Richard then went to Papa and requested the use of the Corvair as substitute small mammal storage, and Papa agreed . . . or maybe not. Regardless, *mus musculus* ended up spending a night in the Corvair Motor Inn, enclosed in a cardboard box on the rear seat, car doors shut, windows up.

The next morning Richard went to retrieve his whiskered prize, but lo and behold, the furry little Houdini had checked out early. *Mus* was nowhere to be found, not in the box, not under the seats, not under the dash, not in the glove box, not under the sun visors, not in the ashtray. Nowhere. It was the *Mary Celeste* all over again. The bits of cheese and jar lid of water were in the box, the comfy cloth bed was still warm. But no mouse. So Richard, not missing a beat, moved on to other enterprises, and that was the last of *mus*.

Except for—with a nod to the noted Paul Harvey, but without the commercials—the rest of the story. Years later, Richard called the Corvair out of retirement by ordering a replacement engine from J.C. Whitney. The engine arrived, complete with clinging remnants of grass and sod, no doubt having been salvaged from another veteran vehicle. Richard pulled the original motor out, and *Sacre Bleu*! There between the aluminum cylinders lay the mummified remains of his old friend *mus*. It had escaped the box and fled through the grill of a heater duct and as far back as it could go to its waiting "*mus*oleum." Where, I might add, unbeknownst to us passengers, it had become part of the fumes emanating from the Corvair's heater over its years of service.

Richard eventually had his fill of the Corvair. He then took up with Volkswagens, first a Beetle or two and then a microbus. One day when he was a junior in high school, he and the white Beetle he'd bought from Daryl Smith, with its J.C. Whitney standard American rim adapters and tires, disappeared down the hill past our house to the flats—off-roading with a two-wheelin' Bug. An hour later he showed up at the house and said he needed help. Papa, Peter, and I followed him to the VW. He'd gone onto the flats, up into the woods to ford O'Brien Creek, around the pond, then back onto the flats and up a low slope into the trees. We arrived to see the Bug clamped between two small birches. We pulled on the trees to separate them enough for Richard to back out of their grip, and off he zoomed for the flats once more.

But the Corvair was just a Corvair, when it wasn't trying to be an ice breaker or snowplow or mudder. It carried us faithfully back and forth to school; on a basketball trip or two; through my high school prom and graduation nights; and on the round trip for Papa, Mom, Becky, and me to my UAF graduation. It was eventually sold to Bob Lucas, who owned an automotive business on Lucas Road, west of Wasilla.

Hal Post's '47 Ford Flatbed

A REGULAR PLAYER ON THE HARBESON lot in the '60s was Hal Post's 1947 Ford ton-and-a-half flathead V-8 stake bed truck. It was dark green with a vertical grill and faded ivory trim and had a four-speed tranny and duals. The duals proved useful to us and to Hal on more than one occasion. We sometimes removed one of the tires, tied a cable to the tire mount, and winched the truck out of whatever difficulty we had encountered. Cables were tricky, though—they could snap and do unpleasant things to one's body. I was always wary around such efforts because I'd seen a cable break. If the rear end mired down, shoving a sapling between the duals would cause it to lift out. Hal loaned the Ford to us occasionally and we ended up owning title to it, but he would still stop by to drive it to and from the Post homestead in the Goose Bay area.

One time Hal came by and borrowed it from us borrowers to help seed his and Burt Lum's cleared homestead land of twenty acres each. They also borrowed eleven-year-old Richard, with my parents' permission, at 0% interest (other than feeding him, which could be considerable). At the Post residence, Hal started the truck in neutral, pointed it toward the far end of the field, and set Richard in the driver's seat.

"Richard, keep it aimed straight at the far end of the field. When you get to the end, turn the key off," instructed Hal. "Burt and I will be sitting on the back of the bed scattering seed."

"What about shifting, brakes, things like that?" asked Richard, nervously trying to figure out if he could see the path ahead better by stretching up to peer over the top of the steering wheel or leaning off to the side to look over the dash.

"Don't worry about that," Hal answered. "It'll drive itself." Hal put the truck in low gear and ran around to hop up and join Burt, who was already grinding away with a seeder.

And it did drive itself. At the end of the run, Richard turned the key off and the truck stopped. Hal then turned the truck around for a new run back the other way, turned the wheel over to Richard, and put it in gear. Across the field they went once again, Richard steering mostly straight and true on one of life's many unexpected paths.

Much of the time Hal's Ford sat at the edge of our field, performing sentinel and bird perch duty, but in the early '60s it transported the milled cottonwood logs and rough spruce rafters and beams that we used to build our house. The eight-inch-diameter cottonwood logs came from a small mill situated on the hill that rose out of Palmer on the Palmer-Wasilla Highway. The mill utilized a lathe to round the logs, which were heavy when wet but almost featherweight when dry. We loaded the truck with logs, some projecting considerably past the rear of the bed, then pulled onto the highway and headed to Wasilla and home, Papa driving and me riding shotgun. Soon I noticed he was having minor difficulty with the steering wheel going up the steeper hills.

"Something wrong with the steering?" I asked with growing concern. It was a warm summer day, but staging another broken-down-along-the-roadside drama definitely did not appeal to me.

"Strange," he muttered, and turned the steering wheel slowly back and forth. There seemed to be a disconnect between the wheel in his hands and the wheels on the front of the truck. "I wonder if there's something wrong with the shocks...."

The front end of the truck swayed and actually seemed to float, bouncing gently up and down as we drove along at forty miles per hour.

"The wheels are coming off the ground," he observed, as the front end drifted lazily into the air, like popping a wheelie in slow motion.

We approached the top of the rise and the front end drifted back down to caress the road with a soft thump, then bounced up forcefully, accompanied by an unnerving scraping from the rear. I twisted around and peered through the rear window, envisioning a nightmare of logs spilling across the road into any traffic that might come along behind us.

"I think the logs are a little too long, and we're riding a teeter-totter," Papa said, grinning. "Gettin' a little 'tippage' here." I saw the logs repositioning themselves on the bed, jockeying for alignment.

I jounced downwards on the seat, trying to add weight to the front end.

"Do you think this'll help?" I asked, only half kidding. I knew the physics didn't add up, but anything for the cause. Papa chuckled and jounced a little himself. He hung onto the steering wheel, steering the truck back on course when the front wheels dipped to the road.

"Why not? Can't hurt," he agreed. "You'll have to jounce harder, though," he said. "You're not jouncing heavy enough."

We progressed over the rise, us jouncing and the wheels dipping while I watched the load, but the logs had settled down and we arrived home without incident. We even surmounted the hills of our driveway, despite the rear end of the logs dragging on the ground and the truck front end rising up to look at the scenery.

Richard Gets Run Over

On November 3, 1963, ten-year-old Richard became the subject of a family trauma involving the Ford truck. It was one of those damp, dark days when near-melting ice and snow cast a pall over a person's mood. We had run out of gas with the Ford truck on Knik Road near what is now Settlers Bay, and we stood around on the edge of the narrow gravel road debating what to do. I stood near the front of the truck, and Papa and Richard were in the ditch at the rear.

As we discussed courses of action, Ed Carney approached from Knik in his beater pickup and swung out to go around the Ford. At this point we and Ed saw another vehicle coming from the Wasilla direction. Papa waved and tried to get the other car to stop, but it kept coming. There wasn't room for three vehicles on the road, so Ed swerved into the ditch behind the Ford to avoid a head-on with the oncoming car. Unfortunately, that was where Papa and Richard were standing. Richard remembers it well.

> Papa had me stand out of the way in the ditch when we first ran out of gas, but I saw the pickup coming at us. I ran up toward the tree line in my slick-soled bunny boots, and then back toward Posts' truck, trying to get out of the way. Papa stepped toward me and tried to pull me from the path of Ed's pickup, but he missed, and he himself barely avoided being hit. Ed's right front fender sent me flying spread-eagled into the ditch. Then the pickup rolled backwards over where I was lying in the "V" of the ditch—the "V" saving me from worse injury. As I lay there, I saw the muffler and rear axle pass overhead in slow motion, and then the right front tire ran over my right leg, snapping the femur.

> It was like my life passed before my eyes. I wasn't very old, and it sounds corny, but it was true. When everyone came over to me, my leg hurt like a sledge hammer was hitting it. I went into shock and I felt like I was burning up while the others covered me with coats.

> ⁃ ⁃

ED'S TRUCK CAME to a stop, he jumped out, and we all scrambled over to Richard. By then the elderly couple in the other car also had stopped.

When we took Richard to the Palmer Hospital, Dr. Hume, our family doctor, was out of town, so Dr. Brown set Richard's leg, but problems resulted with the setting or casting. Two weeks later the cast had to be taken off, the leg re-broken and reset, and a new cast installed, as Richard ruefully remembers.

> They said I would feel no pain, gave me a shot which made me drowsy, and took me into the operating room. Even with the shot, it seemed like my eyeballs bulged out of my sockets from the pain. They tried several times to set it, but couldn't seem to get it right. They said I had healed too fast. Finally, they put me in traction, like in the comic books or movies, with my leg up in the air with a weight hanging on it. They discovered I was allergic to the tape when I started to get blisters the size of silver dollars on my leg.

> While I was in the hospital, I was just a country kid from Sunny Knik and didn't know about bed pans. They told me to ring the buzzer when the urge struck, but I was totally embarrassed to do that. So after three days of increasing discomfort, I finally grabbed the button and held it down until they arrived with a bed pan.

> The nurse then said, "Hey, you're not going to the bathroom enough. Here, take these pills." The pills must have been Ex-Lax, because I was pretty busy after that.

> ⁃ ⁃

AT THE TIME we still lived in our flat-roofed basement, still hauled water, still heated with wood, and still had no electricity except for the intermittent portable generator. Richard endured several months of recovery encased in a waist-high plaster of paris body cast, with a broomstick rod connecting the two legs. Casts today are considerably lighter in weight, but just the weight of Richard's cast caused aggravation. It was especially difficult for him, for he was such a physically active kid. His five weeks of bedridden immobility and associated problems included the use of a straightened coat hanger to reach inside the cast to scratch the almost unbearable itching of his leg. Papa got a hospital bed for him, which allowed him to sit up more comfortably. The accident resulted in Richard's right leg being one inch shorter, requiring him to wear a shoe lift for the rest of his life. He was given the option of cutting the leg bone and lengthening it by growing bone between the cut ends, but having already undergone the earlier re-breaking, Richard understandably chose not to go that route.

The concern and support of our friends and neighbors was appreciated and helped to ease the strain on our family. Richard recalls a time in the hospital when two of his friends, Kathy Kalmbach and Alison Betts, brought him a Revell model car kit of a red Model T Ford, which he greatly appreciated because it gave him something interesting to do to fill the long hours. The accident surely was a source of anguish for Ed, and it proved especially hard on Papa and Mom, but it served in the long run to strengthen our family ties, and things worked out for the best, considering. Richard says that automotive insurance paid most of the bills, a total of $86,000, with a $1,500 no-lawsuit payment for him to attend a year of college, which he later did at the University of Alaska in Fairbanks. Kids are remarkably resilient, but such trials when young can lead to lifelong problems. Richard has avoided those pitfalls. He has led a very active life and has been an easy-going, positive and caring person, rarely complaining and always ready with a helping hand—a source of strength and compassion in our family, for which the rest of us thank him very much.

As for the '47 truck? It continued to be of use to us and the Posts, and even Richard drove it at times, having grown more than tall enough to see over the steering wheel.

The '66 Scout and More Tippage

I DEPARTED HOME IN THE FALL OF 1965 for the university in Fairbanks to take up a curriculum of intramural basketball, work-study poker, beer-and-pizza seminars at the King's Cup, field trips to Gold Hill's liquor store, and a double major of English and Education. This was when the next vehicle in line to join us Harbeson homesteaders and our wacky machines rolled into the yard—a 1966 International Scout that Papa bought brand new in late fall. Champagne Gold with a white top, it was basically a metal box with few of the cushioned amenities of the Corvair. Bigger than our old Jeep, it was still on the small side, especially when compared to today's in-your-face standards. It had four hardworking cylinders, substantial ground clearance, and impressive four-wheel drive capabilities, particularly in four-wheel low with chains all around. Being new, it was treated with some care—but soon was churning trails through seriously deep driveway snow or mud, for that is why we needed it.

I returned home from UAF on the train to Wasilla for Christmas vacation that year. The Scout was our only reliable vehicle, but Papa generously allowed me to use it to go on a date. My snowy evening travel to and fro passed without misadventure and at eleven o'clock I was a minute from home. I cruised up and down the hills of our snow-narrowed driveway and had reached the bottom of the dip between The Big Hill and The Hill After the Big Hill when snow snagged the Scout's right front wheel. No big deal. Except that it was the bluff side and one of the Drop Off spots along the drive, with only three feet of deep-snow shoulder before the descent into the trees on the slope.

I hit the brakes and stopped before going farther over the edge, then climbed out to set the hub on the driver's side and climb down over the bluff edge into the snow to engage the other hub. I got back inside, dropped the Scout into low reverse and tried to back out, but the snow showed a stubborn reluctance to let go of the bluff-side wheel. After some careful jockeying back and forth I began to feel the uncomfortable sensation of . . . tippage.

This gave me reason to pause, in light of the time Al Rousey had snow-plowed the drive with his small open-top dozer. He had gone over the edge backward and slid down the slope. Somehow he managed to make it to the bottom without flipping the dozer over on top of him and immediately charged back up to continue plowing. Brave little Scout though it was, I decided to walk my red-faced self the rest of the way to the house and get help.

The following morning, Papa, Richard, and I coaxed the old Jeep into life, snaked our way around the Scout, and hooked up a chain to the rear bumper. With the well-instructed Richard steering and me pushing at the front, we proceeded to try to work the Scout out of harm's way. However, a tug of war ensued between us and the bluff-side snow. Maneuvering room was limited, so when Papa and the Jeep pulled, the Scout's left rear tire and bumper rose alarmingly into the air, tipping the vehicle further toward the drop off. I quit pushing on the front end to quickly run back and leap onto the left side of the bumper, concentrating on making myself weigh five hundred pounds—and trying to convince the Scout of that. I calculate I must have attained three hundred pounds worth of wishful thinking, because the snow released its grip and the Scout slowly teetered back onto the drive. We were safely back home in a few minutes, none the worse for wear, except for the smirk on the Scout's grill and another gray hair on Papa's head.

Asparagus? In Alaska?

Remnants of the hopes, dreams, and toil of others revealed themselves to us in the land around our homestead. In our hunting and other explorations, we occasionally stumbled onto long-grown-over house pits. As the sun rose one September morning, I stood in a small four-foot-deep outline of such an excavation, the original structure long disintegrated. Faint tendrils of those unknown lives seemed to dissipate in the pockets of low-lying mist scattered among the fall birches. I envisioned the long-vanished inhabitants looking forward as I stood there looking back, our lives joined in the traces of mist. Their endeavors had become part of our endeavors.

One remnant was the abandoned sickle mower we'd found near O'Brien Creek. I remember climbing onto the mower's broad rusted seat and wondering who, decades before, had warmed that cold metal, whose hands had gripped and guided its levers, whose eyes had calculated the height and sharpness of its chattering blades. But such musings were cast

Lug Nut Theater

TEAMWORK, JULY 1972: *Peter beside the 1966 International Scout, George Jr. driving, George Sr. on the salvaged mower.*

aside when the Scout jerked me and the mower forward into action, and practical considerations like staying aboard and managing a reasonable facsimile of an evenly mowed trail took precedence.

Another relic of a bygone era was a plow similar to the ones Papa's family had used on their farm. It was a walk-behind, horse-drawn single bottom steel-beam plow, although the term "walk" was woefully inadequate for the stumbling, scrambling, arm-wrenching effort required to follow the insistence of the mechanical horse called Scout. The plow had one broad moldboard on its right side that would lay the ground over to create a wide furrow. When the speed of the Scout, or our other horse-imitating vehicles, increased, so did the flow of the sod over the blade, and the speed of our scrabbling feet. Attention had to be paid to foot placement, plow guidance, and draft, and fun was had by all: the hapless soul behind the plow, the mirth-filled Scout driver, and bystanders drawn to the scene by the commotion.

Papa, raised on that New Jersey farm, retained a passion for gardening. He grew vegetables in a large plot and maintained a spacious greenhouse, and he once grew "square" tomatoes developed by the Japanese to better fit into shipping containers. He planted rows of strawberry and raspberry plants. Uncle Davis, Aunt Evelyn, and our cousins came to visit and brought Concord grape cuttings for him to try, but these froze out during the ensuing winter. At one point, as a matter of curiosity or as a means to help fulfill the homestead requirement of clearing and planting a certain percentage of the acreage, Papa decided we'd try plowing up a portion of the flats below the house and plant asparagus. It seemed an odd choice to me, but the prehistoric-looking plant grew in salty soil, and the flats were salty. So we gathered up the crew, the Scout, the plow, and down to the flats we went.

The Pat and May Carter family owned the parcel adjacent to our homestead, and Pat Carney, an Alaska state legislator for several years, had mowed the grass and other plants growing on our and the Carters' portion of the flats to feed his cows. The cows loved it, perhaps due to the salt. But plowing and tilling and cultivating the dense, damp, silt-laden ground proved to be daunting. The sod flowed and flopped ponderously beside the broad furrows as Papa and I and Richard took turns driving and hanging onto the handles of the plow. Relation of power to load?

Up-pull, down-pull? Heck, we just chained the hitch end of the beam to the Scout's rear bumper and plowed away. After struggling along for a time, we had two one-hundred-foot long rows. When we stopped for a break, Papa discovered to his staid embarrassment that his false teeth, which had always given him discomfort and which he had stashed in his shirt pocket upon our commencing to plow, had gone AWOL.

We immediately conducted a door-to-door search of the Scout, but the wayward teeth were nowhere to be found, so we began heaving the long slabs of turned-over earth back into the furrows, working our way to the starting point, no doubt recreating a scene similar to that of Van Gogh's "Peat Field" painting. Finally, with the Scout and plow patiently biding time, we rolled over the slab at the beginning and there were the teeth, whitely grinning up at us. We exhumed them and, although soiled, they were evidently none the worse for their brief, albeit intimidating, interment.

It was at that moment that we laid our asparagus plans to rest, tucked away in the family file labeled "Misbegotten Dreams." We kids gave off a collective aura of relief. The prodigal set of false choppers was rinsed in the creek and took up residence once again in Papa's shirt pocket.

Attempting to plant asparagus on the flats may have been a waste of time, even foolish, but young Richard and I had had the opportunity to toil behind an old-time plow, to pull it with a vehicle from our own era, and to participate in one of Papa's enterprises. I wish he were here today to share in the memory he gave us.

Scouting the Power Line

In the mid-1960s the Matanuska Electric Association quoted us a stiff price to run the power to our place, being that we had the only residence in the projected area and thus no neighbors to share the cost. Eventually it was established that we could save money if we cleared the line ourselves. It was half a mile straight through the woods to the Redington compound, the nearest source of power. This distance included three good-size hills. The cost under this arrangement was affordable for us, so Papa put in a bid that MEA accepted for the summer of 1964.

Papa, Richard (in eighth grade), and I (a senior) headed into the woods in the direction of the line, following MEA's flagging. Since this was a considerable job, Papa hired Ed Carney and Associates, with Ed's young son Mike and Ed's teenage brother David, to assist us. We cleared a wide swath, brushing and bucking the birch, spruce, and cottonwood into ten-foot lengths, which we stacked along the edges for later retrieval. It was an honest day's work every day for a good part of the summer. We made do at first with our Jeep and Ed's old Chevy pickup, except for the time its left front king pin or ball joint gave way and it collapsed, and Ed had to administer first aid. When we acquired the Scout, we used that. We cut up the ten-foot sections, loaded the Scout to the roof, and hauled the wood back to the house where we cut and stacked it for firewood.

Eventually the Scout labored its way to retirement in our field, where it overlooked the trails of its glory years until Mom had Richard sell it for parts to mechanic Mike Strang on Knik Road. Even as its dented body rusted, its motor still valiantly rose to an occasional work order.

Miles to Go

PAPA BOUGHT SEVERAL VEHICLES AFTER the Scout. One was a used blue '67 Impala with 37,000 miles. Once in the early 1970s, with Peter and Richard on board, Papa was driving along the Palmer-Wasilla Highway where the road went by the Patrick house. They encountered a car going the opposite way, each vehicle moving about fifty miles an hour, when the lug nuts on the left front tire of the oncoming car came off, flew through the air and sprayed across the Impala's windshield like machine gun bullets. No injuries resulted, but the windshield was a total loss.

Another Impala memory for Richard was driving past the Settlers Bay area once when the engine was running rough, misfiring, and some bikers—maybe The Brothers—blocked the road. Papa stopped and the bikers tossed a Frisbee back and forth over the car and looked at Papa and young Richard, inviting a challenge. But Papa patiently sat there and waited, and the bikers backed off and waved them on.

At one point Papa tied the Impala's choke open and got higher mileage out of it—nineteen miles per gallon—than any of our other cars, keeping in mind that roads had improved. The Impala lasted several years, until April of 1975, when Papa and Mom went to visit Lee and Bea Turner on Fishhook Road. Mom—no doubt reviewing our previous automotive history—had been predicting that the Impala would break down, but Papa said, "No, I would even be willing to start down the Alcan with it."

They left Turners' and had gotten ten miles down the road toward Palmer when a piston went. Papa called Bob Lucas for wrecker assistance. Bob sent one of his young sons, who lifted and attached the Impala's rear end to the wrecker, but found that he had no tie for the steering wheel. In the interest of progress and cab space, Papa sat in the Impala to hold the steering wheel straight. Lucas's boy hopped in the wrecker with Mom in the passenger seat and took off, wasting no time going down the road. Mom, not liking the looks of things, said the exhaust fumes were so thick in the cab she could hardly breathe.

Papa wrote later: "There I was, being dragged down the road backwards at sixty miles an hour and looking through the windshield at the cars following us. I don't think I've ever been in a weirder situation." Papa was not prone to exaggeration, but in light of his many unusual experiences I would say things were just par for the course.

In May that year, Papa bought a new blue '75 Datsun 710, which went 87,000 miles in four years. Later came a tiny white '67 Datsun 1300 pickup that we bought used from Turners and that Becky drove to high school in 1974. It wouldn't start one afternoon, so Papa pulled it and Becky around and around the school parking lot with the Impala to get it started.

"It had carburetor problems," Becky reports. "Papa told me what to do to try to get it running again. When it wouldn't start, he always had me drain the little float, put a dime in there and screw it back up, and that usually got it going."

There you have it—the Harbeson sure-fire method for starting old Datsuns, interpreted by Becky. When the '67 pickup's motor went, Peter and our cousin Jim Marshall, visiting from New Jersey, rebuilt it, but it went out again on its first trip to town.

Some of our later experiences happened on two wheels rather than four. A standout for me occurred when I was home from college one summer and Stephen Ede borrowed Terry Toomey's well-used black Honda 350 motorcycle and rode it to our homestead. Richard rode it out to the end of the drive, unexpectedly meeting one of the occasional inquisitive strangers driving in to see what was to be seen. He managed to avoid a collision but laid the bike over on its side, with no damage to the bike. When he returned to the driveway between the front of our house and the edge of the bluff, I donned the black Bell helmet and hopped on, ready for my first ride on a mid-size bike, a step up from our Honda 70. I figured out the shift pattern and shifted into first, then gave it gas, but the throttle proved to be more sensitive than I had reckoned on. The machine jerked forward, causing me to slide backward, which in turn spun my grip on the throttle even more, which in turn sent the bike into a bit of a wheelie, throwing a rooster tail of dirt and gravel backward from the rear tire. This sent me and the bike on a very short trip toward the bluff, and tossed me into the air to fly head first over the edge. The bike declined to follow. I sailed through the air upside down, totally relaxed, very calmly thinking to myself, "Oh, $#?%!" as I disappeared from their sight and landed in the brush unhurt, but with dented dignity.

This in turn, after some momentary concern, caused great merriment among those watching. Mom, looking through the front window, was not one of the ones amused, at least not at the time. "Mom was mad because Richard was laughing," Lee Anna says, laughing still. ("I wasn't laughing," Richard denies. "I was saying, 'That's *fantastic!* That's *spectacular!*' and, 'My god, that's the most Evel Knievel thing I ever saw!' I was awed. I didn't know how George did that.")

"Well, *that* was different," I thought as I climbed up out of the trees back onto the drive. "I have to try that again—without the detour." Which I did, this time without aerobatics. I rode the bike out and back on the drive and was hooked on motorcycles, later owning two of my own. Years after Papa passed away I read his notes on his own childhood riding days: "I was a small boy in the '20s when I first learned to ride a bicycle. I borrowed Jimmy Conway's one day and set out to ride. The bike and I got to wobbling and I careened down their lawn, flew into the peach orchard, and crashed into one of the peach trees."

There have been many vehicular members of the family across our homestead years and beyond, and many of them, per tradition and economics, "experienced" or "pre-owned," as they say these days. Chevrolet, Impala, Datsun, Subaru, Volkswagen, Dodge Superbee, Land Cruiser, Ford, LeMans, Fiat, Toyota, Nissan, Sunbeam Tiger—the list goes on. (George Gore, the neighbor who had served as a witness for our homestead application, drove a DKW, but we never had one of those.) Alaska life then, for better or worse, was a close integration of people and machines with the land, and even today if one searches the brushy nooks and overgrown yards, the backwoods and tundra, there are old crates and jalopies of all denominations to find and reminisce with.

George Jr., age eight, *fishes on the Willow side of Hatcher Pass, August 1955, dreaming of 20-inch rainbow trout.*

7

Subsistence for the Soul and Stomach

As early as I can remember, fishing and hunting were an integral part of our family activities as we grew to be seven in number. We supplemented Papa's teaching salary with resources garnered from the land and water, both around our homestead and ranging afield on the Glenn, Richardson, Seward, and Big Lake highways, even to netting hooligan in the Twentymile area near Portage.

Other people had it tougher, and did what they had to do. The population was minimal in those days, the land bountiful, and the regs looser. Papa was a firm believer in law, moderation, and conserving the numbers, so we acted accordingly, with minor aberrations. Sorry, but no tales of us with nets across streams and hundreds of salmon trapped. No multiple moose per season or out-of-season poaching. No dozens and dozens of ducks in the freezer—when we had a freezer. (Plucking and gutting even one dozen was enough!) No Boone and Crockett grizzlies devouring our house and friends. Just a family working to help stock the larder. This meant that while hiking or otherwise traveling, seeing the rest of Alaska, and meeting other people, we were also learning the ways of animals living within the natural world, and getting work-study anatomy lessons.

Fish On!

I don't recall ever using or hearing the now popular cry of "Fish on!" when I was growing up. Maybe it's a city-folk thing, or maybe it wasn't as crowded. In our sphere it was the still popular "I got one!", or "They got one!", or "Aw, man, it got away!" Our family plied the streams, lakes, and inlet with snarlsome bait-casting reels, a much-abused fly rod that I used, and later on, spinning rods. We used the old string-on-a-stick a time or two, which was translated in later years to include "hooking" for tom cod on the frozen Selawik River and Kivalina Lagoon, using a short piece of whittled lumber and a dab of ivory with a bent nail and a red bead. It was a tried-and-true, traditional method in the Iñupiaq culture and worked quite well for this *nalaugmiu* as well. A few times in Kivalina, Kathy Schwartz (my wife then) and Roger and Mary Ellen Bliss and I lined the cod up on cookie pans and baked them whole for dinner.

In the '50s and '60s on the homestead, we hopped in our Chevy or the tiny battle-worn Jeep and headed for Willow and Little Willow creeks. At the Big Lake "Y" the better road ended and became more dirt and mud than gravel. We went to the Willow area many times. Once when I was eight, I traipsed my hit-and-miss way down the Little Willow, pausing for a quick try at a deep eddying hole. Orlando Byers, accompanying Papa and me, settled in at the hole after I had moved downstream in the excitement of exploring farther. Orlando patiently fished there for an hour or two and reeled in three magnificent 20-inch rainbows. I pulled in a few ten or twelve inchers, but I caught a lesson of life on that day: If you get in a hurry, think of Orlando and 20-inch rainbows.

We fished there for salmon—silvers, reds, humpies, and dogs. A railroad trestle spanned the stream and we used it to cross without getting wet or swept away; the current could be waist-deep at times. I remember crossing ten or fifteen feet above the current, peering down between the creosote ties to the stream, and seeing huge red shadows gliding upstream, king salmon on their way to spawning, some of them almost as big as I was.

In the years of renting Byers' place we hiked past fields and the adjoining stump rows where burn fires could persist underground for years. I went by myself sometimes—into the woods behind the house and on over a small butte to Cottonwood Creek when the salmon runs filled the stream with schools of undulating silvers. I never thought of them actually taking bait or lures, so we usually snagged them, a practiced art in itself, what with the tree roots, submerged logs, clumps of submerged grass, overhanging branches, and the occasional beaver dam. For the most part we stuck to the limits and hook size—I think the personal limit on silvers was six—but we had "time on task" fun. Occasionally we'd meet a neighbor on the stream, but much of the time it was just us and a once-in-a-while black bear.

One day we stumbled upon a neighbor who was a classmate at the time, standing in the middle of the creek, hard at work for his family's needs. He was tall even then and meant business, wielding a parachute cord hand-line with a soldered treble hook that seemed as big as my fist. Subsistence was what it was in those days, and I imagine his catch was welcomed at their table during the winter months.

For a year or two, I used a long yellow fly rod for salmon but just dabbled with flies, going mostly for snagging. This made for unusual fishing, considering how limber the rod was and the closeness of the trees. Wild times were in store when I hooked into a silver. I wasn't a purist; a river didn't run through it in this boy's life. I spent time fossicking for others' lost lures: Daredevil, Luzon, and imitations. It was a treasure hunt, and it saved buying our own.

After we moved onto our homestead, we frequented Fish Creek, the one past Knik toward Goose Bay, for trout and runs of salmon. It was there I first encountered a what-the-heck-is-that-butt-ugly-thing of an Irish lord, or sculpin. Salmon filled areas of the stream and associated sloughs much as they did in Cottonwood Creek. One of the first times we went trout fishing there, Papa took us in the Jeep and, not interested in fishing himself that day, sat on the hood and read while we kids fished. Read, that is, until the game warden happened by and asked for his fishing license, at which time there commenced an earnest discussion between the two men as to why Papa would need a fishing license since he wasn't fishing, but merely reading and watching over his kids, neither of whom required a license. Most of the game wardens we met were reasonable, and this one eventually succumbed to Papa's multifaceted argument and went on his way, and Papa returned to his book.

Once I chased a silver up a tiny tributary of Fish Creek and grabbed it with my bare hands, but Richard one-upped me when he stretched atop a small beaver dam—and later a log in Cottonwood Creek—and trailed his hand in the shadows to grab a few salmon behind the gills and throw them onto the bank. He says one even leaped up on top of the dam and flopped about before he grabbed it. In any case, being the eldest son, it is my duty to ask him why he never caught any trout or Irish lords that way.

As far as trout tales go, Neil Thomas, a student in my father's classes, babysat Richard a time or two. The Clint Thomas family had smoked some trout, a change from the usual salmon, and Neil offered Richard some.

"I thought it cool that it was trout, not salmon," says Richard, "and it was delicious. I especially loved the crispy tails. They were tasty, like potato chips, which we didn't see too often in our family. I started catching more trout and frying them in a flour and milk coating, so I could have those trout-tail chips."

Mom said that when I was a toddler I liked trout better than ice cream, and I still find it delicious.

Set Nets in the Mud

AFTER WE MOVED ONTO THE HOMESTEAD, we obtained a subsistence permit and set out a gill net for salmon, several times in front of our house, twice a mile up the inlet, and once above the mouth of Fish Creek. I think the permit allowed three hundred fish a season, but we never caught that many. We salvaged gill nets washed ashore and put them to use again. They came in torn, twisted, matted, twig-and-stick-ridden tangles that had to be cleaned and repaired. We'd cobble two or three remnants together to get one overall net by repairing the gaping, ragged holes in the mesh and splicing the float and lead lines—tedious work. We'd attach the net to a barrel tied to a stake anchored in the muck a hundred feet out and string the net to shore, where we tied it to another stake above the high water mark and then waited for the tide to do its work.

Sometimes we used an eight-foot-long "Fold-A-Boat," a collapsible, waterproof canvas and wooden affair that could be broken down and carried in a smaller bundle. When the floats jerked and bobbed in the tide with the struggles of the salmon caught in the net beneath the surface, one or two of us seafarers cast off in the little boat to pick them. We pulled ourselves hand over hand along the float and hauled the fish up to the flimsy gunnel, then picked the entangled fish from the net, all the while trying not to capsize the unstable craft and to keep it and us from being shoved under the float line by the strong current. The silty mud and salt water roughened and dried our hands and the salmon teeth raked and scratched our broken-nailed fingers.

When the current was too strong, or we were on a site when we didn't have the little boat, we picked the net where it rested on the beach as the tide retreated. Until the mid-'60s we had to contend with the Lake George Breakout flooding, an annual event for many years. Meltwater trapped in the valley where the Knik Glacier butted up against Mount Palmer would enlarge the lake until the water forced a channel along the face of the glacier and a massive springtime deluge of water, big trees and driftwood would rush into the Knik River and Cook Inlet. The debris threatened us in the little boat, and even carried the net away once, which meant more beachcombing and patching. But the beach parts store was open 24/7 and so were we.

FRIENDS AND NEIGHBORS TAKE A BREAK *from mending a net found on the beach that will be used for subsistence salmon fishing; from left, Mrs. George Gore, Lee Anna Harbeson, visiting author Louise Potter, Mr. Gore, and George Harbeson Sr. (Peter Harbeson crouching behind Mr. Gore), August 1963.*

Gill netting was an enterprise that produced at most a hundred and fifty fish a year, shared with the Byers, Gores, Coghlans, and Turners. It wasn't in the range of what many Alaskans did for a living, but the fish that Mom canned and Papa smoked helped fill our pantry, sated the ravenous appetites of us growing boys, and gave us a feel for what people dependent on the resource experienced.

The nets also furthered our interaction with the natural world and added interest and challenge to our lives. At the site up from Fish Creek, I remember being fascinated with salmon hearts when I cleaned the fish. When a fresh fish presented itself for cleaning, I immediately extracted the pastel reddish-brown heart and placed it aside to see how long it would beat. I was amazed at the stubborn endurance of that brave bit of muscle. Even after the best part of an hour, it still might beat out a twitch of its programmed code when I poked it. I have always thought salmon to be beautiful fish and us lucky to have them, and my respect for them grew during those experiences.

At low tides when we didn't work the net, I would grab a rod, run down to the flats, and make my way across the mud to the bottom of the deep inlet channel near where tiny O'Brien Creek emptied. At such times, the current and water volume slowed to the size of a small shallow stream. "V" ripples marked the occasional wayward salmon forging its way up inlet and gave me a snagging target. They were few in number and difficult to hook because of the treacherous footing, so I caught only one or two. In the excitement of the chase I always had to watch where I stepped and see whether the mud would support me. On more than one beautiful summer day I stood alone casting down by the channel bed, where the high mud banks rose on either side to push against the sky and block out the rest of the world. Several times I suddenly discovered the incoming tide had quietly risen to isolate me on a small, softening islet of mud, forcing me to leap quickly to solid footing.

The muddy expanses of Cook Inlet are deceptive and ever fraught with risk. Richard says he heard of some soldiers duck hunting, and possibly drinking, on the flats near our place. One of the soldiers shot a duck, walked out to retrieve it, and got stuck. When the tide came in, he tried breathing through a shotgun barrel to survive but failed and drowned. Richard says, "After hearing that, I went swimming in Knik Lake, dove underwater, and tried to breathe through a garden hose. It's really hard to do. And cold water and stress make it worse."

There's also a tale of two men crossing the inlet in a small wooden boat from Knik. Before they reached the other side, the tide ebbed and stranded them on a mud bar. One of the men went to sleep while awaiting the incoming tide but awoke to stop his companion, who had gotten cold, from chopping up the boat to build a fire. However, all ended well that day, and the two lived to tell the tale to their barstool buddies.

I suppose we were lucky to have avoided tragedy, considering the time we spent traipsing around in the inlet. The fine silt combined with water makes for a composition resembling quicksand, but with a denser grip. Many times I stepped onto a hard section of mud and had it liquefy under my weight and movement. I can only imagine what occurred during the '64 earthquake. A person doesn't have to be in very deep; ankle deep gets your attention, up to the knees is real trouble, and the tide makes the rescue time frame very short. Using a compressor or a pump to inject air or water around the trapped leg or body can help but is no guarantee, and we didn't have one anyway. Many times one of us got caught in the vacuum grip of the muck and had to work loose or slide out of our boots to escape, not seriously in danger but close enough to sense that dark shadow that travels with us.

A'Hunting We Went

WHEN I RECALL HUNTING IN OUR HOMESTEAD days, I think of Papa's old model 1917 Erfurt 8-mm sporterized German Mauser. He used it for moose hunting, but where and when he got it is a mystery. He never said and I never thought to ask while he was alive. Was it used in World War I? Was it a World War II souvenir that he brought home from the Pacific? Maybe he bought it after his military service. Did the Chinese or Japanese use it? I look at its rich wood patina, weathered metal, and strange markings, and hear distant mutterings of war and blood in a foreign language. The power of its history lies just below its surface, but I can't break the code.

We carried it through the woods every fall. Its bolt action worked reasonably well, but it had a tendency to jam, and its sights were loose. Papa and Richard went moose hunting one fall on the Post homestead, and the rear open-sight adjustment joggled on a longer shot that missed. Richard heard Papa muttering under his breath as he tried to stay on the fleeing moose and push the sight back into place.

Much of our hunting took place on the tracts of land adjoining our place. One area, bordered by tree-covered hills rising around three sides, was the meadow, pond, and grassy slope where O'Brien Creek exits the woods. It was the site of three successful hunts. Moose liked the feed and the protected southern exposure. One year we shot a young bull in the trees at the top of the slope overlooking the pond. I remember helping Papa slice through the heavy hide of the animal's throat to end its suffering. Another kill was an unexpected fall encounter in the area below the slope. Orlando Byers needed a place to store his fishing boat during the winter, so we gathered to run it up the creek on the high tide. When the boat was in place near the pond, Orlando saw to the final storage details. He was coiling a white rope when we noticed a bull moose step out of the woods onto a grassy stretch between the creek and the pond. The moose looked at us and tossed its head from side to side like a dog, curious about our activity.

Papa told me to run up to the house and get the Mauser, so I edged behind the boat and surreptitiously took off for the house, a half-mile away. Everyone else kept still and Orlando kept coiling the rope while the moose browsed and watched him from its vantage point a hundred feet away. I sneaked back through the open grass to the boat with the rifle and slipped it to Papa. He shot twice and the moose went down, kicked a little, then was still. Papa set the Mauser aside and we waited and watched the moose for a few minutes, but it showed no sign of life. Then Papa slowly edged a few feet closer, with eight-year-old Richard deciding to trail him. Suddenly the moose lurched to its feet, snorted and shook its head and horns, and staggered slowly toward them. Richard still remembers it clearly.

"I grabbed hold of Papa's leg and held on for dear life, and he was running, hobbling as fast as he could through the grass toward the boat with me glued to his leg. He hollered, 'George, get the gun! Quick!' and George ran over with the gun. The moose had gotten within twenty-five feet of Papa and me, but then it fell down again. Boy, that scared the livin' tar out of me!"

Papa shot again, just in case, and that time the moose stayed down. We dressed it out and packed it up to the house with the Jeep. A day or two later, Papa, Richard, and I went back to the gut pile to see if anything had been eating on it. It was sunny fall weather and the stomach had ballooned impressively. Catching us by surprise before we could stop him, Richard grabbed a stick, ran up to the carcass and poked the stomach, breaking it open. The stench was truly formidable, but the expression on Richard's face as he hurriedly backed away was worth it.

Caribou on Forward Control

In October of 1961, the year Dennis Calhoun stayed with the Turners, Lee, Papa, Dennis, and I embarked on a caribou hunting trip to the Denali Highway in Lee's blue-and-white 1958 ¾-ton, FC-170 Willys Jeep. The Turners had driven it to Alaska in their move to Seldovia, where Lee had been principal-teacher and coach before moving to Wasilla. It was a cab-over-engine design, the "FC" standing for "Forward Control." This, with its platform stake body, gave it a bulbous-headed caterpillar look, similar to a VW pickup on steroids. It had a six-cylinder L-head engine and was a skookum truck, but driving and riding in it were strange experiences.

We headed up the Glenn and Richardson highways, past Eureka and Lake Louise, through Glennallen to Paxson and the Denali Highway to the Tangle Lakes area, where we'd heard the caribou were lined up and waiting for us. The Jeep's small cab was designed for the driver and one passenger, with the engine compartment in between, so Lee and Papa, in deference to Dennis' and my youth, generously volunteered to ride in the cushioned seats and warmth of the cab and allowed us to ride behind in the luxury of the wooden bed. Lee had covered the top and sides with canvas that blocked the view but not the cold or wind or exhaust fumes that buffeted us from the rear opening. The two of us had no idea of the scenery ahead but rode blindly along facing backward with a tunnel view of where we'd been.

Dennis and I each had a cast-off army surplus sleeping bag in which we buried ourselves. The insulating quality of these Made-For-Florida bags required heavy use of our imaginations, which, at below-zero temperatures, was limited to visions of the two of us frozen stiff upon our arrival in Paxson. Desperate, we turned to the first line of defense of teenage boys—food. Unfortunately, the only item available in the rear of the Jeep was a package of stale pork rinds, AKA pig skins. But, breathing Willys exhaust fumes and being bounced around on the Jeep's floor boards, the two of us stalwartly consumed those sixteen ounces of greasy crackle in the below-zero temperature. Eventually we warmed up and had a hot meal in the Paxson Lodge, before proceeding on to the Tangle Lakes area and the caribou. In the end, we ended up getting one caribou and a similar return trip home, where we vehemently eschewed pork rinds and took forward control of our real purpose in life: playing basketball.

- -

PAPA WAS FRIENDS WITH CLINT THOMAS, and Clint had taken Richard under his wing. One year, Clint hired Papa and helper Richard to pour a four-foot concrete wall under a house; I had helped Papa build a basement for Henry and Ester Hansen on Fairview Loop near the Dinkel family farm, and now it was Richard's turn. On Clint's job, Richard was kept busy with a wheelbarrow, excavating dirt and moving the sand for the cement Papa mixed by hand and with a small portable mixer. At one point, while Papa watched in amusement, Clint offered Richard a chaw of tobacco. Earlier in life, Mama had offered little Richard a sample of the foam head on a glass of beer, to minimize Richard's insatiable curiosity. Richard had found the foam to be "different" tasting, but he politely declined to take Clint up on the tobacco offer. Richard laughs, recalling the incident after all these years, and says, "No way was I going to put that nasty stuff in *my* mouth!"

In 1969 it was decided that sixteen-year-old Richard would go hunting with Papa and Clint, and the three of them traveled up the Glenn Highway north of Palmer, past Sutton and Chickaloon, in search of caribou. They headed off the highway onto the Hicks Creek Trail, also known as the Pinochle Creek Trail. The trail winds its way through rolling country, with steep ascents, boggy areas, and treeless alpine expanses. They drove Clint's big-tired, modified-for-off-road, blue '56 4x4 GMC pickup, and trailered Clint's small gas-powered John Deere dozer behind it. Clint had a straightforward, no-nonsense manner and a crusty personality, perhaps due in part to increasing back trouble from operating heavy equipment for the Alaska State Highway Department.

They made their way back into the hills, some of which had thousand-foot drop-offs, and bagged a couple of caribou along the way. One morning Richard discovered bear tracks twenty feet from their tent and decided he'd sleep in the GMC after that.

As they camped, they met an Alaska state trooper traveling in a red Weasel who told them he was going in to check on a report that someone had been shot. Later that evening, he returned on his way out, transporting the body of a camp guide who had been shot by a client. The guide had been tending to the party's horses and the client mistook him for a caribou. Richard says that was the first dead person he'd ever seen. But not the last. Many years later, Richard flew into the Rainy Pass area in his Aeronca Champ on a hunting trip with two friends. Each flew his own plane. At one point Richard and one friend flew over the other's plane, which had landed on a sandbar, and saw the other hunter lying beneath it, killed when he'd tried to start the plane by hand-propping it.

Once back in the hills on the Hicks Trail trip, Clint, Papa, and Richard came upon a ram standing on a high bluff. Papa shot it with his old Mauser, but the sheep went over the cliff, leaving traces of blood along the rock edges. They spent the next six hours scouring the area below, before dark set in, but never found the animal.

Otherwise, things went reasonably well until the return leg, when the three of them came to one of the steeper slopes. Clint wanted to give Richard experience operating equipment in difficult situations, so he had Richard driving the dozer. Richard did okay until he tried to maneuver the machine up a particularly steep grade, where its tracks kept losing their grip on the shale. Clint took over, but when even he couldn't get it up the grade, he drove to a less steep section and zigzagged the machine up backward. As the trip progressed toward the highway, the GMC's brakes failed and its rear axle broke, so Clint tied on to it with a thin cable and pulled it with the dozer up another thirty-degree gradient along a steep drop-off. Papa sweated it out in the GMC driver's seat with the door open, ready to jump as Clint gunned, geared, and clutched the dozer. Richard scrambled on foot up the hill twenty feet off to the side. In the process of all this, a front shackle bolt on the GMC broke, and the front axle tore loose.

Richard was sent home to get parts for the GMC. He walked out, tired and dirty from camping, and bloody from gutting and skinning caribou. When he reached the highway, he hitchhiked, but no one wanted to pick up such a disreputable-looking character. Finally, an older man in a pickup gave him a ride, but as the truck wove its erratic path down both lanes of the highway, it dawned on Richard that the driver was three sheets to the wind. Once back in Wasilla, Richard procured the necessary

CLINT THOMAS *(left) and* RICHARD HARBESON *with Clint's gas-powered John Deere dozer on a successful caribou hunt on the Hicks Trail, 1969.*

parts and drove his VW Bug back to the Hicks Trail, then hiked back in to where Clint and Papa waited. Additional jury-rigged repairs were made, and it was homeward bound again for the intrepid hunters.

A few years later, Richard and Clint made another trip along Hicks Trail, this time with a 2WD bulldog of a low-geared Arctic Cat Cub motorcycle with a Kohler engine and wide, fat tires. Richard drove for a time with Clint perched atop the camping gear behind him, then he walked while Clint drove. They came to a swampy spot where a big swamp buggy had dug a large hole that had filled with water. Leaves and grass floated on top of the water, disguising it. Clint, maneuvering the bike and walking his legs and feet alongside as one does with motorcycles, drove into it. The bike promptly turned over on one side and partially submerged, trapping Clint by his leg. Bubbles rose in the dark water around him as Richard rushed in and pulled Clint to the surface. The two retrieved the bike and motored on their sodden way.

The Hicks Trail was littered in those years with abandoned broken-down equipment, scattered along the way like a graveyard of mechanical steeds. They passed a couple of Army six-by-sixes, a diesel Cat that had churned and buried itself into the mud up to its seat before throwing a track, a battered homemade dune buggy, an assortment of axles and wheels, and other discarded remnants of fading dreams.

Turned Around and Upside Backwards

IN THE FALL OF 1961, CHANGES WERE occurring in Alaska as elsewhere. The former territory had been a state for almost two years. Bill Egan was governor and our population was 226,000 and rising. Elvis was swiveling his hips in his military service for the country. Johnny Horton's recording and the John Wayne film of the same title, "North to Alaska," were big hits. Sputnik had beeped into our consciousness. JFK was asking what we could do for our country. A coming proposition to move the state capital from Juneau was a little over a year away from defeat at the polls. The U.S. nuclear attack sub *Thresher* had been launched but not yet sunk. U-2 spy-plane pilot Francis Gary Powers was in a Russian prison—to be swapped in February 1962 for Soviet spy Rudolph Abel. Blanche Louise Preston McSmith had become the first African-American member of the Alaska State Legislature. Amoco and others were moving into offshore oil in Cook Inlet.

It had been a year and a half since we moved to the bluff overlooking Cook Inlet near the historical town and port of Knik. And now—with my eighth-grade graduation gift, the amazing Sears, Roebuck and Co. "Made In U.S.A." Silverstone 6, MODEL 1205 BLACK, pocket-size transistor radio and cylinder shaped nine-volt battery—I was riding the small bore tide carrying me and my classmates into our freshman year at Wasilla High School.

At the moment there'd been a hard frost, it was moose season, and we were in the woods with guns.

"Shh!" Papa suddenly turned and pointed to his left. Following along behind him, I'd concentrated on scanning the early morning September woods and keeping my feet free of the terrain's damp clutches, so his sudden halt threw me into a stumble to avoid bumping into him.

"There," he cautioned. "Behind those alders. . . ." He crouched low and held the battered Mauser in front of him with both hands, waist high and ready. We both peered and listened with held breath, searching a broad tangle of alder that still held half of its fall foliage, fronted by a maze of spine-armored devil's club stalks hung with red berries and drooping yellow-brown prickly leaves the size of pie tins.

191 ·· *Subsistence for the Soul and Stomach*

GEORGE HARBESON SR. *sets off on a moose hunt in August 1961, with his 1917 German Mauser over his shoulder.*

My eyes jerked to the left to join his line of sight, my breathing stilled with his, and the silence of the trees thundered in our straining ears. Father and son, poised on the up-close-and-personal edge of a skirmish with an Alaskan moose.

"There! I saw something move," he whispered, breaking the spell. He shifted his stance and adjusted his black-plastic-rimmed glasses against his face with the back of his hand. I let out a slow, tense breath.

"I don't see anything," I whispered back. Which wasn't exactly true. I saw all sorts of things: dark shapes, shadows, angry moose, a *bear*—like Southeast Alaska's legendary Old Groaner—lurking within the tenebrous thicket. I gripped the old bolt-action single-shot .22 that Papa had bought me in Vermont, and tried to convince myself, unsuccessfully, that it was a 30.06.

"Where's Lee?" Papa glanced at me, then around our periphery, and to our right. "Can you see him?"

"Uh, no," I whispered. "Wait! There he is. Over there by that big stump that looks like a, I don't know, a rocket launcher?" I pointed through the paper birches at two o'clock where Lee Turner stood, thirty yards distant, his short stocky figure leaning against the stump, his lever-action .270 held in one hand, his bald head covered with a black beret. Gone bald at twenty-three—had he said that, or someone else? A few foolhardy kids called him "Chrome Dome," but they were long-ago-and-far-away out of his earshot when they said it. I disgustedly tossed such stray thoughts aside as my mind bounced back to the alders, then returned to Lee. I waved my hand to get his attention.

Papa caught Lee's gaze, pointed to the alders, and slowly stepped off in an oblique angle toward them. As he skirted their edge, shadows exploded in a burst of thrashing. A massive bulk on the move appeared briefly through the branches and faded into the trees to the west.

"Didn't see any horns!" Papa called out, as Lee made his way toward us. I lowered the .22 and waited for the ensuing analysis and a new plan of action, which turned out to be give it another half-hour, trudge on, stay alert. For the last two hours we had meandered through the low rolling terrain of dense birch, slender aspen, occasional large cottonwoods, scattered spruce, alder, willow, red carpets of low-bush cranberries, scattered orange and white *amanita muscaria*, and the ubiquitous devil's club. A few minutes more and we'd call it a day and "head for the barn."

― ―

PAPA AND I went moose hunting several times when I was in junior high and high school. In addition to hunting and raising our garden crops, we gathered cranberries, rose hips, wild raspberries, watermelon berries, and a few black and red currants, all of which Mom froze or made into jams and jellies. But our family of seven always needed the meat, like many families in the Valley in those days.

We'd set forth early on this particular hike from the Turner residence off the Knik-Goose Bay Road, five miles southwest of Wasilla, opposite the Hayfield Road turnoff. Now, mid-morning, a heavy overcast was approaching. After flushing the cow moose from behind the alders we continued for half an hour without encountering any others and decided to head back toward the house.

Papa and Lee were accomplished hunters and proficient in the woods, but after a short time a certain "ambiguity of direction" gradually dawned on us, which can happen when you're not carrying a compass. This hunt was to have been a quick morning jaunt through the backyard woods. The occasional traffic on the Knik Road kept us oriented—it would take idiots to become seriously, ah . . . well, okay, lost. We decided, in a unanimous vote taken over the sandwiches we'd brought for a snack, that we were merely temporarily "confused." Lee offered up one of his homespun assessments—"a tad miscomfabulated"—but revised it as the morning progressed to "turned around and upside backwards." The sun, still obscured by heavy clouds threatening snow, was no help. Papa gestured in the direction of the faint sound of intermittent traffic, and Lee nodded. I, a young novitiate in the presence of sages, also agreed. It was difficult to argue with our ears—the traffic noise drifting through the woods was incontrovertible.

As a final thought, I ventured the idea that moss was supposed to grow on the north side of trees. A quick survey of nearby trees led to the discovery of a vile-looking mushroom/fungus that Papa insisted was edible—not the *amanita muscaria*—he since youth being personally familiar with the questionable practice of actually picking and eating things he called morels, puffballs, and field mushrooms. Oh, great, I thought. Headlines flashed through my mind: "*Young Lad Poisoned by Father and Coach While Hunting!*" or "*Boy in Woods Starves in Midst of Mushrooms!*" or "*GIANT AMANITA ATTACKS TRANSISTOR BOY/ELVIS SINGS AT FUNERAL!*" At any rate, we soon parted company with these dubious culinary delights and proceeded to follow the traffic's Pied Piper summons, to make our way back home.

Or so we thought.

Late morning elapsed around us, then began to stretch uncomfortably long behind us. We meandered through the trees, around patches of devil's club with those malevolent red berries, following occasional faint game trails, climbing over fallen trees, wading through open areas of dead grass, and all the while still searching for any sign of moose. The thought of shooting a moose when uncertain of the direction in which to pack it wasn't mentioned, but some things are best left unsaid until the need actually arises.

Eventually we arrived at a wet area bisected by a small stream. We thought we were headed "back home," of which the "back" part was not supposed to contain a stream crossing, but there it was. This was when Lee updated his assessment to "turned around and upside backwards." The road still called, louder and more insistent, so regardless of true direction we were committed. We leap-waded the stream and soon came upon another surprise element: railroad tracks. With the sight of the rails, our mental compasses adjusted. We had started out from Turners, knocked around in the woods by trudging north and then east, and had reached Lucille Creek and the Alaska Railroad. We now saw a small lake and the Coghlan residence, located off the Big Lake Road. Which goes to show (or as I once heard Larry Teeland express it in speaking to a school assembly, "shows to go") that "No matter where you go, there you are" indeed rang true.

Standing wet-legged and stumble-footed on the tracks, the three of us were presented with a choice: 1. Follow the tracks into town—easier walking, but three or four miles nevertheless—and, carrying our rifles, surreptitiously use someone's phone to call family for a ride, or, 2. Walk around Jacobson Lake and present our abashed selves at the Coghlans' door and humbly beg for assistance. Somehow I remember the dreaded mushrooms and not how we got home that day—but the Coghlans being good friends of ours, and knowing the Coghlan hospitality and straightforward approach to life (and Violet's cooking), I would say that we ended up with a sumptuous lunch spiced with good-natured teasing.

And that was not unusual. For all our faults and individual eccentricities, and through the times of being "turned around and upside backwards," we gave each other true direction and compass in the small rural community that was Wasilla and the Mat-Su Valley, as the '40s and '50s yielded to the storm surge of the '60s, the Cold War, political assassinations, the War on Poverty and the Civil Rights Movement, Big Oil . . . and something called Vietnam.

THE WASILLA WARRIORS OF 1961-62 *practice in the old Wasilla gym, with Lee Turner coaching (hooded sweatshirt); players visible, from left, are Larry Teeland (54), George Harbeson Jr., Pete Hjellen (43), Pat Patterson, Richard Ingram, Dickie Carl, Jerry Bouwens (45), and Lary Hill. Photo from the 1962 Wasilla High School yearbook.*

8

The Game Is the Thing

Basketball has long occupied a special place in the annals of Alaskan high school sports, binding small rural communities together, cementing lifelong friendships and memories, helping to broaden provincial perspectives and giving students an avenue into the adult world. It gave me real-life geography lessons, playing wherever, whenever, against whomever. In high school the gyms were in Wasilla, Palmer, Homer, Seward, Cordova, Valdez, Glennallen, Fairbanks, Chugiak, Fort Greely, Copper Valley, Anchorage.

Later it was Selawik, Noorvik, Kivalina, Alakanuk, Kotzebue, Dillingham, Nome, Shishmaref, Kiana, Shungnak, Kotlik, Wrangell, Alcantra Youth Camp, Sutton Prison, Elmendorf Air Force Base, Fort Richardson, city leagues across the state, UAA pick-up games, UAF dorm league, the old Anchorage school/city gym, village school decks, Florida State rec league, Lewiston City Park, Fur Rendezvous tournaments, alumni games, student/teacher school spirit games, coaches' pick-up games, and a Harlem Clowns game.

And in back yards, on lawns, ice rinks, paved driveways, tennis courts, in school hallways, on gravel pads, tundra, root-infested dirt, in snow and mud. City side-streets. A Chukchi Sea beach. Off a trampoline. From the top of the family cars. In our house . . . (George! Stop bouncing that ball!)

The game has been part of my life since I was seven years old. Though never a "jock," I was a player, aficionado, occasional self-styled critic, coach, spectator. I like some teams, but appreciate good plays and players no matter the team. Skill, teamwork, and sportsmanship. But body paint, major food group headwear, half-time gossip—not for me. Over the years playing was the thing for me—court time.

Our family was television deficient in the early years. We had to leave Alaska and go back to New Jersey for those two years, 1956–58, to watch The Lone Ranger, Roy Rogers, Gabby Hayes, and Lash LaRue—all the oaters—and an occasional NBA game on Grandma Hazel (*née* Witty) Bartholomay's black-and-white set. But in Alaska in the '50s and '60s we listened to basketball on the radio, along with Bill Haley and the Comets ("Rock Around the Clock"). I listened to the Bun Drive-In shows from Northern Lights Boulevard in Anchorage with a KFQD deejay named Ron Moore. Another favorite was Lamont Cranston as "The Shadow"— "*Who knoooows what Evil lurks . . . in the hearts of men!*" (Evil was capitalized then, and not just in radio mysteries—*COMMUNISM* stalked the land, and Elvis was a hip-swiveling son of *SATAN* accusing us of bein' nothin' but a hound dawg.)

But my highest priority was listening to high school and occasional NBA basketball night-cast games. Who can forget the noted 1960 37–17 halftime deficit comeback tournament victory of 59–58 over the defending state champion Fairbanks? If I knew the teams, or players, or sometimes for Wasilla games, I would lay out a score book on notebook paper and keep statistics from the announcer's running commentary. In that NBA era, Jerry West, Elgin Baylor, Bill Russell, Wilt Chamberlain, Hondo, Big "O" and Cooz were the players I admired.

Little did I know as a third grader chasing basketballs around the Wasilla Community Hall practices in 1955 that it was early preparation for coaching the Selawik *Amaġut* (Wolves) in 1973. We held practices in an elementary classroom while eagerly anticipating the completion of the new high school. Slipping on a pencil was a fast-break hazard. It was common to "dunk" the ball against the letter "K" (for Koala, or maybe *KinnaQ:* fool, or crazy person). Perhaps this was the precursor of the little known Sesame Street offense.

The Early Years

DISCOUNTING MASCOT DUTIES IN VERMONT and a fifth-grade Lakers stint in New Jersey, my initial basketball arenas were open to the sky, namely areas beside our tarred flat-roof basement. The roof would have made a great court, but flat = leaks even without basketball traffic. (One leak filled a 15-gallon drum in a couple of hours.) My first homegrown "court" was a vehicle turnaround on our driveway. It was a dirt area twenty by thirty feet square with a homemade backboard, sporting a simple hoop and a sometimes net, nailed to a birch tree. Low mounds of dirt behind the backboard and on the two sides provided a measure of ball containment. Brush and trees on the bluff across the drive offered a small degree of over-the-bluff protection on long rebounds and missed passes. This was the scene of many hours of dirt-floor dribbling and leaf-caressed shots for me, with free admission for occasional spectators motoring past on the driveway. The terms "driving to the bucket" and "filling the lane" had their own meaning for me in later apprentice years. "There's too much traffic in the key. You got to fill the lane!" Coach Turner exhorted us in my freshman year. "Move your feet!" he commanded. "Stop their drives to the bucket!" Visions of our homestead vehicles loomed in my head, and into the traffic I rushed.

Eventually, this playing area morphed into my sister Becky's vegetable garden. Yet ghostly footfalls, thudding basketballs, and cries of "Foul!" echoed through her rows of lettuce, carrots, broccoli, potatoes, Brussels sprouts, and cabbage.

When the twenty-foot-high mountain of excavated basement gravel finally had been utilized elsewhere, we pried the weathered backboard off the turnaround tree and transported it to a grand thirty-by-forty-foot expanse of gravel and dirt, where it was nailed to a similar tree next to our log home. There Richard and I, Peter the Great, often Papa, occasionally Lee Anna and Becky, and even Mama once or twice, honored Mr. Naismith's creation: Horse, Pig (short version of Horse), Round-the-World, One-on-One, Two-on-Two, Three-on-Three, Two-on-One. Once we even played with a medicine ball—suspending, of course, the relevant rules on dribbling and making accommodations in several other aspects of the game. It's amazing how light and small a basketball seems after using one

GROTON GREMLINETTES VETERAN AGGREGATION — With four of last year's starters and four reserves back, the Groton High Gremlinettes are looking forward to the 1956-57 hoop season and a chance to improve on last season's dismal record. Coached by George Harbeson, the Groton girls include (Front l to r)...... Ruiter, ... Robitzer and

"GROTON GREMLINETTES VETERAN AGGREGATION—*With four of last year's starters and four reserves back, the Groton High Gremlinettes are looking forward to the 1956-57 hoop season and a chance to improve on last season's dismal record. Coached by George Harbeson, the Groton girls include (front, l to r) Jackalyn White, Marylin Gray, Alice Orr, Capt. Delia Heath, Myrna Ruiter, Bonnie Robitzer and Janice Hatch. (Back) Priscilla Clark, Lyn Robitzer, Ann Main, Lucille Clark, Coach Harbeson, Betty Playful, Nanetta Crown, Donna Gandin and Kay Moulton.*"

"GROTON HIGH GREMLINS SET FOR OPENER—*Under the direction of new coach George Harbeson Sr., the Groton Gremlins will open their 1956-57 hoop season on Tuesday night at McIndoes Academy. The Gremlins, who number eight boys, lack size and experience, but have plenty of spirit. Composing the squad are (l-r) Robert Wernecke, Lawrence Daniels, Duane Haskell, Mascot George Harbeson Jr., Coach Harbeson, Creston Ruiter, Wendell Darling and Capt. Hollis Vance. Missing are Loren Daniels and Gordon Page. The latter is recuperating from an appendectomy." These photos appeared on the same page of a newspaper presumably published in Groton, Vermont, clipping undated.*

of those! Tree-climbing dunks were popular. For me and other enthusiasts this back-to-nature environment meant basketballs attired in: a. mud, b. slush, c. sand, d. dust, e. tree sap, f. tar, g. peanut butter/cranberry jelly, h. dog slobber (or worse!), and i. grease or other automotive substances.

In the hours spent in this arena, dusk and dawn and daylight-midnights included, we endured such home court disadvantages as tree roots and protruding rocks, tree-branch blocked shots, self-substituting dogs, and the much dreaded chase-the-rebound scramble to keep the ball out of the trees covering the eighty-foot-high bluff. Compounding this issue, the ground sloped gradually downward from the basket to the bluff. Sprinting desperately, we flew out over the bluff and tumbled down into the trees in frantic attempts to stop the errant ball.

Batter Up!

BEFORE THE BACKBOARD RELOCATION, I also spent many hours batting rocks from atop the gravel mound with crude stick bats scrounged from the surrounding woods. As a boy Papa had carved bats from pignut saplings that he smoothed with pieces of broken glass. He and others played in fields and back yards, and a glove was a prize possession. Sometimes they played with broomsticks and tennis balls, but mostly with baseballs, which were expensive. When the covers came off, the balls were wrapped in friction tape. Catchers' masks were unknown in their pick-up games and once Papa was hit in the head with a foul tip, after which he pitched or played infield. As he grew older, he played on a Hi-Y team and a town team. In one game—no batting helmets or Little League then—he was beaned by a pitch and the ball went almost to second base.

Papa's baseball heroes were pitchers Schoolboy Rowe, Carl Hubbell, and Dizzy Dean, and first baseman Lou Gehrig. Papa's Uncle Elmer gave him his old dry and flaking pitcher's mitt and taught him how to throw curve, drop, and knuckle balls. Papa treated the mitt with Neatsfoot oil and Vaseline and used it for many years. Elmer took him to see the Giants and Yankees several times; Papa saw Babe Ruth and Lou Gehrig play, and attended some of the first night games in Brooklyn. When he worked on Wall Street after high school, he and other law firm office boys went to see the Brooklyn Dodgers play. When the Yankees were in the World Series, the boys slept on the soft leather couches of the partners' law offices and were up and at the stadium at five in the morning to wait for the bleacher tickets to go on sale at 10 a.m., and then to wait for the start of the game two or three hours later.

Papa took me to a game in New York City when I was five or six, probably a Yankees game, and I continued to be a Yankees fan for several years. But on the homestead, I had to settle for listening to games on the radio and acting out fantasies of batting clean-up for Mantle and Maris.

> World Series, bottom-of-ninth, two outs, bases loaded. . . .
> There's the stretch . . . the ball slides toward the low outside corner. . . . YES! . . . I step into it swinging, smash the ball

(well, okay, the stone) square on, and it rockets in a high arcing path far out over the bluff, over the reaching tree branches, onto the flats, toward the waters of Cook Inlet . . . and it's GONE! . . . A BASES LOADED HOME RUN! . . . THE YANKEES WIN THE SERIES!. . . I jog the bases, the multitudes go wild, and I give them a sweeping cap bow. . . .

ALAS, IT WAS merely multitudes of seagulls and ravens and I never could slug one quite as far as the inlet, but, "Say hey, man!"

In high school we had annual school-wide comprehensive testing known as "Achievement Tests." In my latter years of teaching and on into today, testing and all of its satellite activities have multiplied like ravenous rodents in search of cheese. But in the days of yesteryear only that one session of tests was held, in—you guessed it—October, World Series time. Those who finished test sections ahead of the allotted time were allowed to listen to the Series on transistor radios—with an earphone, of course. We kept our classmates and some teachers apprised of scores, highlights, and play-by-play during testing breaks. Out came my Silvertone special. I plugged in the single tiny earphone, the equivalent of one of today's ear "buds," and it was "Take Me Out to the Ball Game," play-by-play, and the roar of the far-away crowds, all music to my ears and funneled through the earth's atmosphere down to the little box seat next to my eardrum. Those, indeed, were the days!

By the way, if anyone reading this knows what happened to my shoebox of baseball cards of Mantle, Maris, Mays, Jackie Robinson, Yogi Berra, Elton Howard, Bill Skowron, Bobby Richardson, Whitey Ford, Boog Powell, Hank Aaron, Mel Ott—okay, no Mel Ott—collected in the '50s and '60s, *please* feel free to contact me.

On the homestead I went through dozens of various-sized rocks at a time, contributing in my own small way to the leveling of the pile and seeding the flats in the process. The stones had to be chosen and sorted for size and shape from the mass of gravel. A stone too large sent a hand-wrist-and-radius/ulna-jarring shock through both arms as it landed with a thud in the drive. Stones too small were light in weight and hard to hit, and fell short of the towering line drives I so desired. Many of my line drives came to an abrupt halt when they scored a direct hit on a tree trunk. Some flatter stones buzzed as they flew skyward and others streaked aloft with the voice of a ricochet.

A stick bat with a curve built into its length complicated matters. And bats of dead birch, spruce, or aspen were softer than the rocks, so inevitably they took on a beaver-gnawed appearance, occasionally splintering and breaking. This aggravated the problem of misdirected pop fouls threatening our windows—at times careening off the side and roof of the house and increasing the angst of my poor suffering parents, whom I love dearly for nervously tolerating my dreams of glory and "The Show."

Home Court Advantage

THE FIRST MEMORIES I HAVE OF PLAYING ball in a gym in Alaska are of the old Wasilla School gym, beneath the creaky wooden structure where I had attended Sybil Woody's second grade, and where I started ninth grade in the fall of 1961. Remodeled in 1955, the gym was notorious but nevertheless a great improvement, and people were thrilled to have it. It resembled a gladiator pit in a gymnasium's clothing and provided a considerable home court advantage. I noticed other schools had individual characteristics of their own, such as Cordova's larger and more standard gym with its noticeable ground swell in the center court area, and Copper Valley's abrupt absence of distance behind the backboard on a lay-up.

But the Wasilla gym was in a class of its own. It was tiny, as gyms go—the 1953 plans show the dimensions to be 63' x 33'6"—but a harrowing aspect (one of several) was the walls surrounding it. Other than falling over the bleacher railing, entry was provided by two stairways (with a locker room on both sides of one) that led down to open doorways set into the gym's side walls. A few rows of permanently attached tiered bleachers, running three-quarters the length of the gym, were located on the building's north side, about twelve feet above the floor. A three-foot protective wall and a horizontal steel pipe were sufficient to restrain enthusiastic spectators, much as a similar arrangement may have done in Nero's day. Visiting teams were disconcerted by the home crowd fans looming high over them. The court's narrow width and short length also proved unsettling to visiting teams. Man-to-man defense was restricted due to limited space. Zone defenses were smothering. I conducted experiments for science class extra-credit. The floor was so short that it was possible to stand in front of one basket, throw a full-court pass, and race to the other basket in time to catch the pass yourself and score.

The gym's low ceiling, about twenty feet above the floor, added to the boxed-in effect. It cut down on full-court passes by teams unaccustomed to interceptions by light fixtures. I was chagrined to see my free throws hit the ceiling and fall short several times before I learned to drop the arc of the ball. Like others along the way, I had a flat shot until I corrected it years later. All this led to a planetary shift when the rest of the Warriors and I traveled to the relatively huge Buckner Field House on Fort Richardson in Anchorage. At Buckner I spent much of the game trying to see if the field house had a ceiling up there, if those were stars or gym lighting, and to find the other end of the court, since GPS wasn't available.

Papa sympathized and recounted *his* early trials in a small vintage gym in New Jersey. It had two open-air support beams crossing perpendicular to the court halfway to the baskets from the foul lines, at top-of-the-backboard height. I didn't ask if the goal was a peach basket, but listened attentively as Papa told of how he would dribble full-speed away from the basket to above the free throw line, leap into the air, twist around and loft a two-handed shot up over the beam and down into the basket, with an increasing accuracy that came with practice. At first I took this in with a certain dubiousness, but in view of other corroborating testimony I came to believe it.

Papa had played ball in high school and on YMCA teams. The games were held in church halls, or basements with twelve-foot ceilings. Back then, everyone shot two-handed set and jump shots and two-handed lay-ups. A jump ball at center occurred after every basket. In a game played in his youth in the New Jersey town of Denville, Papa's team won by a score of 32–28, with him scoring 29 points. Once his team lost 80–12 in a game played in a low-ceiling basement room, but he said scores rarely went beyond thirty points, that most scores were in the high teens or low twenties. So things had improved by my time.

Each opposing end of the Wasilla gym had a row of three large windows behind and partially below the backboards. These let in daylight, darkness, or headlights from the window-level parking area. Covered with a protective mesh, they contributed a caged, "gray-bar hotel" feeling to the ambiance. I guess if the power went off, cars could pull up to both ends, shine their headlights in through the windows, and we could play by shadow-light.

Scorekeepers and timers were situated above, in the bleacher area, but team seating was of particular note. The home and visiting teams sat on folding metal chairs in a concrete bunker-like opening built into the wall at floor level, below the bleachers. Visiting players and coaches quickly learned that exuberant team spirit could result in a score of *Concrete, 1, Head, 0. Game Over*. It prevented players and coaches from seeing the crowd, except when they—perhaps on a dare—leaned beyond the plane of the wall and looked up in moments of foolhardiness or bravado, at which time they confronted the faces of exuberant fans. I know of no instance of a player's lap being despoiled by a falling body, but I cannot say the same for containers of popcorn and soda, or articles of personal attire.

Behind the player seating was a "room" ten or twelve feet deep, providing storage for folding chairs and equipment. My brother Richard, a fellow veteran of 1950s "Duck and Cover," tells me that this area reminded him of a bomb shelter. But it was an excellent use of space, for storage in the gym was nonexistent. Consisting of concrete sides, floor, and ceiling, the dungeon-like bunker was utilitarian in nature. Light struggled to survive in the shadowed recesses. The ceiling, at most five feet high, was so low that Mickey Rooney would have had to stoop. This aspect was compounded by low-wattage electric light fixtures jutting down. For those interested in forensic matters, there yet might be dessicated residue of hair and blood remaining for DNA testing and genome research. If one quietly crouches there for a long enough time, echoes of pain-caused invective and epithets can be heard. Having read Edgar Allen Poe's "Cask of Amontillado" and envisioned the red-eyed rats in his "Pit and the Pendulum," I was attentive to all possibilities when in the bunker vicinity.

In spite of its limitations, I've always had a fondness for that gym. As early as sixth grade I tagged along on Papa's vacation and week-end school newspaper and yearbook work sessions with his high school students. I got to join in the high school players' pick-up games when they took a break from journalism—heady stuff. Today I remember the times I practiced by myself in that gym, and savor the memories of the faint voices of the students underscored by the metronomical rhythm of the mimeograph or ditto machine, and the echoes of my own lay-ups and shots and the basketball bouncing on the gym floor.

My brother Peter the Great missed out on much of that particular nostalgia but tells of when he was a third-grader and diphtheria shots were being given in the gym. The kids were lined up in the staircase that led down to the gym doorway, with Peter a reluctant first in line. The inoculation instrument was a gun-like device, a fact duly noticed by the apprehensive kids standing in harm's way. Peter stepped to the altar, took his medicine, then staggered back along the waiting line.

"Oh, it hurts! It really hurts!" he moaned, exaggerating the pain and letting his arm go limp as he passed the line of remaining students. This, Peter relates gleefully, caused great consternation among the rest of the little lambs and resulting irritation on the part of the teachers in attendance. Wouldn't you know it—a teacher's kid!

Decades later, the old gym was remodeled once again. The witches, goblins, and white sheeted ghosts of its Halloween carnivals, its drama farces and sports rivalries, its educational programs that entertained and enlightened us, have faded into the past. For all its idiosyncracies, the gym was much appreciated and served its purposes well. The dreams, experiences, and memories of those who shared this time and space were nurtured within its embrace. And the drama goes on: It is now the site for Wasilla City Council meetings.

Errant Directional Inclinations

WHEN I WAS IN JUNIOR HIGH, THE gym's size seemed respectable. After the knock-around hole-in-the-trees games at home, I was thrilled to play in the gym. I could play in the winter without gloves, mittens, or bunny boots. The junior high boys formed into two groups: the eighth grade Blackhawks and the seventh grade Braves, with each split into two teams, and we played in prelim events before the high school contests. The Blackhawk Red Team roster my eighth-grade year was: Danny Adcock (#9), Gene Huston (#6), Melvin Belden (#10), Arnold Neilsen (#5), and me (#7). The Blackhawk White Team roster was: Burton Kohler (#8), Danny Karnofsky (#2), David Bryant (#11), Keith Lovejoy (#12), and Pat Patterson (#5). We were privileged to have cheerleaders, too: Judy Bergman, Shirley Neal, Ricky Platt, and Janet Michelson. We played shortened quarters, or halves, usually with a running clock. Our novice, scrambling enthusiasm was the cause of pride and amusement among the friends and families filling the overlooking bleachers.

One game stands alone in my personal Hall of Infamy. It was the third quarter and I was on the court near the foul line at the west end. My team had possession at the wall facing the bunker and the bleachers. Everyone was scattered on the far end, and I was alone near the basket. I yelled and waved, calling for the ball, eager to take advantage before the defense descended. I was duly thrown the ball, and then proceeded to turn and drive in for an easy lay-up.

A short silence settled across the gym. Then the other team's defense—and offense—did descend, *en masse*, to shake my hand, slapping me on the back, thanking and congratulating me, their words swarming around my head like a flock of tumultuous ravens.

"Hey, thanks a lot!"—"Nice shot!"—"Way to go, man!"—"Hoo-Whee!" I sensed that my teammates, scattered and silent, took no part in this. My satisfaction turned to puzzlement, then to confusion, then to a dawning horror, and finally to dazed mortification, as I realized what I had done—and why there had been no defense. *Aaaaaaahh!* I had just scored two points for the other team!

Somehow the world kept turning, the game ran its course. The other team won, 18 to 16. I had given them the margin of victory. I dejectedly walked off the floor, trying to apologize to my teammates. I had lost the game for us. Later, I was told that I had scored all 16 of our points, which I found hard to believe, but if so, it came as scant consolation. I had learned two of life's valuable lessons: "If something looks too good to be true, it probably is!" and "Look a gift horse in the mouth!"

Many years later, I heard the "Wrong Way (Doug) Corrigan" story. He flew to Dublin, Ireland, from New York, instead of to the West Coast as planned. There's suspicion that this may have been a deliberate attempt to overcome government bureaucracy. However, there was also a "Wrong Way" Roy Reigels who ran sixty-nine yards toward his opponents' goal in the 1929 Rose Bowl. And a "Wrong Way" Jim Marshall of the Vikings who ran for sixty-six yards to pull off a safety in 1964, with a mere eighty million watching. The Vikings won anyway.

I drove only fifteen feet for a lay-up, with two hundred people watching. Still, I claim some small, rueful camaraderie with such lost souls as these. Happy Trails, Roy, Jim, and Doug (if so be the case), wherever you may be. "Wrong Way" Harbeson feels your pain.

EIGHTH-GRADE GRADUATION IN THE OLD WASILLA GYM, MAY 1961.
The four adults in the foreground, from the far right, are Mr. and Mrs. Cadwallader, Patricia Newcomb, and Mary Bergman. Others recognized are Gene and Violet Coghlan, to the left of the post in the center of the upper level, front row, and Linda Carney, third to the right from the post in the same row. No complete list of that year's graduates has come to light, but study of the photo with several friends from the time has yielded 20 names; roughly left to right on the lower level, with several gaps in identifications: Dan Adcock, Gene Belden, Judith Bergman, Cynthia Blissard, David Bryant, Susie Budbill, Sherman Eves, George Harbeson Jr., Donna Harvey, Frieda Hulke, Eugene Huston, Barbara Kelton, Janet Michaelson, Burton Kohler, Roger Lincoln, Ricki Platt, Sherry Walker, Pat ("Floyd") Patterson, Elizabeth Wright, Kay Yates.

High School Commences

THE WORLD SPUN ALONG IN ITS ORBIT, even if one had occasional fits of errant directional inclination. Eighth grade graduation found our class standing proudly alongside the bunker and listening to Alaska's Senator Ernest Gruening promise us a swimming pool, although this didn't come to pass for many, many years.

As I worked at becoming acclimated to freshman status it was determined that I needed eyeglasses. Reading several shelves worth of science fiction books in the small Wasilla Public Library had probably contributed. During summers I checked out eight or ten books each Friday and read them the following week, on rainy days, in the Alaska midnight twilight, and in the eerie shadowed flashlight world under the bed covers.

So I was introduced to wearing plastic and glass objects on my face, an on/off adaptation process. One off period came in the school library on my first day with glasses, when I had stuffed them into my shirt pocket. I was anticipating the upcoming basketball season with my schoolmates, and exuberance was running high. In a fit of spontaneous energy, I leaped into the air to touch the ceiling. The glasses in my pocket jumped with me, but contrary to the laws of gravity didn't fall to earth at the same rate that I did. They lofted out of my pocket before rejoining the rest of the planet by crashing to the floor to sow glass fragments and cracked frames across the fields of learning. For every action there is a reaction, and that night dismay and disappointment shadowed Mom's face; Papa, not saying much, dipped into our meager funds and resignedly ordered another pair. Nick Carney, a past Wasilla High graduate, writes of his early sports days and his uneasiness about breaking his glasses. He played without them and had trouble seeing the basket. I didn't want that, so I became more careful with mine.

Coach Turner declared a prerequisite to basketball season that year: If we desired to participate, we needed to show up with a crewcut.

"It is a matter of personal hygiene and efficient use of time and water," he said. "A swipe or two on the head with a washcloth after practice suffices, thus allowing you to get home sooner to your waiting families." As the son of a teacher man I discerned that this would also lessen the time he had to waste waiting for the Brylcreem crowd.

"But the girls dig it," the older players said, of what has been designated the "wet look."

"They like to run their fingers through your hair, drives 'em crazy."

I pondered the validity of that argument with my friend Dennis Calhoun, and after thoughtful consideration we arrived at the conclusion that girls, stereotypically of a more fastidious nature, would not rank getting their hands greasy high on any list of priorities. The Brylcreem inducement was filed for review at a later time.

Mr. Turner's edict was met with annual consternation—resentment by some, trepidation by others. Squirming ensued: Was a longer "flattop" allowable? It went without saying that a longer "flattop DA" was out of the question. (This was when I learned of the fashionable connection between one's head and the rear part of waterfowl anatomy. I hadn't yet heard of the "Pope's nose.") Older players Larry Teeland, Billy Gilbertson, Richard Ingram, Pete Hjellen, and Dicky Carl ventured the "silly millimeter longer" approach of a flattop, no doubt accorded some leeway in light of their returning veteran status. But the crewcut was the only option for us rookies, I, encumbered with a shy nature, feared mirth and ridicule and underwent a brief period of anguish, but love of the game won out and I was inducted into the Butch Wax brigade.

This wasn't the only pressing concern in my high school athletic years. There was also the painful matter of plantar warts—*Verona plantaris*, to be precise. Hyperkeratosis lesions on the plantar surface, if you will. These afflictions grow in the sole of the foot. Ten percent of teenagers got them, it was said. I just wanted to get rid of mine. Richard in his time after me got them. Peter the Great in his time after Richard got them. The virus lies in ambush areas such as communal showers and locker rooms.

Papa took me to Dr. Vincent Hume, our family doctor in Palmer. Hume had serious problems in later years, but for us he was a good doctor. He delivered Peter the Great into the world. He removed my tonsils, using ether for the anesthetic. (I can still taste the stuff and see the metal mesh of the mask; I made it to 93 in the countdown—and it's true what they say about the ice cream.)

"What's the problem?" asked Dr. Hume.

"George has some kind of foot growth—a wart, maybe," Papa told him. We went into a back room, where I removed my shoe and sock.

Doc Hume looked at my foot, readied a needle, and told me to hold my ankle with both hands to keep the foot from jumping around.

"This will deaden the area—might hurt a bit," he advised, and slid the needle into my foot. After a few minutes of waiting for the anesthetic to take effect, he burned the wart out with an instrument that resembled a soldering iron. I listened to the sizzling, saw and smelled the smoke, felt no pain, and it was done in a matter of minutes.

"It'll take a little time for the hole to fill in," he told us. "Not long. Keep it covered and dry for a week or two. There'll be soreness, but not much. Any problems, come back."

And the bill? Something like twenty bucks. Or less. No *Verona plantaris* until twenty years later. That time I went to a clinic in Anchorage. Can't remember the doctor's name, nor the nurse's, nor the assistant's, but it entailed three visits, getting naked with the open-back gown, signing statements promising not to sue anyone over any possibility, and getting the laser treatment. Same healing procedure. Oh, yes, that will be 500-some-odd dollars, thank you very much.

After another couple of decades pesky *Verona* once again rose to the surface. This time it was one visit, no shot, no gown, no statements to sign. I had considered the duct tape procedure, duct tape being the Alaska Standard for all things mechanical, medical, cultural, and masculine, but opted for a cryosurgery application of liquid nitrogen. With a small round Band-aid in place I was off to the races again, to the tune of eighty bucks. In medicine, like basketball, it's a roller coaster ride, a carousel caravan, a muskrat scramble on a one-life gamble, this world, it is.

The '62 Season Begins

ONCE UNDER THE BASKETBALL AEGIS OF Mr. Turner and the Wasilla gym, with an inkling of what was coming, Dennis and I became cook's helpers in the school lunch program, where we performed general bus boy and dishwashing duties, provided fodder for teasing from the good-natured cooks, Ilah Senske and Fay Riley, and *ate*. In those days school lunches were real food, meals actually cooked, baked and prepared on site, with glasses, silverware, steel trays. Dennis and I took full advantage of the bountiful fare, and Ilah and Fay saw that we were well nourished. To this day I recall the soul-stirring spaghetti, which provided fortitude for Mr. Turner's regimen. People today might say that we were bulking up, but I think we were just hungry teenage boys.

It wasn't long before we were feeling the effects of practicing with experienced players. My ribs and arms seemed to have established an uncomfortably close relationship with Dicky Carl's elbows; my court vision was filled with the larger-than-life front jersey numbers 42 and 45, those of Lary Hill and Jerry Bouwens; and I had the sinking feeling that high-waymen Pete Hjellen, Billy Gilbertson, and "Leaky Greek" Joe Leone constantly lurked behind me. We all looked to the august presence of our impressively knee-braced senior and team captain, Larry Teeland.

Somewhere in a fray I knew there would be Richard Ingram (#55). Richard, good-natured, friendly, and powerfully built, had a jump shot style that included kicking his legs almost horizontally in front of him. While not deliberate in any way, on two distinct defensive occasions I was the surprised flat-on-my-back recipient of two large footprints that abruptly appeared on my jersey. On each occasion, I looked up to see Richard's smiling face, with his hand extended to help me to my feet, he being always the gentleman. It was a pleasure to see him forty years later in a restaurant in Homer, where, true to his nature, he smiled broadly and extended his hand in friendship and the spirit of old schoolmates. After he'd departed, I noticed that I was still standing, with my shirt front undisturbed. Here's to Richard and old times.

Life in the Fast Lane

THE ADVANTAGES AND DISADVANTAGES OF THE old gym were most apparent during one David and Goliath contest during my first high school basketball season. The Kenai Kardinals journeyed north to take on us Warriors in January of 1962. Kenai was a Class "B" school, with a larger student body to draw from, and had taller, older, more experienced players, with Coach Evenson at their helm.

Lee Turner, a fan of Kentucky's Adolph Rupp, had coached quite successfully in Ohio and Indiana and had been assistant coach at South Bend with runner-up placement in the state tournament—not something to sneeze at. There was also the rumor that he had employed the coaching technique of chasing players down the court in practice with a paddle. The kind and size of paddle wasn't specified, but that in no way diminished our healthy respect for him. Ping-pong, croupier's, or canoe: a paddle was a paddle. Although small of stature, Lee was a formidable force. So the Warriors were in high spirits and ready to battle Goliath.

High school basketball scores at all levels of play in those years saw wide point margins, sometimes with major reversals in contests that followed. The Kardinals had swept the Warriors four out of four in the previous season, by scores of 57–38, 62–39, and worse—or better, from their perspective—60–26 and 60–28. But there was always the possibility of a Jack and the Beanstalk event, with a certain amount of humiliation on the part of the giant.

Our gym became a disadvantage for us sometimes—for example, when spreading the floor in an area with little space to spread, and when a zone defense by a taller team could be impenetrable, and when a full court press might go either way. The disadvantages of our home court faced by the Kardinals were the low ceiling, the high close walls, the narrow, short floor where their offensive and defensive strategies might not fit, the looming hometown crowd and its overwhelming noise, the barred windows, and the ghostly menace of the bunker. Like some other small gyms of the era, the wall was considered the out-of-bounds "line," except when the ball was being thrown into play, at which time the defense had to honor a three-foot lane running around the gym's perimeter. But they were aware of this.

A court's "over-and-back line" is normally the half-court line, but each half of our small floor had an additional line between the free throw line and the top of the key. Once the ball advanced past center court, the extra line in the back court became the over-and-back boundary, thus creating a larger forecourt. Added to the lane rule, this compensated for the smaller overall floor size.

Confusing? It was actually quite simple, once the concept of quantum entanglement had been taken into account. All of this no doubt added much frustration, anguish, and premature aging to the referees' lives. Ed Carney and Rod Cottle were among the referees over the years. They were certified and did a credible job, in spite of the complicated lines.

Occasionally, for obscure reasons, Association refs from Anchorage were requested by visiting teams, or even by us. They braved their way through snow and ice to tread up and down our hardwood, make whistle noises, eat the snacks, take showers, and chat with the stat keepers, who were teacher volunteers—Papa, Katie Noonan, Warren Jones, Ray Holtz, and others.

Some of us underclassmen played J.V. and subbed for the Varsity as well. We had won the J.V. game against the Kardinals on Friday, 48–46, and lost the Saturday J.V. game 58–30. Kenai had won Friday night's Varsity game 36–20, a closer, lower-scoring game than the previous contests. Memory of the Class "C" Warriors coming from a 37–17 half-time deficit to beat the defending state champion Fairbanks in the Anchorage Class "A" tourney two years previously may have given us extra encouragement.

The possession rule wasn't in use then, so jump balls were actually jumped, and quarters started with a jump ball at center. No jumper was allowed to tap the ball until it had reached the apex of the official's toss, an observance that has deteriorated considerably in today's infrequent jumps, almost to the point of knocking it out of the official's hands. We—our starting five with the rest of us guarding the bunker—lined up around the circle with the Kardinals, maneuvering for position. Up went the ball and Saturday's varsity game was on.

Although the Kardinals had a substantial edge even on our floor and held the lead as the game progressed, our fast break was giving them difficulty. We managed to sneak through the timber from time to time, and there may have been just a bit of "stalling." There was still value to stalling then, but it was less effective than in basketball's early days, when scores might consist of single digits. As might be expected, this tactic on our part met with disapproval, but we were open to all options.

At some point, in his infinite wisdom, Mr. Turner put me in to rest a starter. Other freshmen such as Dennis and Pat Patterson also got a chance, perhaps more than I, because they were bigger or taller. (My "little brothers" Richard and Peter the Great grew to be a formidable six-five and six-four respectively. The only way I can account for this is our family tree history of an 1800s grandfather, Carl Boston Porth, born on the sailing vessel *The Boston* on the way to the U.S. from Germany. Uncle Bill said this ancestor stood seven feet tall.) At any rate, there I was, all five feet eight inches of me, lacking my later additional height and weighing in at a hefty 130 pounds. I was developing my ball handling and shooting skills, but I suspected that at that particular moment Mr. Turner was interested in a less sophisticated role.

"Harbeson!" he commanded down the line of seated players, his famously bushy black eyebrows furrowed, his bald pate aglare with the lights. Players sat with their feet teasing the out-of-bounds line, so I slid along the line of knees and knee pads and crouched next to him, gathering my white canvas Converse All-Star Hi-Topped feet under me, and trying not to disrupt the floor action.

"What's our defense?" he barked, his eyes following the play.

"2–3 zone," I quickly answered, as the players rushed back and forth. I'd learned to pay attention to "small" details like that. Man-to-man could get us in foul trouble against a taller team.

"You're out front. Get in there for the Greek and keep 'em from gettin' into the key!" The thought crossed the back of my mind that I was an odd choice for a hatchet man. But I snapped to attention, my head narrowly missing the concrete edge of the bunker ceiling, and yelled up to the scorekeeper. Soon a ref whistled an out-of-bounds call against the Kardinals. I heard gentlemanly protest plus disagreement of the playground sort from the vicinity of the Kardinal bench concerning the wall-as-out-of-bounds rule, with conjecture offered about the legitimacy of someone's parentage, and some intriguing vocabulary I had not yet encountered at home or in English class. Mr. Turner continued to take note of the action, calling out occasional instructions. No doubt he, with his long career in coaching and having gone to the Indiana State Finals, was more familiar with home/visitor conversation than I.

With the ball dead, the ref waved me in, and I entered the mix, well aware of which basket was ours and which was theirs due to my earlier "Wrong Way" days. I rushed to my spot on defense, then scrambled into the offense, then back to defense. I caught the ball unexpectedly and passed it to another white uniform. My head swiveled like an owl's, this time with my new black-framed glasses securely fastened to my face by an elastic eyeglass strap, or "ear brassiere." My over-sized feet avoided becoming co-joined with each other, or with any of the other twenty-two on the court, including the refs'.

Suddenly I crouched on defense, right arm raised, left lowered, on the balls of my feet. Balanced and alert, I pushed off left, then right, sprang forward, then back, and there it was! An empty area above the foul line! Off to the far side, I saw Gilbertson or Hjellen tangled up with one of the Kardinals. At mid-court, an ominous figure appeared, driving the ball across the half court line, headed straight down the middle toward the Warrior/Kardinal ruckus under the basket. In a flash I pushed off to my right, toes stretching to get planted in time. Then the world of lights and color and roar of the crowd spun crazily, and I skidded along the floor on my back, feet and arms outspread, my lungs searching for a prodigal breath. My ear brassiere and eyeglasses frantically clutched my face. A whistle sounded from beyond the pale as a striped shirt blurred into view.

"Number 44, white! Blocking foul!" I heard the declaration rise above the abated roar, saw a blurred hands-to-hip motion, and a beckon to the sidelines. The familiar face of Joe Leone loomed over me; his hand grabbed mine and pulled me staggering to my feet.

"Wha . . .?" I asked.

"Way to go, George! Good 'D'! Stopped 'em cold!" He aimed me in the direction of the bunker and added, "I'm in for you." I stumbled toward the bunker and tugged at a sagging knee pad as the Kardinal stepped to the free throw line. I saw Mr. Turner's lips moving.

"That's the way. That's what I wanted. Might make 'em think a little before they try that again." Overall, it seemed to me that most of his words matched his lip movements, which was good. "But next time, be quicker. Get there first." His praise jumped into my ears as my floor-bounced butt found an empty metal seat, and teammates on either side congratulated my shoulders.

I regained my equilibrium, and tuned to the game's action again, slightly confused, but with a growing sense of accomplishment. I'd stopped him! Well, yeah, he got to shoot free throws, but he'd missed the first on the one-and-one, and Dicky Carl had grabbed the rebound. Next time, I vowed to myself, I'll get there first.

Players and coaches had to sit just inside the opening of the bunker because the out-of-bounds was the wall, and while the game progressed, an unfortunate Kardinal may have snagged himself on one of the bunker door hinges adjacent to the player seating. (The heavy doors were removed for the games, but not the hinges.) This added to the tension. Evenson may have jumped up too quickly a time or two, and found the concrete ceiling resistant and unsympathetic. Adding to the excitement was Kenai's Erickson stunning himself against the wall on a lay-up, despite the mat—forgetting about the short backboard-to-wall distance—and their loss of Cooper, who was ejected on a technical foul call.

With three minutes left in the game, with the score reading 45–32 in the Kardinals' favor, a time-out turned into a Kenai exodus. The game action ceased. The Kardinal players and manager rummaged around their side of the bunker, gathering their gear, while coaches Evenson and Turner, the referees, and the scorekeepers conferred. Confusion emanated from the spectators. Our five came over to mingle in the swirling potpourri in front of the bunker.

"What's goin' on?"

"Beats me."

"You can take this crackerbox and shove it!"

"Somebody get hurt?"

"Hey! Where you guys goin'?"

"Look at those punks. They're leavin'!"

"Damn right we're leavin'!"

And so they left. Forfeited the game. Their bus high-beams slid across the barred windows as they pulled out of the parking lot. The Kardinals and Coach Evenson were staying with the Turners, who had a large basement with room for many players. It was too late to drive home to Kenai. Bea Turner says things were "tense" at the Turner residence that night. Subsequently, Kenai canceled their upcoming season games with us and didn't play Wasilla for years afterward.

In the week after the game, Evenson was quoted in the *Anchorage Daily Times* as saying he had understood that the new Wasilla gym across town had been scheduled for completion by that weekend. Unfortunately, the construction had been delayed, and the old gym, the scene of basketball contests for many years before Kenai even had a gym, still had life left in it, and that's the way the ball bounced on January 20, 1962.

Bea says the *Times* called Wasilla school about the incident. Jane B., the school secretary, answered the phone, sent for Mr. Turner, and listened to his end of the conversation from her desk. She found discrepancies in the ensuing article with reference to what she had heard Turner say during the call, which added to the local confusion.

In their defense, the Kardinals were the better team, and our gym *was* a problem. They were in the classic big school/small school situation, where the larger school has little to gain in league standing by winning, and much to lose in reputation if defeated. Playing in an unequal contest also is difficult because the better team wants to play its best players, despite the chance to give the second string experience. There is also the risk of injury for a win that may not count for much. The better team might pick up bad habits, and appear mean-spirited. The underdog team can face humiliation and also become mean-spirited. When the chemistry is right and restraint is exercised, such a game is well worthwhile for both teams, but the odds are often against this.

It may have been a scheduling requirement; I don't know. But it was generous of Kenai to play Wasilla and good for the sport, and good for the communities involved. Big schools need a touch of humility at times to appreciate the overcoming of long odds by a small school, and small schools need a taste of glory and an appreciation of the higher caliber of play of a larger school.

Looking through the season records in my yearbooks, I see that there were several lopsided scores in the years that followed, in our newer, more standard gym. My junior year, with Wasilla in Class "B" and Milton Wetherington coaching the '62–63 season, shows us beating Copper Valley by 20 in each of the first two games of the season, them clobbering us by 41 and 26 in the last two. Cordova beat us in one game 99–47, Eielson 98–58. In my senior year we beat Glennallen once 91–36. But no other games ended with a walkout.

Tales of Adversity and Courage

As my freshman year progressed, the small gym was a classroom like the academic ones, where lessons were taught and learned. Or not learned, as the case may be. Friendships grew, or faded. This hope, that dream, blossomed while others withered on the sidelines. And basketball season continued.

One unique player stands out in my freshman year memories of the old gym. His name eludes me, and I'm not sure of his team, although Valdez comes to mind. He was of average height and strong build, and one of his arms had been amputated just above the elbow. Yet he played well, holding his own. His shortened arm helped hold the ball, and he dribbled and passed with the other. He blocked out, rebounded, screened, and I quickly learned to respect his shortened arm, as he employed it effectively. I respected his courage and will and wondered how I would have handled such an adversity.

I also remember watching girls' basketball, as a sport and in PE, before Title Nine days. The girls had different rules from us boys, with positions that included "roving" guards. Some players on each team couldn't play the full floor but had to stop at half-court. This seemed much too complicated, especially in the old gym with its extra over-and-back lines. Eventually the girls' rules were changed to resemble the boys' rules.

Organized girls' basketball was in its early stages during my Wasilla High years. At first there were no contests with other schools, but the intramural program was popular just the same. In 1962–63 the girls were coached by Billy Gilbertson and Pete Hjellen, with referees Richard Ingram and Dicky Carl, and at times my father. Patricia Noonan was the faculty sponsor. Players included Karen Andrew, Barbara Kelton, Judy Bergman, Georgia Starr, Shirley Neal, Frieda Hulke, Nancy Mitchell, Marilyn Gilbertson, Kelly Palmquist, Phyllis Edwards, Colleen Carter, Kathy Coghlan, Ida Hjellen, and others.

Girls' basketball brings to my mind the year of 1979, when I was teaching in Kivalina and coaching the Kivalina QaavIks (Wolverines), both the boys' and girls' teams. The girls' team was eventually dissolved because of the rough style of play of some of the girls and their obstreperous attitude toward taking instruction.

Kivalina was a small school with small rosters, so four girls who hadn't caused problems were assimilated into the boys' team. The boys, after some mumbling and grumbling, accepted this, even becoming protective of the girls when playing other teams. There were a few games left in the season, so it was a process of convincing our opponents that, no, it wouldn't be so difficult; that they could use girls too; that a girl/boy on-the-floor-at-any-one-time formula could be worked out. I argued that playing meant a great deal to these kids and to their schoolmates, and that they deserved the chance to play. We may have agreed to forfeit for the sake of AAHSA regulations and win/loss records. After an initial reluctance, the few coaches and teams left in our season understood and obliged.

Thus the season ended, but the state tournament in Dillingham had to be considered. I duly sent in rosters and the required paperwork, including a casual footnote of, "Oh, by the way, we're bringing a co-ed team." I continued with practices, worked up strategies, held a pep assembly, and imagined the principal-to-principal, principal-to-AHSAA, AHSAA-to-principal phone calls taking place. Kivalina principal Calvin Baker supported us, so that helped.

When tournament time came, we flew to Dillingham, played as the only co-ed team, and both boys and girls had a great time. It was a new experience for the other teams and the refs as well. Someone told me later that the coaches' meeting preceding the tournament and our arrival saw "dissension in the ranks" until somebody asked a dissenter, "What's the matter? Afraid they'll beat you?" We were treated the same as any other team, with no special consideration except a dressing room for the girls. We played two games without winning, but we were more successful than some teams. One game at the tournament resulted in a score of 90 to 2, a truly sad affair, but without noticeable controversy.

I made it a point to give all team members a chance to play. One of the girls was Janet Swan, a senior, who liked the Bonnie Tyler song, "It's a Heartache." In our games, I substituted Janet several times, maybe started her once. She was actually a better player than some of our boys, and she had greater court composure than the other girls, one of whom was too nervous to enter the game when I gave her the chance to play. Janet quickly adapted, becoming at ease in the action, making a steal, advancing the ball, rebounding, taking shots: nothing spectacular, but competent in her role. At one point she was fouled by an opposing boy who was uncertain of how to guard her, and who apologized in embarrassment. She smiled at him, they shook hands, she stepped to the foul line and made one of the free throws and then a later basket to become, as a newspaper reporter later informed me, the first girl to score in an Alaska high school boys' state tournament. If that's true, I think Janet's record may still stand today.

THE WASILLA WARRIORS *with* **COACH LEE TURNER** *and their Class C tournament trophy in Valdez in 1962: team members were (in back, from left) Richard Ingram, George Harbeson, Dicky Carl, (and front, from left) Pete Hjellen, Pat Patterson, Larry Teeland, Gerald Bouwens, Bill Gilbertson, (Coach Turner), Dennis Calhoun, Joe Leone, and manager Lary Hill (not pictured).*

Of Champions and Moose Droppings

A HIGH POINT OF MY FRESHMAN YEAR, the last year the high school used the old gym, was winning the Class "C" State Tournament held in Valdez. Later that spring we would move across town to an entirely new high school and a new gym.

Led by our sole senior, Larry Teeland, we set out in a caravan of cars with volunteer drivers using their own cars, the standard mode of athletic travel for most small schools then. The caravan held the drivers and Coach Turner; ten of us players and manager/sometimes player Lary Hill; our spirited cheerleading squad of Linda Carney, Ida Hjellen, Joyce Patterson and Marilyn Gilbertson; and sponsor Patricia Noonan. We stuffed ourselves, our luggage, and our equipment into the vehicles, cranked up the heaters and headed for Valdez, a six-hour trip. Up the winter-attired Glenn Highway north of Palmer to Moose Creek, then past Sutton and the Jonesville area, Chickaloon, King Mountain, on up the rising elevation past Long Lake and the vast panorama of the Matanuska Glacier— the glacier much larger then than it is today. Then Meekins Roadhouse, Lion's Head outcrop, Sheep Mountain Lodge (pit stop), the notched crag of Gunsight Mountain, and onto the high plateau and Eureka.

The stunning scenery, then as today, rivals the best in the world, and we were young and on the road, and the snow-streaked miles streamed beneath our tires. On to Tazlina we went. We rolled past the Lake Louise exit where caribou scattered across the hoar-frosted landscape, then followed the long straight lines of passing-lane yellow into Glennallen and the junction with the Richardson Highway. Glennallen provided a chance to stretch our legs, restore circulation, and empty our bladders. We also replenished our snacks, checked with the Brylcreem and Butch Wax mirrors, and gassed up the vehicles. And strutted a little—after all, we were the Warriors.

Then it was south on the Richardson. We glided by Copper Center and Willow Creek and past the Edgerton cut-off that leads to the Chitina/Kennicott/McCarthy area, then continued through Tonsina and along the Tiekel River to Thompson Pass. The roadside snowbanks rose higher, to six feet at times, as we luged our way through the straights and curves in our combustion-engine sleds. Along the trail we halted for a moose taking advantage of the easy snow-free traveling in the roadway. Wary of its hackle-raised scan of the lead vehicle's front end, we conceded the road to the moose. Our convoy fell into line behind the north end of that south-bound moose and followed its rambling rear for a half-mile or more until the animal vented a nugget-laced opinion of us, made a tremendous leap over the left berm, and disappeared into the brush.

Then it was up into the pass and across its windswept tree-dotted expanses. Today, this route from Glennallen is punctuated by views of the Trans-Alaska Pipeline, but then the oil boom was years in the future. We sped onward, down into the twisting curves and ice-fall-laden sides of Keystone Canyon, and emerged via the open Lower River delta and Valdez Glacier drainage into Valdez.

Papa, coaching Wasilla basketball in 1954, had brought the team here, with Mom making the trip also. This was the old town of Valdez, before the post-'64 earthquake relocation. It had snowed heavily in 1954 as it did when we made the trip. Papa said snow was piled up to the roofs of the houses, many of which were connected by high-walled alleyways and in some cases tunnels. Bea Turner stayed in a two-story house in Valdez in 1962, and she says the snow was so deep she had to walk up an outside flight of stairs to the second floor to get down into her first-floor room.

In any event, regardless of snow, the '62 tourney commenced. We played hard and won our game on Friday and were slated for the championship game on Saturday night. Papa, Bea, and a few others drove to Valdez to cheer us on. Mom generously sacrificed her wish to attend and volunteered to stay home with seven energetic Harbeson and Turner kids. Red and Nelda Calhoun came from Homer because their son Dennis was a Warrior that year. Nelda provided us with Polaroids of the awards presentation. We took the championship by beating the host Valdez Buccaneers 65–50, after leading at halftime by 37–25. Larry Teeland connected for 28 points and a tourney All-Star award. Dicky Carl had 14 points, Billy Gilbertson 13, and Pete Hjellen 10. Dicky and Billy also were chosen for All-Star honors, as were Marvin Totemoff and Bob Day of Valdez, Ft. Greely's Alan Gibson and Bill Armstrong, Cordova's Dick Shellhorn and Mike Anderson, and Copper Valley's Ron Peltola.

Winning in Valdez gave us a slot in the Class "A" tournament in Anchorage, so we played there next but lost to the East High team of, I believe, Terry Gose and his teammates. Around this time I remember an eligibility controversy over a West High player, who had gotten married while still in high school, which incited a minor ruckus.

We freshmen weren't playing much but were definitely along for the ride, and for me it was a meaningful way to end my first season. I had learned a lot, had fun, made new friends, traveled a new section of Alaska, even learned to play poker as I chalked up experiences in life's scorebook.

A Long, Long Ride and a Rough Flight

IN THOSE DAYS WHEN WE RARELY TRAVELED to school events in buses, and mini-vans were still far down the road, it was station wagons, early Suburbans, a '59 Chevy, our Corvair, a Merc, possibly even a Cadillac that took us where we wanted to go. Lee Turner, Al Martin, Papa, Milton Wetherington, Marvin Richardson (with his black Mercury nicknamed "The Trashy Merc") and others drove us to our away contests. We were crammed into the vehicles, surrounded by luggage and equipment, never knowing what might happen along the way. Buses didn't enter the picture until later, when I discovered that traveling to away games on a bus seat with the lovely Sharon was vastly preferable to being jammed into a car with sharp-elbowed, chip-munching, irreverent and flatulent teammates.

One winter trip up the Glenn Highway on a cold, cloudy morning we began the steep southern descent to the Caribou Creek bridge and came upon a man traveling with his gear on a Flexible Flyer sled. We stopped briefly to chat, to see if he needed assistance.

"Thank you very much, but I'm doing fine," he told us. "Matter of fact, I'm headed to Whitehorse." We all looked at each other, at him, at the substantial downhill grade in front of us.

"Uh . . . *Whitehorse?*" we exclaimed. "Whitehorse, as in the Canadian city Whitehorse?"

"Yep. That's the one." He smiled from the recesses of his parka hood. "I was just sitting around and got to figuring, why not."

He waved good-bye as we continued on our way. The steepening road down to the curved bridge was covered with patchy snow pack but had areas of bare pavement, and we wondered about such trivial concerns as brakes and steering. And a possible sparks-flying, twisting, tumbling, terrifying flight off the road into the guard rail and over the steep drop-off on the right. We topped the rise on the far side and craned our necks for one last look but didn't see him. And so it was that this intrepid stranger, nameless and cryptic, became one of life's mysteries for us. Did he make it to Whitehorse? Did he crash at the bridge? We never heard, but we wished him luck. Many years later a semi traveling down to the bridge from the north spun out of control and wrecked, and the driver was killed. Even now whenever I hear of this area, or drive through it, I sense the spirits of those who travel the Alaskan journey with me.

Alaskan road conditions, then as now, took command on road trips. Returning on one trip through the Caribou Creek section we slid into the narrow snow-filled ditch at the rock face opposite the precipitous left-hand drop-off, but dug out and continued home. Returning from Homer on another occasion we encountered rain and black ice on the straight stretch through the Kenai Burn, several miles to the north of Sterling. We lined up along the sides of our family's Corvair station wagon and advanced like a strange red centipede down the ice-covered crown of the roadway for a hundred yards until we came upon wet pavement again.

- -

VISITING CORDOVA REQUIRED OTHER MODES of travel: There are no roads to it. It was Valdez by car, then a small ferry to Cordova. Sometimes the water was rough, but I never got seasick. My first ventures into the penny-ante poker world originated on these trips. I learned beginner's luck from Turner and my older teammates, who were determined to separate my little copper cents from me as we chugged along on the waters of Prince William Sound past a small blip known as Bligh Reef, made infamous by Exxon many years later.

But once, in the '61–62 season, we flew to Cordova on a DC-3. Dennis Calhoun remembers it better than I do, even though it was my first plane ride.

> We flew into Cordova on an Alaska or Wien DC-3 for a mid-season week-end of basketball. This was an exciting change for us from the usual car trips and spirits were running high. The trip down was uneventful and we were looking ahead to the coming contests, host families, and new sights to see. I don't recall who won, but we had a good time, staying with our host families, and checking out the town. The big deal about this trip was the return leg.
>
> When it was time to return home, the plane was undergoing engine problems, and we were delayed in the airport for a couple of hours before departing. We made our own entertainment:

snacking, sleeping, wandering, messing with basketballs. The weather wasn't that great, and it deteriorated as we waited. Finally, we got to board and roared off into the stormy skies, headed for Anchorage.

As we flew over Turnagain Arm prior to landing at Anchorage, I sat in the window seat on one side of the aisle and Jerry, a teammate, occupied the corresponding seat on the other. Some of us craned our necks, trying to catch a glimpse of Anchorage. I think Jerry was dozing or reading. We had encountered occasional mild turbulence along the flight, but abruptly, without warning, the plane hit a very long downdraft. I had my seat belt securely fastened, but Jerry had unlatched his. By chance, I happened to be looking in his general direction, so I witnessed the action.

Jerry soloed out of his seat, straight up in the air as gravity went south, then aviated hell-bent-for-leather horizontally through the air beneath the overhead rack, and sailed across the aisle for an unannounced visit into the lap of the person sitting next to me. The pilots evened the plane out and the DC-3 recovered. After the initial shock of realizing his uncomfortably close proximity to the guy in the seat under him, Jerry hit the deck scrambling, zipped back across the aisle, dived into his seat, and performed the fastest demonstration of seat belt operation that I've ever seen, its punctuating click cutting through the hubbub to be heard several seats away.

Get Me to the Game on Time

IN MY JUNIOR YEAR PAPA WAS RETURNING from one of his MSEA work sessions in a gathering midwinter snowstorm late on a Thursday night when our Chevy, now advanced in age, made an unscheduled stop a mile south of what is now Settlers Bay. Papa hoofed it the rest of the distance, about five miles, and arrived home in a heavy snowfall in the wee hours of Friday morning, to Mom's anxious relief.

She awakened us kids as usual at six that morning. I grabbed a flashlight and pulled open the basement door, foolishly thinking to use "The Fortress," our birch pole outhouse, eighty feet away in the dark. That was overly optimistic: Snow in the stairway leading up from the basement blocked the lower third of the doorway.

This led to a family discussion that awakened Papa from his all-too-short slumber. Two main problems took center stage in the overhead propane light's illumination of our breakfast table: Problem #1: Even if school were to be called off later in the morning with no students in attendance, as a teacher Papa had to show up to get paid; and Problem #2: The Warriors were scheduled to travel with Coach Wetherington to Glennallen for basketball that weekend. My realization of problem #2 altered my assessment of the snow against the door.

"Snow's not that deep," I interjected into the conversation. "Just drifted a little on the steps." Mom did not look convinced.

"There's three feet of snow out there," she said. "How are you going to get to school?" The Jeep wasn't running, and the Chevy sat on the road where it had stalled the night before. The Chevy's status being news to me, I admitted she had a point.

Papa stirred his coffee and drew on his cigarette, no doubt considering problem #1 and the possibility of a smaller paycheck, and cleared his throat.

"He'll walk."

Mom and I looked at him. Lee Anna and Richard looked at him, their eyes widening over their homemade toast and cranberry jelly. The hiss of the propane light filled the silence.

"I'll walk!" I proclaimed. Of course. That was it. "I'll walk." Visions of Glennallen's gym grew stronger in my mind's eye.

"He can walk out, get the Chevy, and drive it back to meet us at the drive. If it's too deep, Lee Anna and Richard can stay home today, but I have to get to school." Unstated was the fact that he needed more sleep. "The Chevy should start after sitting there for a few hours; it probably stalled from sucking snow into the carburetor, or from water in the gas." He looked at me and added, "I poured a can of HEET in the gas tank before I left it last night." And so it was decided. I gulped down a cup of hot cocoa, finished off two slices of toast, and quickly bundled up. I was off—neither snow nor cold nor sleet nor dark of night would stay a Wasilla Warrior from his appointed rounds.

The walk out the driveway to the Knik Road was just under a mile. The snowfall had abated, and the dark was giving way to daylight. The snow was thigh deep, at times to my waist. A myriad of white-weighted birch trees overhung the narrow drive, forming an archway, almost a tunnel in places, and bits of snow fell sporadically from their bent limbs. The temperature was 28 degrees with little wind. The snow and moist air muted most sounds, creating a peaceful hush of a sort experienced too rarely. I stopped for brief rests, and breathed in the silence like a life-assuring fragrance.

But a Warrior must keep to his task. On I trudged, my steps plowing a furrow through the snow for the others to follow. I reached the end of the drive and started on the Knik Road toward the Chevy when a snowplow went by me, headed toward Knik. The cleared lane spurred me on and I soon reached the Chevy, parked on the edge of the road near the Ulrich place, a home with an envied artesian well. I brushed the snow from the Chevy's windshield and hood, clambered into the driver's seat, dug beneath the layers of clothing for the . . . *Oh, no! The key! I forgot to bring the key!* I dug frantically in my pockets.

Whew—there it was. Gratefully, I gripped the thin piece of metal, placed it in the ignition, shifted to neutral, pulled the choke out halfway, gave the gas pedal a couple of quick pumps, began reciting fragments of the over-the-top William Ernest Henley poem "Invictus," which I had memorized in school. "In the fell clutch of circumstance/I have not winced nor cried aloud./Under the bludgeonings of chance/My head is bloody, but unbowed. . . ." and "I am the master of my fate;/I am the captain of my soul." I slid my foot onto the spring-loaded starter sticking up out of the floor near the gas pedal, and shoved down.

"R-rr-rrr-rrrr-rrrrr." I let up, then tried again. The "fell clutch of circumstance" drew nearer, hovering.

"R-rr-rrr-rrrr-rrrrrrrr-rrrrrrrr. R-rr-rrr-rrrr-rrrrrrr-rrrrrrrr-cough, spit-rattle, cough . . . *Vroooomm!*"

Success. Sweet glorious success. I was the master of my fate, the captain of my soul!

I drove the Chevy on the one plowed lane back to our driveway, to where Papa, Lee Anna, and Richard were waiting. Papa took over, and we sailed off to school. Eventually, the rest of my teammates showed up. We had to wait for J.V. player Frank Jackson who, because the Willow bus hadn't shown, had caught a ride in the back of a pickup all the way from Willow. Coach Wetherington seemed reluctant to let him go with us, even after Frank's nearly freezing effort, but in the end we loaded up the cars and hit the road for Glennallen, Frank included.

Thus, on that long-ago snow-fallen morning, I got my wish to play ball in Glennallen, and Papa's paycheck remained intact.

Wasilla vs. Seward, 1965: *from left, Warriors George Harbeson and Dave Bryant; Seahawks Ray Gillespie and Bob Dunphy. Photo from the 1965 Wasilla High School yearbook.*

Host Families

On away trips, with the exception of tournaments, we stayed with the families of the host team's players or staff, or with other residents. This arrangement, long since abandoned, seemed a beneficial one to me. The host families' hospitality was warm and friendly and served to bring people of different locales closer together. This is not to say that there wasn't an occasional mildly awkward time for visitor or host family, or the one-of-a-kind Kenai dust-up. I remember being nervous about staying with people who were strangers, but it was interesting and educational.

Some players I remember: Mike Pate, Jack Collie, Ray Martin, Jack Alexander, the Selle twins, and Brad Nixon from Homer. (Mike went into insurance. Ray became a pilot and died in a plane crash years later. Jack showed up a few years ago to install Homer Electric Association power to my then under-construction home. Jim and John Selle did student teaching with me at Lathrop High and have been longtime friends.) From Valdez I recall Bobby Day, Jason Wells, and Ed Irish. Jim Estelle and Mick Petit from Palmer. (I was teaching in Kivalina years later when I heard that Jim had been killed in South America while on a Peace Corps mission.) Ron Peltola and Ross Schaeffer from Copper Valley. (Ross later became the magistrate in Kotzebue.) The Mielke brothers, Bill and Bob, and Jim Kohring from Chugiak. (Bill and Bob played city-league ball with me.) And Jerry Behymer, Chip Lamb and Dick Shellhorn from Cordova. Others I can envision upon hearing the names.

We were housed in pairs with the host families, sometimes three or more of us, or occasionally by ourselves. Once I soloed, the privileged guest of honor. I regret that I can't recollect the names of all the families that housed me, other than the Calhouns, but one name I do recall is D.J. Moon, of Cordova. All in all, the experience gave us a first-hand perspective of how other people lived, what was important to them, and the differences and similarities to our own homes and lives.

Overtime Medley

As might be expected, the move to the new school and gym in the spring of 1962 signaled the end of an era, just as the first gym had done in its time. With the '62 move came a larger gym and hallways, and more classrooms.

The new school also came with new gym lockers—and combinations to be learned. Mine was the first number into the second number equals the third number. Or the third number into the second number equals the first number. 3–39–13. I did manage to memorize it before graduating. I checked it out years later when playing Community School ball, and it still worked. Even today it is chiseled into my fading brain cells, to the point where I may adopt it as my epitaph.

3–39–13.

Let 'er RIP.

This combination inspired me to select #13 when we received new uniforms, in a fit of reverse triskaidekaphobia. Omens are omens, and in one high school ball game we played on Friday the 13th and I wore #13 and scored 13 points. Michael Jordan played for 13 seasons. And Wilt Chamberlain had his #13 retired by three different teams.

We were avid in those days. We shot baskets before school and at lunch time, and lofted sideline heaves between classes. On hall passes, we cajoled gym class students into letting us take a shot from the doorway or sideline. If we missed, we wheedled another try.

Once in P.E. class I was bringing the ball down in the back court, guarded by Dan Karnofsky. Harassed by Dan's defense, I let fly a long down-court pass to someone under the basket. Dan leaped for the ball and it smacked him right in the eyeglasses. Which happened to be attached to his face. Which was connected to his body. Which went flying head-over-heels backward to the floor. The ball careened in the opposite direction to hit the backboard behind us, and almost went in the basket. But he took it well and accepted my apology. He may have claimed an interception and shot attempt. But what goes around came around when I taught P.E. in Selawik. I was talking with a student under the basket during a gym class when another student's three point scud-missile flew out of the lights and struck me full in the face, flattening my glasses. The

239 ·· *The Game is the Thing*

THE WARRIORS HUDDLE AT HOME IN 1963: *from left, Patricia Noonan, scorekeeper; George Harbeson Sr., timer; coach Lee Turner; and players Jerry Bouwens (seated, left), Pat Patterson, Joe Leone, Dicky Carl (5), Pete Hjellen, Gene Belden (51) and George Harbeson Jr. (13). Photo from the 1963 Wasilla High School yearbook.*

surprise, shock, and immediate reactive anger gave me a clue to what Dan must have felt.

One winter night, the East High J.V.'s arrived from Anchorage for a game, several of them wearing sunglasses. Strange breed, city people. And this was before *The Blues Brothers*. They got to whoopin' 'n' hollerin' in the locker room, getting themselves all stirred up, and busted out for the pre-game warm-up one-lap strut around the gym. Well, *one* of them did. The rest stayed in the locker room. The guy hadn't noticed that his teammates let him go it alone. Maybe it was the sunglasses. His teammates then joined him for the warm-up, but their three-man weave kept falling apart due to fits of laughter. After that I noticed that a few of the Warriors who liked to be first through the door to break the spirit banner were more cautious when it came to leading the charge.

In 1963–64, Milton Wetherington was our coach. Janie Nunley, Shirley Neal, Judy Bergman, and Jean Hartman were leading the cheers. We had a less-than-enviable season win-loss record of 8-17, but we hosted the Class "B" State Tournament, and there were exciting games. One was Homer vs. Barrow. Barrow was a smaller team but had speed and an amazing shooter.

The game was beset by fouls from the start. Homer had scored 50 points by halftime, but because of Barrow's hustle and their shooter, and the great number of fouls called on Homer, the score was down to the slimmest of leads by Homer in the last seconds of regulation. So many of Homer's players had fouled out, including Mike Pate, one of their taller players, that their manager, Phil Brudie, had been put into the game. Homer may have been down to four players at the last. Homer's Jack Alexander had the ball in the last seconds, surrounded by the frantic down-by-one Barrow team. Out of the scrum, scant seconds left, with no fouls called, a Barrow player came up with the ball and sprinted for his basket for a successful lay-up. A controversy erupted over whether the buzzer had sounded before the shot, but the end result was that the shot had counted, and the Mariners had lost to the Whalers by one point.

It was one of basketball's ups for Barrow. For Homer it was one of those downs that stick for years. Almost half a century later, Mike Pate and Dennis Calhoun still recall that game. I imagine that Jack Alexander and the other Mariners might also. As for us, we took fourth place in the

"1968 Bell Tournament Champions—*as shown above. From left to right are McIntosh's Tony Vaska, George Harbeson (capt.), Mike Kompkoff, Lynn Kritchen, Chuck Clement, Howard Fennimore, and Jim Huston. Absent from the picture is Jason Wells. Photo by Ray Collins.*" From the Polar Star *at the University of Alaska Fairbanks, April 10, 1968.*

tourney. We beat Copper Valley 49–42, lost to Monroe 61–52 and by one to Ft. Greely 59–58, with Dave Bryant and me making the All-Tourney team.

In my senior year, we improved our win-loss tally greatly over the previous year, earning a season record of 16–5. The Class "B" tournament was held in Fairbanks at the UAF's Patty Gymnasium. This was a far cry from our old gladiator gym, but in the three years since we had moved we had played on larger courts, and a larger floor wasn't the disadvantage it once had been. In fact, I liked the larger size; it provided room to maneuver and less advantage to taller teams.

With fans and cheerleaders Judy Bergman, Colleen Carter, Phyllis Edwards, and Shirley Neal, the Warriors drew a bye and sat out for the first round. In the second round we beat Monroe 67–63, and thus faced Nome in the championship game. It being my senior year, I was desperate to win and choked. I scored five free throws and only one field goal. I had two fouls at the half but fouled out three or four minutes into the third quarter. Nome ended up winning 76–55, and we took second place. I think Dave Bryant and another Warrior received an All-Tourney team honor, so that was one bright spot. Again, basketball has its ups and downs, but that was a major low point for me.

But it was on that same court three years later, in my junior year at UAF, that our McIntosh Hall dorm team won the intramural Bell Tournament, the first time for McIntosh, and brought the trophy back to campus after five years of town team victories. I played on this team alongside younger players from schools that we Warriors had played in high school. My teammates were ex-Wasilla Warrior Jim Huston, Mike Kompkoff (who told me his leaping ability came from hours of trying to touch a cross-beam in a barn) and Lynn Kritchen from Cordova, Howie Fennimore from Wrangell, Tony Vaska of St. Mary's (the Nanooks' manager for a time, who later earned a doctorate from Stanford and was elected to the Alaska Legislature), Chuck Clement from Southeast Alaska, and Jason Wells from Valdez.

We beat the Lathrop High Seniors by five, then Nerland A team by thirteen, and met the Lathrop High Faculty, which included Joe Tremarello and T.D. Dumas, to lose by six. Since it was double elimination, we then beat the so-named Chemps in the loser's bracket, 43–40, to set up a rematch against the still undefeated Lathrop Faculty for the championship. We stayed alive by a score of 66–58 against them, which gave each team one loss and forced an extra play-off game. We of McIntosh Hall prevailed, 52–47. Mike Kompkoff and I made the All-Tourney Team. This brought some belated consolation for me, after my senior year tournament disappointment, and maybe for Jim Huston, but not for the other '65 Warriors.

If the UAF intramural league was anything it was entertaining. One team had a player with a black belt in karate. His martial arts skills were better than his basketball prowess. During a game, he inadvertently ran into another team's player and knocked him unconscious for several seconds. I decided that when we played that team, we'd play it safe and stick to a zone—the end zone!

BACK IN THE 1960s, one or two things about the new school didn't involve the gym or basketball. One was the student council election when I was a senior. Several students campaigned for the office of president. I garnered the most votes but no one came up with a majority. A run-off election followed, and a question arose concerning the counting of write-in votes in a run-off. I consulted John Shaw, an attorney in Palmer, and for the grand *pro bono* fee of one dollar he wrote a letter of opinion stating that according to the school constitution I was the winner, which carried the election for me. I had gone with Papa a time or two to visit M. Ashley Dickerson, a noted attorney who had a place on Hollywood Road, so I had a big-time legal backup in reserve. Ms. Dickerson, a friend of Rosa Parks, was a remarkable woman with several "firsts" in her field, including Alaska's first African-American attorney, admitted to the bar in 1959.

WASILLA WARRIORS CHEERLEADERS, 1967: *from left, Linda Andrew, Norma Newby (in dark sweater), Sherry Burrow, Lee Anna Harbeson (captain), and Sharon Reeder.*

9

Encore Sports

In my sophomore year we faced an irksome "request" by Mr. Turner, one of his standing ones, that those going out for basketball first had to participate in cross-country, for reasons of "training." Lee Turner, along with Bill Wiltrout of Homer and Anchorage, had been influential in organizing the sport, with Papa contributing. Lee Turner's son Tom had won the Small College State Cross-Country Championship for Ball State several years earlier.

So I joined the mandatory after-school roadside jaunts down to the Williwaw Lodge on Bogard Road. I enjoyed the fresh air and the chance to meet the cross-country team runners coming back as I was still headed out, those stalwarts including Bob Bunker, Joe Leone, Dwayne Fowler, Lary Hill, Ted Hadfield, Pete Hjellen, and Bob Hardcastle.

Soon it was time for the state meet, held at the old Palmer school. All of us were stretching, warming up, high-stepping, jumping our jacks. The wind picked up—it was Palmer, after all—and termination dust, as Alaskans refer to the first autumn (or late-summer) snowfall, shone on Pioneer Peak. Actual dust clouds rose off the Knik Glacier, and the temperature registered in the upper thirties. The course started near the high school, wove its way around the outskirts of town, through fields, on dirt trails and paths and gravel roads, and back to the start.

We were off and running, our numbers pinned to our chests. I loped along in a pair of new spiked cross-country shoes someone had handed me earlier, size 12's—I had small feet then—thinking, "Hey, this isn't so bad." I knew I wouldn't place, but I thought I might capture a low-respectability slot. I moved along and the runners stretched in a loose line. A mile or two slid by and Jay Sellens came up beside me.

"Hey, George. You notice anything about these shoes?" he asked.

"Yeah, now that you mention it," I replied, "it feels like I have pebbles in my socks." I'd thought it was the way these shoes felt, since I'd never run with spikes before.

"No," he informed me, "it's the spikes. They're coming up through the soles."

He and I continued on our rambling way and politely allowed those behind us to pass. We pronated on the sides of our feet, hopped on our heels, sought softer ground. Eventually, we stopped, sat down, pulled off the shoes and, sure enough, the "pebble" hypothesis was revised in favor of "Man, these are cheap shoes."

We forged on, since we were closer to the finish than to the start (which confused us temporarily because both were in the same place). We carried the shoes, wended our stocking way across the last mile or so of field stubble, commiserated on our misfortune, and discussed the upcoming basketball season. We arrived at the finish, where a very patient race official waited for us and the few lost souls behind us. Others found trouble with the shoes, too; I think Dwayne Fowler finished the race in his bare feet, and placed.

They say every end is also a beginning, and years later, when my now former wife Kathy Schwartz and I attended Florida State in Tallahassee for graduate classes, she persuaded me to take up running. In the many summers that followed—basketball occupied the winters—I ran thirty-plus miles a week, in places like Morro Bay, California; Seaside beach in Oregon; Cache Creek, B.C.; on the Alcan highway bordering Kluane Lake in Yukon Territory, and along the east coast beaches of Australia. I ran in many Anchorage 10K races (never with spikes). I stayed with the shorter distances, whereas Kathy ended up running a few marathons. I thank her for getting me started on all those miles that passed beneath my feet over the following twenty years. Good on ya, (ex)mate.

The Trials and Tribulations of Brother Richard

AFTER I GRADUATED, RICHARD JOINED Lee Anna at Wasilla High. Vern Cherneski, Wasilla Warrior basketball coach in Richard's high school years, has a thing or two to tell on Richard. Some of the Warriors then besides Richard were Dave Patrick, Tim Bell, Tom Roth, Bud Starr, and Gary Buchman. Richard, a sophomore, played center. One story of Vern's happened in a 1969 Kenai Tournament. Richard and Dave had forgotten to bring their uniform trunks and so were stuck wearing plain white practice trunks. Those were the days when basketball trunks were trunks and not loosely partitioned skirts. Richard, duly mortified and modified, was heard to comment, "Well, we can't have Coach think for us all of the time."

During the game, Vern told Richard to run back and forth on the baseline, to elude the defense and free himself up for rebounds and shots. Richard dutifully complied, inadvertently bumping into the referee twice in the process, apologizing each time. Finally, Richard collided one last time with the ref, knocking him down.

"Number 44! Why do you keep running into me like this?" the annoyed ref inquired, regaining his whistle and his disheveled dignity.

"I'm sorry, sir," Richard replied contritely, "I didn't mean to bump into you, but Coach told me I'm supposed to run back and forth on the baseline." The ref was so amused that he went to Vern at half-time and related the affair of the polite Wasilla Warrior. And run back and forth on the baseline Richard did. In his later high school years he grabbed 19 rebounds in a game, put down 38 points in another, and more, all by running back and forth on the baseline, proving that while it's not advantageous to knock down a ref, running back and forth on the baseline may be good for the score.

Oh, and the ref? He was Jim Palin, father-in-law of Sarah Palin, who later was elected governor of Alaska and presidential candidate John McCain's pick for GOP vice-presidential candidate in 2008.

Faux Beer, P.D.A., and Pancakes

COACH CHERNESKI TELLS ANOTHER RICHARD tale: The Warriors were on their way to play Ninilchik on the Kenai Peninsula, traveling in a forty-passenger school bus driven by Cherneski. Vern says the bus heater near the driver's seat cooked his left leg, yet on his right side the gas pedal froze at times—more to think about while he was driving a commercial vehicle down Alaskan roads in Alaska weather with his back to a load of high school kids. They motored down Tudor Road in Anchorage, and Vern braked to a stop. Richard stood up and walked forward to stand in the step area to ease an aching knee. There arose such a clatter that Vern looked down at the aisle on his right, where what to his wondering eyes should appear but two or three bottles of beer on the floor, rolling to a stop next to him.

Before Vern could confront the occasion, Richard called out, "They're mine. They're mine." In the tense discussion that followed, Richard managed to convince Cherneski that it was, indeed, beer, but the homebrewed root beer stuff, not the get-kicked-off-the team alcoholic stuff. Richard and sister Becky had each taken some to school that day. Richard took the recycled beer bottles and gave Becky a pop bottle of the stuff, because Rich thought it might be easier for him to explain if necessary. Just the same, Vern put the matter to a taste test. Then it was back on the road to Ninilchik, and another gray hair on the head of Coach Cherneski.

In those more innocent days, athletics being what they were and teenagers being what they are, there always seemed to be the occasional matter of ball players' P.D.A. for coaches to handle, P.D.A. meaning Public Displays of Affection. Thus it was inevitable that Vern and Richard were destined to enter into new areas of conversation. Sure enough, in the hall one day THE COACH espied THE PLAYER place a passing peck on the cheek of his GIRLFRIEND at that time.

The prescribed punishment fell into place. THE PLAYER was benched for one game by THE COACH, which possibly had something to do with the Warriors losing THE GAME that particular week-end. And THE GIRLFRIEND? She eventually went on her merry way, as often happens.

On one ball trip to Homer, Cherneski recalls, he and Richard stayed with the well-known commercial fishing family of Red and Nelda Calhoun and sons Dan, Dennis, and Jimbo and daughter Sally. In the morning Nelda prepared a substantial breakfast of dinner-plate-sized Swedish pancakes, along with other items.

Richard, six-foot-five and a major player at the Harbeson table, proceeded to dig in with appreciative gusto. On his polite inquiry as to the availability of pancake #6, Nelda exclaimed in amazement and creeping apprehension, "*Nobody* can eat *six* of those pancakes!" While "Nobody" wasn't at the table that morning, Richard was. The sixth pancake appeared, then vanished from his plate. Followed by Pancake #7, and Pancake #8.

"This kid doesn't have a stomach!" Nelda observed in disbelief.

The concept of black holes may have been known in a few scientific circles at the time, but it had not filtered down to encompass Swedish pancakes with a breakfast table place setting as an event horizon. There is no doubt, however, that Richard, returning home several years later from his job at Yukon Office Supply, would down a dozen-egg omelet for dinner, and thus, in his own way, qualify for singularity status. In retrospect, while having a hearty appetite of my own, I'm glad I was in college when Richard attained full membership in our family's "What the Heck Are Leftovers Club." When he set off in turn to the University of Alaska in Fairbanks for his one year in college, the rest of the family stood on the porch in farewell. Papa smiled and waved, calling out, "Bye, grocery bill. Bye, grocery bill!" (I congratulate my brother Peter the Great for having the foresight to be born eight years after Richard, long enough later to become a force in his own right in the family food budget, and as a family athlete. Vern says he had an inkling of this when Peter, as a third or fourth grader, would come to watch the Warrior practices and earnestly offer advice to him such as "You might want to do this, Coach," and "Maybe you could try that, Coach.")

Richard tells of a ball trip he made with the Warriors to Cordova one winter, where he was the guest of the owner or maybe manager of the processing cannery, in an apartment on the pilings above the water. His host brought out a large bowl of fresh shelled crab and told Rich to eat his fill, obviously not knowing with whom he was dealing.

Richard took the poor man at his word and polished off three to five pounds of the stuff, played a rousing game, and, lulled by the soothing waves below, slept like a baby that night to awake refreshed and ready for Swedish pancakes and raring to play ball.

Richard once was injured in a game against the Homer Mariners in Homer. The Mariners had a strong physical player who could plow through Wasilla's defense like a bowling ball through ten pins. Richard recalls a rumor that the guy got his strength by carrying a forty-horse outboard motor around under one arm.

> One of the shorter Homer players fronting me on defense suddenly leaped for the ball, rising up and backward and slamming the back of his head into my jaw and teeth. It was a good whack and stunned me a little, so I stood around and tried to clear my head. I spit out a few bits of tooth, wiped away blood, and felt the pain of my breath on the exposed area of my teeth. I realized that no one was paying any attention to me, that people were huddled around the Homer player that had jumped into me. The contact had knocked him out cold. They gave him smelling salts to revive him, and he came to after a bit.

LATER, RICHARD WENT to dentist Dr. McCavit, who tried to glue the main piece of Richard's tooth back in place, but it kept falling off and never stuck.

A Family Affair

BASKETBALL IS A FAMILY THING, IF YOU have enough relatives. Peter and I played community ball together in Wasilla, circa the 1990s, and once we wandered over to the old Palmer gym for a pick-up game. This gym was closer to standard than the old 1955 Wasilla gym. The bleachers and the floor were on the same level, with large screened windows, sideline space, a high ceiling—all the bells and whistles. A built-in stage occupied one end. The basement locker rooms, on the other hand, resembled a gulag—harsh concrete, no nonsense, no frills. Suit up, tape your ankles and knuckles, cup mandatory. Mirrors of stainless steel? Maybe. Benches bolted to the floor. A maze of cloth-wrapped pipes overhead. Black cast-iron ones snaked through them and each other, on their way to Dante knows where. One small ground-level opaque window let in daylight.

On this occasion Peter and I were joined by Richard and his son "Dooner." Richard had had a successful high school career, and his permanently shortened right leg hadn't kept him in later years from carrying a gutted-out caribou for several miles on hunting trips with his stepson, Brian Harris, or wrestling fuel drums out of helicopters onto mountain tops for Soloy Helicopters. But he hadn't played ball for a long time. If Papa had been there, we'd have had a coach or a two-handed jump shooter. Lee Anna's son, Bryan, would have made it a fearsome fivesome, but he was involved with the East High football program or maybe his plans for the U.S. Marine Corps, so we drafted a local for the Harbeson team.

In warming up, Richard slipped on some melting snow on the gym floor and snapped the Achilles tendon in his leg with the shoe lift. He says it sounded like a 30.06 going off. Being Richard, he stayed to cheer us on, replaced on the floor by another local. Dooner and one of the local guys took forward slots. Peter the Great, with his disconcerting habit of straying from the post to hit three pointers, filled the middle. I and a local guy took guard, and Richard held court in the stands. It was the only time we all played together, and we felt mildly tribal.

Pick-up games are loose, call-your-own-fouls, take your knocks affairs, and we Harbesons have a laid-back get-along style, but this local guy had "issues" or something to prove—maybe that the basketball gods should have made him taller. He was increasingly in my face and space with his elbows, shoulders, and hands, on offense as well as defense until finally I confronted him.

"What *is* your problem, man?" I inquired. Suddenly three shadows fell over us—a lanky six-foot-five shadow (Dooner), a truly formidable six-foot-four shadow (Peter), and the substantial six-foot-five shadow (Richard) limping up and down the sideline. It didn't take much persuasion to re-commence the game, this time in Harbeson style.

And Richard? Despite hearing the noticeable pop when he slipped, Richard didn't fully realize what had happened and proceeded for almost a week, through the resultant pain and swelling, to work at his handyman job of building a deck for someone. When his lower leg had become quite swollen, he finally took himself to see a doctor at Providence Hospital in Anchorage. The doctor was shocked, afraid that the tendon might have atrophied.

"My god, you've been working on this? Aren't you in pain?" he asked incredulously.

"Well, yeah. My ankle's swelled up the size of a cantaloupe. Does hurt some," Richard replied, with characteristic Richard understatement.

"I'll have to operate immediately," the doctor said.

"I 'spose so," agreed Richard, adding, "but I want a second opinion."

Result? Same reaction, same diagnosis, that the muscles might have atrophied too much to pull the tendon down for attachment. But this time, with a shot of morphine, Richard was off to the E.R. for a three-hour wait and then surgery. He chose spinal anesthesia for the procedure, so he would be awake and able to watch.

Richard says, "I watched them operate, with the forceps, and the cutting, but I think they gave me a tranquilizer, too. I didn't mind and didn't feel any pain, so I started telling jokes." The medicos were in stitches as they sewed, until they finally told him to shut up so they could do their work.

And it didn't end there. (Author Advisory: The faint of heart may wish to skip to the next section.) With his leg in a cast after the surgery, and a post-op blood clot, Richard's foot began to swell, sending him back to the doctor.

"Cut the cast off!" he demanded, pointing to the flesh bulging out around the ends of the plaster.

"Oh, yes! We need to get that cast off," the doctor hurriedly agreed. The technician wasn't available so it wasn't until the next day that the cast was sawed and pried off, the leg cleaned, and another cast installed. Recovery recommenced.

Eventually it was time for the second cast to be removed. The now skinny leg that presented itself was a sickly combination of dark red, ashen white, and splotchy black and blue. The muscles had atrophied a bit.

"It looks like a broomstick," Richard observed, beginning to have visions of drastic action. "Are you going to cut it off?"

Richard looked at the leg. The doctor looked at the leg. Peter, who was there, looked at the leg. The intern looked at the leg. A powerful odor emanated from the leg. Peter, six-foot-four and 260 pounds at the time, almost passed out; he left the room because of the smell. The intern turned pale and gasped, "Oh, my god!" At that the doctor marched the intern from the room and Richard heard him rip into the man: "Don't you *ever* react like that in front of a patient!"

But Richard recovered, Peter recovered, and presumably the intern recovered. Irrepressible Richard notes regarding the short right leg that if he had been born a girl he could tell people his name was "Eileen."

RICHARD *and* BRUCE THE SECOND *at Byers' place in 1955.*

10

The Animal Kingdom

In today's world pets comfort people in their old age, ease the pain of illness and infirmity, banish degrees of loneliness, help people feel secure, stand in for children or spouses, and apparently sniff out cancer. The human animal's pet menagerie is almost as broad as the range of life on this earth. Cats, dogs, mice, rats, fish, ferrets, bears, seals, salamanders, iguanas, rabbits. Bill Cosby professed to have a chicken. Over the years stories have been told of people in Anchorage owning lions, as well as the usual assortment of reptiles. The mind boggles at the human capacity for bonding.

But with bonding comes bondage. Pets take control. The center of the universe purrs and looks at you with soft velvet eyes as you gag on hairballs and wonder if that insidious odor wafting through the house is the cat box or the refrigerator door left ajar. Vet bills, exercise, feeding schedules, excrement adventures, transportation, the neighbor's flower bed or chickens—all have to be taken into account. Which end of the leash are we on, anyway? But on our homestead the question tended to be rhetorical. We lived in the woods with the nearest neighbors the better part of a mile away. The pets lived outside, and most of them ran free and usually stayed close to home. And we avoided larger animals, such as horses, although Lee Anna rode once in a while at Beldens' and Becky occasionally rode Al and Charlyn Martin's small white horse, named Bolivar Shagnasty after one of comic actor Red Skelton's characters.

Bruce the Second

BRUCE THE SECOND, OUR DOG IN THE early years, was even-tempered and friendly. He replaced an Irish setter that had died of distemper at the Marcella Camp for the Blind before we first came to Alaska. The second Bruce was a lab and husky mix, medium-to-light brown with a white patch on his chest. We got him as a puppy when we came to Wasilla in 1954, and he quickly grew to be one of the family, in affection as well as size—he outweighed me for a few years. He expressed that affection energetically for us, or complete strangers for that matter, by shaking "hands," so to speak, with his two front paws and much of the hundred or so pounds that composed the rest of him wrapped around one of us humans.

Bruce loved to ride in a car. He rode in the small enclosed space beneath the plywood platform in the rear of the Chevy on our early trips to and from Alaska. We kept him tied on the homestead because otherwise he would have been too well-traveled.

In Groton we lived next to the school, and one summer day I went to play marbles in the school yard. As I spun around on my heel to form a hole to shoot the marbles into, Bruce broke loose and commenced to race around the vicinity, dragging his length of chain behind him. I lit out after him, hollering.

"Bruce! Here, boy! Here, boy!" and "Get over here, you dumb dog!" It was like calling a whirling dervish to heel. "Bruce! You come back here!" A small part of him heard me, and panting, tongue lolling, he sprinted eagerly up to me, knocking me down. I grabbed the trailing chain and hung on for dear life as he took off again. He dragged me behind him like the horse dragging Jimmy Stewart through the fire in the old western. I was a fourth-grade lightweight, so through the gravel my face, shoulders, and flailing body plowed. After banging into the school swing stanchions, I snagged one of the posts and brought us to a halt as Papa strode up and took the chain from my scrunched fingers.

"Well, cowboy, how's the dog-taming business?" he said with a grin, then added, "Good thing you stopped him. At the rate you two were traveling, you'd have been in Massachusetts before you knew it."

When Bruce got loose on the homestead, we would pile into the Chevy and cruise up and down the driveway until he came running out of the woods or up from the bluff to jump in when we opened the door. That dog did love to ride in the car!

And he liked porcupines. They were not only smaller animals but they waddled and were easy to catch. And catch them he did, five or six times. Once Papa, Orlando Byers (or Hal Post), and I took him with us when we went fishing in Cottonwood Creek behind the Byers place. After Bruce jumped a porcupine along the bank of the creek, we grabbed him and Papa used a pair of pliers to pull the quills while the other two of us literally sat on him to hold him immobile. He still managed to buck us around, but he seemed to know we were helping him and never tried to bite us. He never did learn to avoid porcupines, though. We'd wake up mornings on the homestead to frenzied barking and find a fat, bristling porky under our vehicle of the moment, or up one of the trees lining the bluff in front of the house. So near, yet so far, eh, Bruce?

(Richard also had his eye on porcupines in his young Dan'l Boone days. He'd shot and eaten squirrels and rabbits, as Papa had done in his youth, and decided to do the same with a porky. "I shot one, but when I gutted it I found it had huge ugly tapeworms and I decided not to eat it after all," Richard says. "I felt sorry about killing it, and because of the worms I never shot another one.")

Once when Mom had gotten tired of Bruce's barking, she laid into him with a broom. Bruce just crouched down with a hurt expression, his eyes saying, "What? What did I do?"

When Bruce was twelve years old, Papa told Richard he thought someone had given Bruce meat laced with bits of glass on one of Bruce's off-the-chain runs. Bruce had trouble eating after that and withered away to skin and bones and pain, before Papa put him down and buried him in our field. I can imagine him looking up at Papa at the end, with both man and dog uncertain of what had happened, and Bruce expressing the same puzzled canine query, "What? What did I do?"

Beloved Blackie

OTHER DOGS FOLLOWED THE TRAIL BLAZED by the two Bruces. King was a small, black, short-haired friend and companion of indeterminate breed. He lived long and prospered, sturdily guarded us from the ravens and the occasional eagle that soared overhead, and followed us around to offer his canine opinions on our various human activities. He ran off in his declining years and may have been poisoned or killed in the wild.

And there was Blackie, called "Boy" by my sister Becky. A shaggy-haired lab-and-spaniel mix, like Bruce with a white chest patch, Blackie was the runt chosen by Becky from a Turner litter. Despite his slow start, he grew to small black bear size but had a friendly disposition. I say black bear because of the time he took me for a walk along our tree-lined drive and disappeared briefly on some canine exploration. Suddenly up over the bank ahead, out of the brush and trees overlooking the flats, burst two black forms running full tilt across the drive in front of me. In split-second reasoning, I figured that Blackie had found another Blackie, one of the ursine variety—but I wasn't sure which was the chaser and which the chasee. Was Blackie bringing a new friend back to meet me where I stood gaping so impolitely? One of the streaking black shapes turned and ran up to me to brag about his find, so I postulated that one was our Blackie.

Sometimes it was taken for granted that it was Blackie. A friend of Lee Anna's once spent the night in a pickup camper by our house, arose in the morning to stumble sleepily toward the house, and groggily greeted Blackie, only to realize belatedly that the dark shape sniffing the nearby ground was a black bear.

Blackie—the dog, not the bear—was also a sports enthusiast. If one of us wanted to play baseball but had no one to join in, Blackie gladly volunteered to retrieve any and all fungos, even over the bluff, thus providing my siblings and me many hours of fun and entertainment. He rarely committed errors, never complained to the press or demanded free agent status, didn't use steroids, and was a willing role model for kids and fellow dogs alike. And cats for that matter, for Blackie good-naturedly tolerated our Gray Cat and Mittens purring and rubbing against his face when he was resting from his sports duties.

As with Bruce the Second, porcupines factored into Blackie's years, but Blackie seemed to learn more readily. One summer day Richard ran from our front yard into the house yelling over Blackie's barking.

"Papa! Blackie's got a porcupine!"

"What? Oh, no! Where?"

"In the yard. I think he's trying to eat it," Richard exclaimed. Young Peter stood in the doorway, drawn by the commotion.

"Papa, there's a porkypine goin' up a tree," he observed. And there was.

Papa grabbed a pair of pliers, and they ran into the yard and collared Blackie. Papa pressed the dog to the ground and threw a coat over him.

"Here, Richard, kneel on this side of the coat. Peter, take the other side."

The boys knelt on the coat and lay across Blackie, and Papa commenced pulling the quills.

"Hold him, hold him!" Papa commanded, for Blackie proved to be amazingly strong, struggling half-out from under the coat, surprising Richard and Peter. Finally the quills were pulled, and Blackie walked around the yard snuffling, licking his mouth, and shaking and pawing at his muzzle, not paying the slightest attention to the portly, bristling critter watching disdainfully from high in the tree. From then on Blackie accorded "porkypines" a respectful perimeter.

Blackie was with us for many years, never failing to joyously welcome me or others in the family home when we arrived after being away, but in his old age he explored a wider range and finally disappeared one day, never to return. Maybe he tangled with the Redington sled dogs at the beginning of our drive, or a bear or moose or wolf got him, or someone shot him. We never found out. But I like to think that he just trotted off one day, found a sunny spot along the bluff overlooking Cook Inlet next to his buddy King and forebear Bruce the Second, and settled down to watch over the rest of eternity for us.

Snoopies

OF COURSE, EVERY DOG-BLOODED AMERICAN family needs a Snoopy to relish the joy in life, and I knew three. One was a beagle owned by George Gore and his wife, who lived in a small house before the Girl Scout Camp exit on Knik Road, a mile before Knik. They were a nice older couple, both short in stature—George lean and quiet, his wife outgoing with a lively sense of humor. We would visit back and forth, help each other out. George and Gene Coghlan witnessed our homestead application papers. We kept the Gores' beagle at our place once. Becky says she thinks the beagle ended up being eaten by one of the grizzlies that wandered through now and then. I don't remember that happening, but time has a way of picking and choosing our memories.

Number-two Snoop was a beagle named Dino, owned by our good friends Lee and Roberta Alward. I house-sat for the Jim and Julie Ede family in the early '70s when I was just out of college, and Dino was part of the deal because the Edes were dog-sitting him when Alwards were out of town. He was advanced in years, and had a propensity for flatulence, especially when snoozing behind the easy chair that I sat in to read and relax. In later years, when visiting Roger and Mary Ellen Bliss, I was amazed to see that Roger's Iditarod dogs had their training diet complemented with a barrel of rotten fish, a road-kill dead horse that Roger and I ventured into a dark, rainy night to collect, and—I'm not kidding—their own excrement. Even stainless metal feeding bowls fell victim to their jaws. But while Edes kept Dino inside, Roger kept his sled dogs outside. Well, most of them, anyway.

Snoop Three was the small waddle that my sister Becky bought during the years of Mom's trials with multiple myeloma. Named Spunky, the little beagle lived up to his name around the dinner dish, for there was no plate that he couldn't face down and lick clean. Once I went to Becky's apartment to visit, when she was taking care of Mom, and decided that the Spunk needed a workout regimen. I scooped up the anxious round mound and plopped him down on Becky's electric treadmill for a short jaunt. Spunk gave it a gallant, albeit befuddled, effort. Mom saw some innocent humor in the little guy through her pain, and Spunk soon hopped off and went to comfort her in his doggy manner. Blessed be the Spunk.

Cats Galore

Our family also had a procession of felines over the years. The first cats I remember were a tabby and a midnight black one with white paws that lived with us when we rented Jim Wilson's place on Fairview Loop in 1958–59. The house had a coal furnace but was chilly in the winter. One morning when I was eleven I descended into the basement to check on our kit kats. Usually the two would pop out from the shadows when I called. However, that morning they didn't show. I looked around the basement and was shocked to see two lifeless furry bodies stretched on the floor against the furnace cowling. Their habit had been to sleep close to the furnace for its warmth, but this time, like canaries in a coal mine, they apparently had succumbed to furnace fumes. So the line of feline succession was not off to a good start.

Papa held a benign attitude toward our cats, despite memories of his family's embattled tomcat Sidney, and his boyhood pet, a big gray cat named Peter. Peter was discovered one day standing on the dining room table with his feet in three pies and eating a ham. Mom barely tolerated our felines, but she grew fonder as the years progressed. After Papa died, Chessie and C.J. would accompany Mom on her walks on the flats and along the drive with their tails in the air.

We kids appreciated any mischievous little ball of fur with claws and raspy tongue, but Becky doted on cats and adopted several into our family, sometimes dressing them in doll or infant clothes. In grade school, a friend told me he had tied two cats' tails together and draped them over a clothesline, and had rubbed kerosene on the procreating parts of others. This gave me greater insight into the human psyche and caused me to look more closely at my companions' leisure activities. But I saved my friend's life by never telling Becky.

The first of Becky's little charges was "Mother," a tabby she sneaked into the house, in violation of Mom's later-to-be-relaxed rule of no cats in the house, and hid under the covers at night. Mother Cat had two litters and became very protective of the second, which she housed outside at the back of the house.

Richard claims that Mother Cat dragged a live rabbit home by the scruff of its neck. "The rabbit was almost the size of the cat," he says. "It was struggling, so Mother Cat had her front legs fully extended in a stiff-legged manner in order to haul the unfortunate prey home. I pulled the rabbit loose and let it run off into the woods." He also freed a young weasel that Mother Cat brought home squirming in her mouth. "I was totally amazed. That was one nasty cat."

Mother Cat's nastiness progressed to the point of sinking her claws into people's legs, even Becky's. This came to an abrupt halt after a couple of months. Richard and Peter were rolling around outside in the leaves in one of their sibling wrestling bouts when Mother Cat came flying out of nowhere, hissing and spitting, and bit at Richard's hair and raked and batted both sides of his head with her claws. The human mother in the vicinity, Mom, waded into the fray wielding a broom and sent feline Mother Cat squalling and tumbling away from the amazed boys.

"Harb, you take that cat out and shoot it!" Mom commanded Papa in a rare show of serious anger. "Right now! I've had it with that cat."

Papa did exactly as ordered, and Mother Cat was history.

Later, when Becky and her husband Mark Chapman and infant daughter Shanna were living in a small cabin on the shore of Knik Lake, Becky had two cats, Nellie and Chessie, each caring for a litter.

"They were good mothers," Becky says, "and helped each other. When one ventured forth hunting, the mama cat at home would watch over and care for both litters."

Becky gave one of the kittens to neighbor and friend Terry Rosevear, who gave it back after ending up in the hospital with a severe allergic reaction. Becky herself, not allergic during her time on the homestead, became allergic, but not enough to banish cats from her life. Her Chessie produced Chessie Junior, or C.J., daughter and companion for Chessie. Fifteen years later, when Becky was staying with Mom on the homestead, C.J. died a natural death at age 15 while resting in Becky's lap. Becky says she sorrowfully put C.J. in a box on Peter's bed, so he could perform the burial. This was a surprise to Peter, who later entered his bedroom intent on a nap and unaware of his mortuarial obligations. Chessie died a year later.

Other feline personalities arrived and passed on over the homestead years, many of them with a superabundance of toes. Taffy and Tuffy—two Siamese or Burmese siblings—joined us for a few years, Taffy was chocolate-colored and Tuffy was a large, friendly male blue-point. There was Gray Cat, who liked to nuzzle our dog Blackie and who died when he chose to sleep in the right rear wheel well of Richard's VW Bug. And of course, Mittens, a long-haired cat with tabby markings, who also would rub the tolerant Blackie in the face. One black and white kitten had an automotive misadventure with our '66 Scout but survived. We drove the Scout to school one morning and upon exiting the vehicle in the parking lot discovered the wayward kitten crouching under the hood atop the battery, unhurt but suffering stowaway psycho-trauma.

Our cadre of cats roaming the homestead yard wasn't enough. We took on boarding responsibilities for friends. Once, we "cat-sat" two chocolate Siamese clones of Disney's Si and Am, owned by an artist, a woman who gave Mom painting lessons. These two demons from hell, the evil twins of evil twins, prowled our basement for a week, living up to their Disney nature, hissing, biting, and clawing. But the week passed and they returned home.

In the '60s we adopted a large, good-natured, orange and white long-haired cat owned by the Rhea family who lived up the highway near Willow. Vince and Larry, schoolmates of mine, had a tale to tell of this cat. They said their father came home late one night, tired from work, and crawled into his sleeping bag while the rest of the family slept.

"All of a sudden we were shocked bolt upright," the Rhea boys said, "by a mighty shout from our father."

"JEEEEE-SUS CHRIST!"

A mad wrestling scramble ensued, their father versus his sleeping bag, with further invectives. The bewildered family watched their father open the front door, fling the family cat in an accelerating trajectory across the yard, and slam the door.

"&*%$#! cat crapped in my sleeping bag!" he snorted in disgust.

The cat had crawled into the bottom of the sleeping bag to snooze and used the bag for a cat box in the process. They say cats have nine lives, and Vince and Larry thought all nine of that cat's were definitely at risk. "And you know," the Rhea boys said, "believe it or not, the same thing happened again a few days later."

So we adopted it, with Mom's demand that Becky not hide it under her bed covers.

ON THE HOMESTEAD PORCH, 1978: *Becky's daughter Shanna and Tabby the cat are almost dwarfed by the produce from George Harbeson Sr.'s garden.*

Bully

Starting when he was thirteen, Richard and his friends Rip, Roland, and Dave Patrick worked occasionally for Tony Vickaryous on his dairy farm for ten dollars a day, room and board, and all the milk they could drink. One summer Tony and Papa made a deal on a calf. Papa and Richard brought it home in the '66 Scout, with the understanding that Richard and inevitably the rest of the family were to raise the animal—this came to mean not only feed and water it but pet it, play with it, ride it. The ultimate goal of slaughtering and packaging the calf in the freezer for eating got lost in the shuffle.

"I'd heard the Greek wrestling legend of the boy Milo lifting his calf every day to build up his own muscles, so I followed that example. I figured it would help me in basketball and in wrestling with Peter the Great, who was growing fast," Richard says. "I heaved Bully up on my back each day until one day I couldn't do it. Then I rode him around like a horse. I fed him potatoes and staked him on the flats to graze, to reduce the feed expenses."

Peter remembers Bully, too. "I moved Bully around on the flats, restaking him (so to speak), and Bully would bump me with his head, which was okay when he was small, but I got nervous when he grew larger—he grew faster than I did."

Richard says, "I expressed my opinion to Papa that I didn't want Bully to die, but when I returned from a basketball trip someone told me that Papa had bopped Bully on the head with a sledgehammer, like they do in a slaughterhouse, and then had shot him with his Mauser to finish him off."

Becky remembers the time as well. "I called Papa a murderer!" she says. "And after that none of us kids would eat Bully."

"Bully didn't taste very good," Richard recalls, "because I fed him potatoes, and because he'd grazed on the salty grass down on the flats."

And so Bully too passed into family history, not with a Teddy Roosevelt-like "Bully!" but with a bang and perhaps a whimper, and a very, very reluctant chorus of "Please pass the ketchup."

Monkey Business

Our neighbor Al Rousey and Papa were visiting the Gores at their place one Christmas, after Al had finished plowing our long drive and the Gores' short one. Richard, twelve years old, went along to check out the rabbits that the Gores kept in cages. The adults enjoyed neighborly conversation and sociable hot buttered rums, and offered Richard a small HBR, but he was interested in the rabbits and declined. Richard hadn't, however, counted on Al's bringing his own pet, a monkey that suddenly introduced itself to him by running over and climbing up Richard's leg. And climbing up his side and arm. And climbing up onto the side of his head, where it clung tightly to his hair and head with both paws.

"I immediately froze," Richard says. "I was looking at the rabbits in their cages, because I wanted to raise rabbits, when in a blink of an eye a brown scrambling thing streaked over to me and climbed up my side and stuck to my head with its sharp claws, pulling my hair and making squeaking noises. It dawned on me, unbelievably, that it was a *monkey* hugging my head. I heard Papa, Mr. Rousey, and the Gores laughing. I thought, 'Where the heck did a monkey come from? This is Alaska!' I was afraid to move because I thought it might bite me. So I stood frozen to the spot, the rabbits completely forgotten, thinking 'Get this thing *off* me!'

"I gradually became aware of something poking in my ear, which I assumed to be the little fellow's belly button. Then I felt a growing anxiety that it wasn't the critter's belly button, but something of an entirely different nature. I still didn't move, because I'd heard that monkeys have sharp teeth. Finally, Mr. Rousey came over and plucked the monkey from my head, and set me free from whatever the animal had in mind."

Moosin' Around

ALASKA HOMESTEADING CAME WITH THE usual assortment of wild animals. An occasional wolf would slide through, a coyote now and then. Moose were common visitors every year, even three-legged ones. We had two of these, on separate occasions. How the legs had been lost—shot off or in a trap or some other accident—was a mystery, but they limped around well enough. One cow even had a calf with her.

We had many close calls with moose on the roads over the years but managed to avoid a serious collision (until Becky hit one with her Nissan a few years ago). We counted moose when we rode to and from school with Papa. They browsed in the fields and woods along the way, and there were many. I counted 150 on one trip to school. Lee Anna remembers about 300 on a round trip, and Richard says 600, but I think he's dreaming. One morning Papa and Lee Anna stopped on the way to school to watch two bulls with locked horns fighting near Vine Road and ended up late for school. That would have been a tardy slip worth framing!

Richard remembers a time on the Knik Road before the Gores', when he was coming home in his VW Bug and encountered a heavy ground fog. He slowed, then stopped as a great albino bull moose strode out of the fog and stood on the road in front of him, its hide and horns a tawny, off-white color. It stood there for a bit, towering over the small car before disappearing back into the fog.

"It was a mystical experience," Richard says. "And, no, I was not on drugs, I never did drugs. It was an amazing happening and I was lucky enough to be there for it." He also saw two or three albino cow moose over the years, one with a calf, on the bad "S" curves below where the Wasilla Theater is now.

Becky, who rode the school bus more than the rest of us, would get off at our driveway. "I walked home using the power-line right-of-way instead of the driveway, because it was five minutes faster, even with snow up to my knees. Lots of times it was dusk or dark, as well as cold, and I used a flashlight. One day Mom wasn't there to meet me, as she sometimes was, but five moose were. I figured six was a crowd, so I scooted faster than usual up and down the hills of the power line to our house!"

"When we stayed at Jim Wilson's place," Lee Anna remembers, "a grouchy cow moose hung around at the top of the driveway where the bus stopped. We could see her from the house and we'd race for the bus and try to board before she chased us."

The straight stretch leading to Fish Creek was where I encountered a cow moose with a slight attitude—or a sense of humor. Headed in the direction of Goose Bay and Point MacKensie, I'd ridden my blue and white Honda 350 MotoSport past Fish Creek to where Jim Barlow, a high school classmate and brother-in-law (married to Lee Anna), had lived with his grandparents, the Gliddens. Returning to the homestead, I topped the rise from the creek and noticed a cow moose standing along the right side of the road fifty yards ahead. It was preoccupied with its grazing, but when I neared, it stepped into the middle of the road and stood staring at me.

I sat on the bike, revved the engine and beeped the tinny horn. The moose flipped its long ears and kept chewing, but didn't move. I turned around and retreated before it got personal, and the animal sidled into the roadside grass. I did a U-turn, swung into the left lane and gunned the bike. Again the moose strolled into the middle of the road, and this time I skidded to a halt ten yards away, man-handled the bike around, and regained the space between the two of us. The moose went back into the grass again, looking at me with that supercilious look that moose can get. This motorized "Mother May I" game had gotten a little tedious, so again I started homeward, with the intent of using the opposite ditch if necessary. As Alaska Governor and later Secretary of the Interior Walter Hickel once commented, "You can't just let nature run wild."

Going about fifty, I zoomed by the moose. This time it just watched from the ditch, no longer interested in traffic control. After a hundred yards, I slid to a halt and looked back. The moose ambled into the center of the road and stood looking at me, idly flipping its high-bush-rabbit ears, and I swear I saw a broad smirk spread across its incongruous mug.

Bear With Me

AND THERE WERE BEARS. MOSTLY BLACKIES, but occasionally a grizzly moved through the homestead, stopping to check out our woodpiles. Once Papa took us blueberry picking and dolly varden fishing up in Hatcher Pass near the Fern Mine. While we were gone a grizzly showed up back on the homestead, giving Mom something to ponder in her solitude. Another time when she was home alone, two black bear cubs broke the outer pane of a basement window. When hunting in the extensive wooded areas around our place, we'd see bear scat, a torn-up log or stump, or rake marks on trees, but generally the bears shied away from us human intruders.

Inevitably, though, surprise meetings took place. One sunny fall day of Lee Anna's high school years, Mom sent her out to the beginning of the driveway, a three-quarter-mile walk, to pick wild raspberries that we'd noticed growing there. It was a great day for a walk, and the view of the inlet from the drive was spectacular as usual. Lee Anna reached the patch where the raspberries mixed with tall tangles of brush and grass and proceeded to fill her pail. She worked her way through, concentrating on the berries, trying not to squash them, eating a few of the really nice ones, all the while keeping an eye out for the yellow-jackets that frequented such spots with their ground nests.

She finished harvesting a particularly nice strand of berries, reached out to part the dense grass directly in front of her—and abruptly revealed the black-snouted visage of a heretofore unnoticed fellow picker. Face to face, the two berry seekers froze, each presumably startled to see the other.

"We were so close, I could have reached over and tweaked his nose if I had had such an inclination, which I certainly did not," Lee Anna remembers. "And the bear could have done the same! In a split second both of us jumped straight up into the air, spun around, and streaked away in opposite directions, me headed for the house and the bear headed for wherever.

"It felt like the bear was right behind me, but I was too scared to slow down and look until I got close to home. I ran into the house, flung the berry pail, which I had hung onto for some reason, down on the floor and told Mom in no uncertain terms, 'I'm *never* going berry picking again!'"

Of course, it was a vow made to be broken, for Mom's jams and jellies were too hard to resist.

On one beautiful blue-sky day after I graduated from high school, I rode my ten-speed bicycle to Fish Creek. I was pedaling along the straight just before the drop down to the creek when I spotted a young golden-hued grizzly in the open grassy area to my left, close to the traffic control moose's hang-out. I stopped and sat on the bike for a few minutes watching the bear as it reared up and looked in my direction. After a bit it took a few steps toward me, no doubt curious about the two-wheeled creature standing on the road. It snuffed a time or two, trying to catch my scent, but the breeze wasn't in its favor. It decided that a closer inspection was in order and moved nearer, but I zipped on down to the creek. The bear was gone when I pedaled past on my return, but I was glad that I had gotten a chance to see it, for it was truly a magnificent animal in full health and color.

While watching the bear that day I remembered a story Larry Rhea had told me about a black bear frequenting their place in the Willow area. He had grabbed a rifle and stepped outside, but the bear saw him and fled through the brush behind the house to the Alaska Railroad, and began ambling north on the tracks. Larry pushed his way through the stand of alders and onto the tracks, where he stood watching the bear saunter away from him.

"I raised the rifle a couple of times to aim," Larry said, "but all I could see was its fat waddling butt with its stub of a tail. Shooting it in the ass didn't seem sporting, so I did what first came to mind: I hollered as loud as I could, 'HEY, BEAR!'"

Larry never had a chance with the rifle. At the sound of his yell, the bear streaked off the tracks and disappeared into the trees.

"Maybe I should have shot him," Larry told me, "but it just didn't seem right."

My brother Richard has his own bear story. When they were still in school, he and Peter rode Peter's old blue Honda 50—a bike so small it was almost hard to see the bike when Richard *or* Peter was on it, and yet the two of them would ride it at the same time. Once Richard popped a wheelie with Peter on the back. Pete flew backward, ripped the bike's tail light assembly loose and dragged it with him. But on this particular day, Richard was by himself near Settlers Bay, riding the Honda 50 on an abandoned section of the old Knik road left over after the upgrade.

"I couldn't get that tiny bike to go full speed because I was six-five and weighed close to two hundred pounds, and because the road surface had stretches of soft gravel that mired the Honda down," Richard says. Suddenly, from the roadside bushes loped a grizzly bear, three-quarters grown. Richard looked over and saw the bear galloping desperately beside him. Its paws flashed and its head pumped up and down two feet away from his left foot peg.

"It was as scared of me as I was scared of it," Richard says. "I gave the little Honda full throttle, which might have increased the speed at most by five miles per hour. I kept trying to give it more gas, to no avail. The little Honda swerved and wobbled in the gravel, engine spitting and missing but, strangely enough, it never occurred to me to just stop. So there we were, both scared as rabbits, trying to get away from each other by running in a straight line, each bent on leaving the other in the dust. Finally, the bear gained ground, pulled ahead of me, then suddenly cut across the Honda's path to the other side of the road, intent as ever on getting into the woods despite the obstacle of me and Li'l Honda."

Papa had a parallel experience with a skunk on their New Jersey farm.

"I was trapping for a weasel by nailing a piece of chicken to a tree with a trap underneath, but I found a small striped skunk in the trap. The skunk was worthless to me, so I reached around the tree and freed it. The two of us then walked parallel to each other, fifteen feet apart, for a quarter of a mile." So, while some people dance with wolves, strolling with skunks and racing with bears is more the Harbeson style.

Like Father, Like Son

OUR MAGNIFICENT COOK INLET VISTA INCLUDED wild animal sightings. Richard has reported seeing belugas in the waters in front of our place when he flew over the area in his Aeronca Champ, but such whales were rare that far up the inlet.

Larger birds shared the woods and the bluff. We had a few nesting eagles around to entertain the ravens, and once Richard found a huge injured raven walking on the ground, possibly a casualty of such teasing. He managed to catch it, since it was unable to fly, and kept it in an unused rabbit cage for a few months.

"For the first couple of weeks I had to wear leather gloves to feed it because it would pinch and bite at my hands with its large, strong beak. After it got used to me, it stopped that," Richard says. "We fed it hamburger, table scraps, and a concoction of Gravy Train dog food mixed with warm water. King, our dog of the time, may not have been pleased to see such a waste of good food, but he showed interest in the bird and didn't protest. After three months, I took the raven out of the cage and it flew thirty feet, landed, flew another thirty feet, landed again, and seemed to be doing well, so I let it go."

Papa once captured a young crow in his younger days on the family farm in Montville.

> *As a boy, I found the crow in a high nest on* the farm and took it home. We had it for several years. My Uncle George gave it chaws of tobacco and the bird's hinged tongue protruded when it spit out the tobacco. Once it took Mama's wedding ring from the window sill, and it wasn't until much later that we found the ring up in the drainpipe. When we worked on our vehicles, the crow would steal the nuts and bolts if you laid them on the running boards. It soared in through the bedroom window and dropped things into the water pitcher. Finally, after its years with us, the crow flew to a neighbor's place to alight on their child's playpen, and Don Abbott shot it.

ONE YEAR IN Alaska, at Byers' place, we raised chickens to save grocery expenses. We cut their heads off on a stump with an axe, and the headless bodies flapped and flopped around spouting blood from their necks. But we never had any geese that I remember. Perhaps it was because of Sir Francis Drake, a belligerent goose of Papa's boyhood.

> *Sir Francis lay in wait for anyone going from* the house to the barn, and terrorized my sister Louise and the rest of our family. We carried a peach basket around and put it over his head to distract him when he attacked. Once, when I was sent to the barn on an errand, I checked the yard for Sir Francis, like I usually did. He wasn't in sight, so I quietly sped toward the barn. Somewhere along the way Sir Francis picked up my trail, but I sprinted madly, frantically jerked open the barn door, and pulled it shut behind me, safe at last—only to realize that Sir Francis had ridden my heels through the doorway! The goose would fly over Changebridge Road to visit a flock of ducks on Montowac Lake. On one such trip he caused the milkman trouble when he flew down Changebridge directly at the milk delivery truck. The driver—perhaps Kevah Konner, who operated a dairy in Pine Brook—slammed on his brakes to save his windshield and smashed a number of milk bottles.

WE SAW HAWKS regularly along the bluff and flats on our Alaskan homestead, which also reminded Papa of his boyhood in Montville. There he once climbed a big hemlock and found several hawk chicks. Two fell to the ground and Papa took them home, where they entertained his family for a year before flying away.

Papa and his family attempted to raise a diversity of wild creatures: opossums, raccoons, skunks, gray squirrels, hawks, snakes, turtles, flying squirrels, a green heron, and even a pigeon named "Sappy Jack," who survived a hawk attack. He discovered a small opossum too young to keep alive, and once when plowing their fields, he dug up two little skunks from their nest, but they, like the opossum, soon died. He had several boyhood experiences with skunks. One moonlit night from an upstairs window he heard a thumping in the yard. When he looked out, he saw a skunk with its head stuck in a mayonnaise jar. His sister Louise ran out, grabbed the skunk and the jar, and pulled them apart with a "Plop!" that Papa heard even from his vantage point.

Another remembrance: "On a dark night, I heard a disturbance among the chickens. I grabbed a lantern and our .22 and ran down to the coop, where I spied the torn carcasses of two chickens stuck in chicken wire. I went into the coop where the chickens were milling around. When I looked down among them, I saw a skunk near my feet, so I held the .22 above his head and shot him."

Shortly before coming to Alaska, when I was four years old, Papa found a number of ring snakes under a board and brought one home for me. I kept it for a time as a pet.

Many of Papa's notes on his early life on the farm show a strong kinship to Richard's exploits. Like father, like son. Papa rarely volunteered such stories when he was alive, but his memoirs reveal that his boyhood experiences resembled Richard's, which must have given Papa fond moments. All I can say is praise be to the providence that kept skunks out of Alaska, or Richard would have tangled with them on our homestead for certain.

A baby seal entered our lives when it became stranded in the soft silt of the channel between our homestead and Frank Smith's cabin, which was located on the point of land bordering the beach down the inlet from us. Richard and Frank took a rope and shiplap boards and, mindful of the serious risk the silty muck posed, made their way to the seal and lassoed it.

"The mud out there is a tricky place to be," Richard says. "People have died after getting stuck in it. Frank and I managed to rope the seal, haul it out, and carry it up to our house. It was pretty far gone, but we thought we could help it."

According to Becky, "We kept it in the bathtub until we got a pen built outside. This caused consternation on Mom's part, but by this time she likely was resigned to our escapades, and also wanted to help the seal. Checking on it the next morning, Richard found that the seal had escaped the pen, and we discovered its body on the flats below our house. It had crawled and rolled its way down the bank to the base of the bluff and died trying to get back to the inlet."

Froggie Stuff

WHERE THERE ARE KIDS IN THE COUNTRY, sooner or later there are frogs in jars, boxes and tubs, for they are fascinating and irresistible to youthful curiosity. We collected black pollywogs from the myriads that swarmed in a small swampy pond in the woods not far from the Redington dog lot. There were plenty of frogs on the flats, along the bottom of the bluff, in the grass beside O'Brien Creek, and in the marsh environment of the larger pond where the creek exited the woods onto the flats. We had a washtub terrarium with as many as twenty or thirty of them in residence. There was always one hopping around to chase down. They were small in size, and there were no bullfrogs, as at our Aunt Mary and Uncle Charles' pond in New Jersey. We didn't have their snapping turtles, either.

Mom declined all requests for fried frog leg entrees, and Becky never mentioned dressing them in doll's clothes. We tried frog races a time or two. I had read Mark Twain's Calaveras County story, but we found our contestants too small for "quail shot," too undisciplined to go in one general direction, and interested only in escaping. Our pet cats, however, expressed great interest in our small captives. As, of course, did Richard.

"I remember finding frogs down there on the flats, three-legged frogs with some of them missing the hind foot, and one-eyeball frogs. I don't know if it was radioactivity, or what the heck was goin' on down there," he says today, still marveling at the mystery of the mutant frogs, although they may simply have been the worse for wear after escaping the clutches of seagulls and other predators.

Sputnik had beeped its way into the skies not too long before, so under that influence we bought elastic-powered rockets complete with small parachutes. Having heard of the adventures of space monkeys, we searched around for similar wannabe travelers. Al Rousey wouldn't have looked kindly on our using his monkey, plus the rocket's rubber band didn't have enough horsepower. Spidernauts were available but too hard to find upon landing and drifted away on the wind. Since the '40s, an assortment of critters had been blasted skyward by different countries: dogs, fruit flies, meal worms, wasps, flour beetles—voyages of the weird! France cast the first rat, naturally followed by Felix the cat. Russia and the U.S. had sent mice (we'd considered mice) and northern leopard frogs.

With frogs plentiful on the homestead, they soon hopped into the line of sight as suitable candidates.

"I removed the parachute from the rockets and put tiny frogs in its place," Richard says. "We fired the rockets twenty or thirty feet into the air. The rockets came down and stuck in the mud, but the frogs all seemed to be okay." Since they had survived to hop another day, we released them back into the grass to spread tales of alien abduction among their compatriots.

The frogs got a small measure of revenge in 1982. Unfortunately, it wasn't against us kids. Papa was chasing a frog around a mud puddle in the yard near our homestead garden, trying to catch it for Becky's four-year-old daughter, Shanna, when he slipped and fell. He gave the frog to Shanna, then came into the house and sat down. He mentioned nothing about being injured but went to the doctor the next day and found that he had broken his ankle.

Mousin' Around

RICHARD, HAVING MARRIED FLORENCE "DOTSY" Harris, began trapping mice to sell to a pet store—proving once again that you can take the boy out of the homestead but you can't take the homestead out of the boy. He had captured wild mice to add to his tame ones and earned extra money by breeding them by the boxful. A modified Malthusian population constraint was put into action to keep the numbers in check—he sold them to a Wasilla pet store as food for the pet store critters. Still, a brouhaha ensued one evening when three or four of his little charges escaped in the house, much to wife Dotsy's dismay. Another time a few of the mice got loose in a bedroom where my nephews Dooner, Brian Harris, and Bryan Barlow had congregated. The kids quickly put a towel across the bottom of the door to keep the furry escapees from scurrying into the rest of the house.

Richard says he made enough money to buy some groceries, milk for his kids, and dog food for their German shepherd, Nikkio. Someone once said that Richard, in his money-making schemes, had a remarkable ability to "make a penny dance." And that penny was certainly tripping the light fantastic that time.

And, so I presume, was Dotsy!

During Christmas season 1982, my wife Kathy Schwartz and I were living in a log cabin in the Hollywood and Vine area off Knik Road, not far from the Beldens' former homestead. Roger and Mary Ellen Bliss, whom Kathy and I had met when Roger taught shop in Kivalina in the late '70s, came over to visit. We'd had mice infiltrate the house to nibble on gift-wrapped peanut brittle, and just as we commented on the ways of Santa's helpers, a shrew dropped from a log rafter onto Mary Ellen's shoulder. Mary Ellen, a future Honda Shadow and BMW Rockster rider, married to dog musher and Iditarod racer Roger and no shrinking violet herself, flung the wee forager away from her. She reclaimed her chair and composure, and the shrew reclaimed its right to join the peanut brittle all-you-can-eat buffet.

In the spring of 1978, while teaching in Kivalina, Kathy and I rented a two-room house from one of the local churches. It was much like homesteading. We chopped and hauled up-river ice for water, used a fuel oil

Richard *and* Dotsy Harbeson *(from left), Mr. Snowman holding a HURLEY campaign sign, Becky Harbeson Chapman and George Harbeson Jr., with Lee Anna Harbeson Barlow kneeling in front, and Mark Chapman behind the snowman. The sign was most likely for Katie Hurley's election to the Alaska State Legislature from Wasilla, District 16A, in 1984.*

seep stove for heating and cooking, and had a honey bucket behind a cloth partition. Kivalina, located on a treeless sand bar bordering the Chukchi Sea, is a windy place with impressive snow drifts. We progressively dug our one exit several yards up through the snow as it piled up, shoring the roof of the tunnel with plywood. The drifts built up to the point where we could walk on the peak of the roof, and the house's windows were completely walled in with snow.

Voles built their outside byways through the snow against the thin window panes, and we watched these fellow travelers pass by, stopping to peer in at us humans. The scene resembled a giant ant farm, but reversed; we were the "ants" and the voles with their quick little eyes were the curious observers that studied our lives behind the glass.

SIX-YEAR-OLD BECKY ("MISSY"), *lost in a book on the bluff edge of the Harbeson homestead drive, summer 1963. The family greenhouse is in the background.*

11

Pastimes Quiet and Shocking

WE WERE KIDS; WE ENTERTAINED OURSELVES. ESPECIALLY when stuck in the woods on the homestead. Mundane things like transforming dirt piles into roads and imaginary communities occupied our hours and our minds. Unlike today, there wasn't the seductive glitter and complexity of toys that leave little to the imagination. Wooden blocks and small metal cars composed the standard. A tiny balsa glider was cool. My sisters liked playing dolls and dressing up cats, too. I played marbles on our driveway and in the schoolyard at recess. On rainy or winter days we played checkers, Clue, Monopoly, Parcheesi, Sorry, Scrabble, jacks, hopscotch, Ping-Pong, indoor hide'n'seek, jackstraws, Yahtzee, dominoes, hangman, bingo, Chinese checkers, and Battleship. And we played cards: slap jack, go fish, war, old maid, spit in the ocean, pig, Authors, crazy eights, hearts, and rummy. Fifty-two pick-up had a perennial but limited appeal. We played casino with a deck of circular cards we'd acquired somewhere along the way.

In addition to some of the games we played, Papa wrote about playing hockey, horse and rider, johnny-on-the-pony, and steal-the-flag. He pole-vaulted over clothes lines using home-made poles and held horse-chestnut-on-a-string duels. Like us, he mashed his feet into empty cans and stomped around with them stuck to his shoes. Like us, he played horseshoes, but unlike us he used shoes from the horses on the farm. He put daisies on top of the pegs at dusk, in order to see them better. And he introduced us to the marble culture—digging a hole in the ground by spinning around on your heel, utilizing two ways to shoot a marble, using your fist to gain height. He taught us terms like funsies, keepsies, spans, groundsides, the pot, steelies, aggies, glassies, cat's-eyes, and clearies. When I was a sixth grader in Wasilla, he suggested I give back the marbles I'd won from another boy, saying I'd taken unfair advantage of the kid's inexperience. I took the hint and complied. I didn't play pool until college, but I guess I was a marble hustler at the tender age of ten.

We were never much for football, but in his elementary grades Papa played football during lunch with no padding or helmets and a ball stuffed with rags. It became so rough that the county superintendent of schools banned these pick-up games. Ironically, during the very next lunch hour after that decree, Jackie Keller, Papa's schoolmate and the biggest kid in the school, suffered a broken leg in a follow-the-leader pile-up.

On occasion, we had firecrackers—sparklers, strings, ladyfingers (odd name for a firecracker), M-80s, cherry bombs, smokers—but rarely bottle rockets or roman candles because they were expensive. We didn't try to make our own, to Mom's nervous relief.

When I was in college in Fairbanks, we made crude blow guns from glass tubing and used wooden matches for darts. From our dorm windows we launched the matches at the sidewalk below, where they ignited and startled passing pedestrians and dogs. I didn't know then that Papa as a boy had used matches as BB gun ammo, shooting them into stones and foundations, and had constructed them into exploding darts.

On the homestead, we experimented with carbide lamps, compliments of Papa, but I was unaware of Papa's boyhood escapades until I read some of his remembrances after he had passed away.

> *I tried to make firecrackers by mixing sulphur,* nitrate, and charcoal. It would burn, but I never could make a good firecracker. I tried to make gunpowder many times, grinding the charcoal, mixing in sulphur and saltpeter, even wetting and drying it to make grains. It would burn quite well, but I never got more than a pop or sizzle. For other pyrotechnics, we took a small press-top baking powder can, poked a hole in the bottom with a nail, put chips of carbide in the can, then watered or spit on the carbide and pressed on the lid. We put the can under our

foot and put a lighted match to the hole—Bang!—a satisfying explosion. However, I'd seen railroad work crews near our farm make two-gallon-sized carbide bombs whose thunder dwarfed our little cannons!

- -

SOMETIMES PAPA GOT involved in others' mischief. As a boy, he'd gone fishing near the farm at a local place called "The Washout," which was part of the old Morris Canal. It had a small outflow of water and was covered with algae and pond lilies, but a variety of fish could be caught there: large-mouth bass, perch, shiners, catfish, sunfish, and occasionally trout. Once Papa had a dozen fish on a string in the water when Billy H. and Watson K., two local boys, came up and began fishing on the other side. Billy quickly tired of fishing and said to Watson, "I'm going to throw this match into that dry grass, and I bet you put it out."

Watson replied, "I bet I won't!"

Billy did; Watson didn't.

Soon the hillside was beginning to burn, and the three boys ran off. Somebody on a passing train reported the fire. Men came to put it out, and Papa, Billy, and Watson came back across the tracks to help. Later that evening, Papa went back to collect his fish, but found that someone had swiped them.

Papa watched his father dynamite holes in the ground on the farm for peach tree plantings, which upped the firecracker ante a bit, and dynamite also played a part in Papa's WWII years on Saipan. Because they missed eating peanuts, he and his pals blasted a hole in the coral to get at peanuts growing there. A chunk of coral from the explosion whizzed through the air and crashed through the roof to the floor boards of an officer's tent. This scattered the cards, money, and officers playing poker inside. The irate brass burst from the tent to nail the culprits but found that everyone was mystified how such a thing could have happened.

As a boy, Papa had made ear-piercing whistles from pignut and willow branches, and he showed us how to cut whistles out of willow and alder. We played Pied Piper and marched in woodwind duets. We picked up on pea shooters on our own, and skirmished with each other using straws, lengths of copper pipe and different types of hoses, usually substituting pebbles or green high-bush cranberries for commercial ammo. Being a teacher, Papa never told us of the time in his sixth grade class at Towaco School when he owned a "pea bean shooter," a device like a straw with a mouthpiece. He shot a bean at another student on the school steps, but the principal, Mrs. Eckhardt, walked into the line of fire and he hit her in the head by mistake. Years later, when Papa was first teaching at Montville, Mrs. Eckhardt supervised a reading library at the back of his classroom and perhaps dreamed of revenge.

When the teacher is your father—even one with a checkered past—you tend to avoid such pursuits. But when I was in high school, we would unobtrusively tie a string from the chair in front of us to a belt loop of its occupant, thereby providing great entertainment when the end-of-class bell rang.

Playing With Electricity

WHEN FIRST ON THE HOMESTEAD, WE had an old army field telephone set that we found somewhere. Papa had been in Army Air Communications in WWII, so he was familiar with it. We strung wires and spent hours talking on the phones. Ten-year-old Richard saw potential in them, too, and conducted experiments on how electricity works. He told trusting Becky to put her fingers on the contacts and gave the phone a crank, which gave Becky a surprise lesson. I knew his ambushing nature, but he got Lee Anna and Becky with another trick. He had them hold the ends of two wires and went around the corner of the house to the hidden army phone and cranked it. He also used a McCullough chain saw with its coil for this. (He says he really heard Becky yell that time.) He regrets these tricks now and says he knows where his son Dooner got some of his ideas for mischief.

Papa got into the act, too, in these "lessons," but his participation stemmed more from a "get-it-done" practicality than mischief. He and Richard would grab the electric fence wire that penned in Bully, our calf. Once when we had Jeep engine trouble Papa told me to hold the head of the spark plug wire next to the spark plug to see if it was getting spark. Unwillingly, I complied and got zapped. He then pointed out the insulating values of rubber. He did the same with Richard and the Chevy. "I told Papa I didn't want to do that. Papa snorted and said, 'Here, watch me,' and grabbed the wire and held it. I could see the current in his arm. Later, I talked to a doctor who said it was the same frequency as your heart signal. You can stand it, but it can mess up your heart."

Nomads of the Night

SLEEPWALKING LIVENED UP A FEW OF our nights. I never did somnambulate, but Richard and Becky did when we were still living in our basement with its flat roof. We had re-tarred it a few times, but it sprang leaks faster than we could get cans, buckets, pots, and pans under them. To catch the drips during rains, we constructed mazes of receptacles, positioning them on the rugs and concrete floor, on the beds, and occasionally on a table or couch. We lived in the middle of a tin-pan orchestra of drip-drip-drips, dings, plops, and plinks—homestead renditions of Handel's *Water Music*. We had to watch where we stepped or sat to avoid knocking over a section of the orchestra. Ballet was worlds distant from our basement, but many a crude *pas de bourée couru* (quick tippy-toe baby steps) was performed of necessity in those days. We utilized the careful, deliberate *pas marché* when caution was required, and the *polonaise* when we felt sociable or wished guidance through the maze. All this, of course, with apologies to Nureyev, Baryshnikov, and other lovers of dance.

One rainy night, Becky started talking in her sleep, got out of bed, and in the dark talked and danced her way through the array of cans without bumping any of them. She made it outside before someone noticed and retrieved her. One October night she sleepwalked outside again and Richard found her wandering around in the snow in her bare feet and helped her back into her bed. Still asleep, she kept telling Richard, "I have to save the cat"—no doubt her personal interpretation of *pas de chat*.

Richard himself somnambulated once after we moved upstairs atop the basement, when plastic still covered the windows. He says, "I was sleeping on the top floor of our log house and dreamed that I had two motorcycles and that someone had stolen them. I woke up when I found myself walking around on the frosty grass in my shorts. The dream was so intense that I still thought I had two motorcycles. I was mad and kept demanding, 'Where are my motorcycles? Where are my motorcycles?' It was five minutes before I realized I didn't have any motorcycles."

Bunk Mate Bugs and BB Guns

During the first several homestead years, we kids slept in metal bunk beds with a metal mesh to support the thin mattresses. The mesh sagged, creating a hammock-like effect. Top occupants suffered kicks and shoves from below and the possibility of sailing off the bed to the floor. Becky tells of one shenanigan that played out after I had gone off to college.

"The four of us each slept in a bunk bed. I walked by my bed one day to find Richard hanging around it. When I asked him, 'What are you doing?' he said he was making my bed. I thought it was odd, but I left him there tucking in the covers. That night when I was in bed, I felt something crawling up my leg. I leaped up screaming, to find that it was one of those big black spruce bugs."

We called them spruce bugs. They were likely white-spotted sawyer beetles (*Monochamus scutellatus*); most of them were black with a few white spots. They were hard-shelled and nearly three inches in length, including very long antennae, and our cats ate them. The bug would squirm around in the cat's mouth, its long antennae flipping. We could hear the crackling and crunching as the cat chewed on them. They had barbed feet that stuck to the cat's jaws and whiskers; if the cat decided to spit the bug out, it would shake its head vigorously and paw at the bug to get it loose.

One of Richard and Peter's jokester agents was itching powder, used in their itching powder wars. When they didn't have itching powder, they used fiberglass insulation, not the best of choices. Richard suffered one clandestine attack by Peter—most of the tricks were perpetuated in secrecy. Peter sprinkled itching powder in Richard's shorts one day, and when Richard pulled on his shorts, he couldn't comprehend what was wrong at first. When it dawned on him, Richard retaliated by adding itching powder to Peter's bed sheets.

That may have led to an incident involving wasps. "Eight yellowjackets had crawled down into the creases of the sheets on my bed, possibly seeking warmth," Richard says. "I slept all night on top of them, but when I started waking up in the morning, all of a sudden they hit—*Bam!*

Bam! *Bam*! *Bam*! *Bam*!—and got me several times on my back. I had been in a deep sleep and was still groggy, but that really stung. Normally, I'm not a violent person, but I shot out of bed and beat that bed to death. All these years since, I thought they had crawled in there on their own, but Peter told me the other day that he had stuck them in there to get back at me for the itching powder. I don't believe him, though."

IT WAS RICHARD'S NATURE TO EXPERIMENT. Once he was playing with a BB gun but had no BB's, so he used small pebbles. Becky was several yards away riding Richard's bike. "I picked up a little pyramid-shaped rock and loaded it into the gun," Richard says. "Peter told me to shoot it at Becky, so I shot it at the back tire as she peddled away, but the rock missed the tire and found an area it wasn't supposed to."

Richard tells of a time when he was on the receiving end of a BB gun, when we lived at Byers' place and Richard was six and I was eleven. He says, "George told me to come to a site a few feet off the barn wall and said, 'You want to do a math experiment? Just stand by the wall and put your leg right here. I'll go over there and shoot into the wall at a forty-five degree angle, and we'll see what happens.' He shot at the wall and it richocheted and bounced off my leg. I went bawling to Mom and George got in trouble."

We stripped the leaves from fireweed stalks to make swords for our fencing matches, just as Papa and his brothers and friends had done with New Jersey weeds. Like Papa, we also made bows and arrows from small saplings and dry sticks. Richard and I were throwing stick spears at each other one day near where our dog Bruce the Second was buried, when one I threw at Richard glanced off his head above his right ear. It tore the skin a bit, and he sported a little bald spot after that.

We did do some stupid things as kids but it was fun, in the spirit of adventure—not mean-spirited at all. Just the same, sometimes we were lucky not to suffer serious injury. One thing we were taught was to keep the mischief at home, to control ourselves in public and in school, and with other families.

ON THE TURNER HOMESTEAD, JULY 1965: *Lin Turner holding "Boy," as Becky called him, known to the rest of the family as Blackie; to the right of Lin are Becky Harbeson, Dena Turner and Peter Harbeson. The names of the two girls on the left are not known.*

Model Airplane Antics

IN THE 1960S, FASCINATED BY AIRPLANES and flying, Richard bought a Testors string-controlled model airplane—a "rock-on-a-string," as some called it. It flew in a circle and used an EverReady 1.5-volt battery to heat the glow plug. It burned Testors fuel, an unusual mixture not familiar to Richard. The engine, a Testors .049, was cantankerous, and he struggled to start the troublesome thing in our basement.

"It would start, sputter, run five to ten seconds, then stall," he says. "Once the prop backfired and the plane took off backwards and wrapped the string around my legs. After working with it for almost an hour, so focused that I didn't notice the fumes, my body started jerking in what felt like convulsions. I bobbed about like a sandhill crane. Becky and Lee Anna took me outside and walked me around until I recovered."

Richard later graduated to radio control models. He and his sons Dooner and Brian sent up mice and frogs as pilots. Richard cut a Windex bottle in half lengthwise and rubber-banded it onto the top of a model plane. They put a mouse in the homemade cockpit for the flight. Mice didn't take to the idea, though. In flight they ran around inside the cockpit, throwing the plane off balance, and left scatological protests behind.

Richard remembers putting two mice in flight once. "They got to scrambling about in the cockpit and threw the plane out of control. I initiated a 'Lomcevak,' a tumbling, free-style maneuver of Czech origin. (It was a term first used by a mechanic comparing his pilot Ladislav Bezák's aerobatics to the hangover movements of someone who had too much 'Jelínek slivovitz' to drink.)" The maneuver quieted the mice down and Richard landed the plane. After that, he grounded the mice.

He went to the gold standard of critter pilots, the frog. He had one particular frog for most of a summer and sent it on many solo flights. The frog was a cool customer, hopped to the front of the cockpit for the flights, and quickly became a veteran with many hours of single-engine flight. After three months, Richard retired the frog and set it free in the swampy area near his house. His live pilots had a perfect safety record—not one animal died in his pilot training program.

Bill Bowers, Richard's friend in Eagle River, built radio-controlled model planes and had Richard test fly them. Bill had a one-third scale Bud Nosen Gere Sport with an 8-foot wingspan, and Richard wanted to send Bill's cat up in it, but Bill refused to allow it—cats and airplanes don't mix well. Richard says that one day at the Birchwood Airport a couple took off in a Cessna 206 but quickly returned to land. They'd had their pet cat aboard, and the animal had freaked out, streaking around the cabin like a motorcycle rider in a cage.

Richard spent many hours with Eagle River's Mosquito Club, a model airplane group that took part in shows, traveling as far as Glennallen and beyond. At one of their flying shows, Richard was sitting in a camper shell on the back of a pickup when someone's radio-controlled model dove straight down and crashed partway through the aluminum ceiling over Richard's head. "It startled the heck out of me, but I understood," he says.

12

Flannel Boards and Grape Juice

IN THE BEGINNING WAS THE WORD, OR WORDS, TO BE PRECISE: Sunday school. I had been sprinkled on when I was an infant, but the first memory I have of religious affairs was in 1955–56, when we were staying at Byers' on Fairview Loop. Lee Anna and I dressed up and rode a church bus to Wenter Harvey's Church of Christ for Sunday school and church.

As background to my experiences, Papa's notes tell of the role of religion in his family when he was a youth in Montville, New Jersey, in the 1920s and '30s.

> *In school we'd get a verse from the Bible, salute* the flag, and sing "America" to start the day. On occasion we went to Sunday School, and more rarely to church, at the Dutch Reformed Church on Changebridge Road. I was in two or three one act plays in this church—Ella, Bill, and Davis were in them. too. The plays were terrible. We never went to dances, but we weren't against dancing. I never heard my parents curse, except for a very rare "Damn," or "Hell," and my older brothers and sisters didn't swear. Most of the boys I played with when I was young didn't either. Even in the Army, where cuss words flew like shrapnel, I didn't swear, but if others wanted to do so, it was okay with me.

RECORDS SHOW THAT my parents were married in New Jersey in November in the parsonage of the Dutch Reformed Church, but were married again the following September in the Church of Saint Joseph. I wonder about that. Was there some sort of sectarian struggle and accommodation that took place after the first ceremony? Was it to placate Mom's parents? St. Joseph wanted equal time?

Growing up in Alaska, I can't recall my parents mentioning religion one way or another. Profane language was nonexistent in our family—my ears were versed in it via the usual social contacts, but my own first oath was a mild one to a friend in my sophomore year of high school—that Elgin Baylor was a "hell of a basketball player"—and it surprised and embarrassed me. (I must confess in the years since, in my private life, I have back-slid a little from the example provided me.) Moral necessities such as honesty and taking responsibility for our actions were made very clear to us kids, through direct guidance and Papa's and Mom's "preaching by example." As for school, my own elementary class days in Wasilla may have started with a small prayer. I can't remember if we recited the pledge or not—Alaska was a territory then—but I think we did, probably with the phrase "under God" in later grades, it having been added in the 1950s era of McCarthyism and the "Red Scare."

Singing had a rich history in Papa's family, likely due in part to the lack of electronic diversions that proliferate in our homes today. They sang and played a variety of music. Papa didn't have a singing voice—although he sang children's songs to us—and growing up on the homestead we didn't sing much. Of course, we couldn't afford a piano, so we settled for a radio. Papa's memories reveal how it was for him.

> ***Music was an important part of our lives. Hymns,*** gospel, and spiritual selections were sung, as well as an extensive variety of international, traditional, classical, and popular tunes. Mama played the piano by ear and could play almost any popular tune. Papa could play a little. Dorothy learned to play the piano, could play by the notes, and Davis, Bill, and Ella sang in the church choir. Louise at the age of three could pick out "My Country 'Tis of Thee," and began to compose her own tunes on the piano. Often, a group of young people gathered around the piano on Sunday evenings.
>
> I learned songs like "The Old Rugged Cross" and "I Come to the Garden Alone," "Rock of Ages," and others. Bill and Davis

taught me the Baptist Sunday School hymns, and in school I learned "We Three Kings of Orient Are." I liked to hear Davis or Ed sing "The Lord's Prayer" and "The Twenty-Third Psalm." Other hymns we sang were "The Church in the Wildwood," "Come, Let's Gather at the River," "Go Down Moses," and "Swing Low, Sweet Chariot." Davis and Ed sang with quartets and other groups and soloed at weddings.

IN WENTER HARVEY'S church, I liked the hymn singing. However, I had inherited even less of a singing voice than Papa, and it didn't improve with age. Small birds fell from the sky and young children fled to their mothers when I attempted to carry a tune. But others could sing and I enjoyed listening, all the while semi-faking it so as not to attract attention—"Lip-syncing: The Early Days." Sunday school was held in the church basement and featured traditional stories like the "Prodigal Son" illustrated on a flannel board, a simple device using picture cut-outs. Even then, I was an avid reader, so I found the tales interesting.

Upstairs, in the main sessions, eventually the sermon and singing drew to a close and communion took place. This presented the first of two events in my introduction to religious practices, the likes of which I had not yet encountered in my short life. I was told that the wafers and grape juice (no wine for us) were the body and blood of Christ. I understood this, since I was aware of what symbolism was, but I was told that in some churches no symbolism was involved, that these manifestations comprised the actual blood and flesh of Christ. I can't recall the position that Harvey's church took, but this brought me up short, gave me considerable pause. How was that possible? Christ had been dead for a rather long time, and why, in a civilized society, would anyone want to consume his flesh and blood? I was just a kid, but this smacked of South Sea islanders' "long pig" and the Donner party's troubles. Many years later, I came across the term "transubstantiation"—and others like it—and realized that I had stepped in a theological hornets' nest. Neither Papa nor Mom spoke of it to me, one way or the other. They just sent me off to church and it was up to me to hash it all out.

Around this time, I attended church camp for a week during summer vacation, located at a permanent site off Hayfield Road. We bunked in cabins, and a dining hall/activity building served for classes and study. A large tent was erected for services. The driveway dropped down through the trees and crossed a small bridge where Cottonwood Creek emptied into a small pond. It was a pretty spot for a camp.

It may have been my first time away from home in a group setting. Some of my classmates also attended, so it was like school without the schoolwork, with different teachers. The food was good and we were taught manners. To wit, anyone uncouth enough to rest his or her elbow/forearm on the table during a meal was met with the gleefully chanted refrain, in my case, "George, George, strong and able/Keep your elbows off the table!" The ditty could be initiated by anyone, adults included, sitting at the tables or serving, so throughout our meals we all kept a crafty watch, waiting to pounce on those poor souls unfortunate enough to lapse into less formal etiquette. Some of us stretched our arms, yawned in sated contentment, and feigned an elbow rest on the table to keep the monitors that monitored the monitors on their toes.

The second formative event in my contact with religious activities began in the camp's large communal tent, situated near the pond. A late evening service was conducted there, with forty or fifty campers of all ages in attendance. I can't recall what the sermon topic was, something backing up the lessons of morality that my parents espoused, but it was effective. Its conclusion culminated in people being called to "accept Christ" at the front of the folding chair and bench seating. As people shuffled to the front, I looked around and was astonished to see that everyone in the audience, I mean *everyone*, was crying or tearing up in some manner—except me. I sat there in my pre-teen confusion and tried to sort it out.

Soon everyone filed out of the tent and stood at the edge of the pond while baptisms commenced. The bunkhouse cabins were visible through the birch trees on the hill that served as a backdrop in the fading Alaskan summer evening light. People waded one by one into the cold, muddy water to be immersed. I wasn't sure how this fit in with my early-in-life holy water rite, but I knew I couldn't swim. Night was falling, the water was quite cold—evidenced by the blue lips and shivering of those participating—and I was still dealing with the tears-in-the-tent thing, so I stood back from the water's edge with a group of campers and watched.

That moment stuck with me, and over the ensuing years the power of words to evoke emotional response, especially in groups, became very clear to me. I learned that emotion can muddy the waters of reason, and that keeping a healthy balance between the two is essential for societies and cultures. I find that over the years my parents' moral and ethical precepts have stood me well, although it is not always an easy road to travel. But I do regret never learning to swim.

I actually spent a considerable amount of time in churches in my school years. My classmates and I attended class in the school overflow use of the Church of Christ building where classmate Donna Harvey's father Wenter presided on Sundays. John Blissard, classmate Cynthia and her sister Colleen's father, was our teacher. Papa came from the high school and taught us history. Later, in eighth grade, we again went to school in a church, this time in the basement of the Presbyterian church located a couple of blocks away, with Mr. Louis Pinkham serving up our education. That was the year that a student's pants (no, not mine), minus the student (no, not me), somehow ended up in a tree during a recess—not exactly pious behavior.

It struck me that Papa was genuinely interested in discussing religion with those burdened with missionary zeal. On several occasions intrepid souls such as Mormons or Seventh Day Adventists presented themselves at our door, foraging for converts in the wilderness and perhaps struggling to maintain a sinking resolve as they wended their way deeper along the formidable drive to the house. Papa greeted them warmly, invited them in, and discussion commenced—usually a lengthy one. Papa's inclination toward taciturnity eased with the onset of a good debate. An hour, two, three, would pass—the visitors had no idea of Papa's wide experience in lengthy professional meetings. Longing glances toward the door and the checking of watches ensued. Eventually they would make it to the door, or even to their vehicle—if they hadn't had to walk the drive—to be engaged further. Once when we visited the Edes a similar discussion took place. It ended with Papa and Jim presenting the departing emissaries with a gift of Darwin's *On the Origin of Species* as a gesture of good faith.

These visits didn't always focus on religion. A few fell under the Willie Loman category. In one instance a vacuum salesman braved our driveway to perform his spiel extolling the advantages of a Kirby or Hoover, tossing dirt on the carpet for effect. Becky and Peter joined the salesman in his high-pressure sales pitch when they heard that all purchasers had a chance to win a vacation in Hawaii. They had never been on a vacation other than on the Alaska road system, so they pleaded, begged, and cajoled Papa to please, please buy one. Papa was a hard sell, though, and resisted both peddler and progeny. The disconsolate salesman wandered back along the wilds of our drive to the Knik Road, and presumably to more propitious locales and more amenable customers.

In the years since, I have resisted those who endeavor to clean my carpets as well as those attempting to cleanse my soul. I have, at times, admired the temerity and, yes, even courage, of those so concerned with my floors and my salvation. But I prefer to handle those tasks myself and forgo the grape juice and flannel board for the writings of Mark Twain and Bertrand Russell.

*The "*Bound for Alaska*" Chevy Carryall, at rest on the homestead half a century later.*

Epilogue

"From the age of nine, to nineteen or twenty, I experienced the Depression, and this experience has shaped my life ever since." As I read, Papa's fluid handwritten words stride across the pages of the memories discovered decades after his passing.

"I was nine and in the fifth grade when the Stock Market crashed. My Aunt Louise worked for a broker in N.Y.C. who killed himself, and she died a short time later."

Papa's recollections swirl up off the sheets of paper like the morning mist rising out of the rows of the family's cornfield, where I ran as a small child. From his writing arise images of skunks in the chicken coop, rats in a hand-dug well, flickering oil lamp and candle-lit evenings. Scenes emerge of flat tires, clincher rims, wooden-encased magnetos, roadsters and touring cars and an old Model A. Wendell Wilkie and Herbert Hoover and FDR. Plowing for twenty-five cents an hour, and picking strawberries all day for three cents a quart. Always life is integrated with the natural environment, as personal as the "goofus feathers" that burned Papa's skin on a hot day in the peach orchard.

The Depression was a strict teacher. People spent long arduous hours making a living. Cars were simply a means of getting from one place to another, an imperfect tool—fix them yourself. Jeans were the badge of a working man, not for designer vanity. Build your own house and repair it; it should look used and comfortable. Sunglasses for medical reasons only. Use things until they can't be fixed, then use them to make or repair something else.

Music helped counterbalance the trials of the times—singing in the evenings around the piano, in church, in the fields, in old vehicles while traveling, in small groups or alone. Papa's list of song titles scrawls a long scrambling score across the pages.

These were lessons for the homestead and for Alaska in the '50s and '60s—for starting from scratch. Somehow from all of it came a belief in the goodness of human nature. A faith in the ability to overcome corruption and poverty through education and teaching and knowledge—by action, by example, and by perseverance. This was Papa's objective.

And Mom believed in her "Harb," even in moments of uncertainty. She took his beliefs to heart. She expanded her horizons by reading, studying art, and breaking away from the housewife role to become a member of the Food Service Division of the National Maritime Union and to work at the Nike Site so she could travel to England—long of special interest to her. She traveled the Alaska Highway to the East Coast in a blue Datsun with Papa and Peter to visit relatives—which surely required great patience and fortitude. She also took a correspondence course in Library Science from Loyola University. She and Lee Anna took a mother-daughter vacation in Hawaii. She listened to James Galway music. She, too, believed in justice for all and in the primary role education plays to improve the human condition. And in her quiet way she guided my brothers and sisters and me along the trail behind my father.

Papa was ever the picture of composure and kept his stronger emotions inside. Yet all these years later, his notes reveal a rare glimpse of his feelings for Mom. In one excerpt relating a time just after they were married, he recalls: "We drove to Boonton and there in the shop next to the State Theater she bought a pastel blue dress of a soft light material. Later, in her sister Mary's kitchen at the Marshalls, I opened the door to see her sitting in a chair attired in the blue dress. Suddenly my chest filled and my heart pushed up in one swelled beat that caught my breath. I had never seen anyone so lovely."

Telling of the time we were building our basement on the homestead, Papa wrote of Mom: "She stood on the scaffold, her smooth, brown, strong arms moving up and down with the sure quickness that characterized her, while she puddled the cement down eleven rows of blocks."

And finally, Papa's observation later in life, after his retirement: "Today I watched her walk up the drive to the house. Her steps have slowed, but her walk is still erect and she is neat and clean and trim, with the colors that have always complemented her, and I feel regret that to someone who has given me so much, I have given so little...."

But despite his regret, I think he gave more to Mom than he realized. I remember one high school literature class discussion when Papa gave us students a possible definition of true love: "True love is an elderly gentleman arising before his wife in the morning to place her false teeth in warm water." Not exactly Elizabeth Barrett Browning counting the ways, but touching nonetheless, and it provided me with one of the rare insights into his personal emotions.

In his years of retirement, Papa's activities were drawing down, yet his and Mom's marriage remained strong. The life they both gave to Lee Anna, Richard, Becky, Peter and me was unique in many ways and was a fine effort. And in all of my teaching career in the state of Alaska, there wasn't a day went by that I didn't appreciate and directly experience examples and results of the effort that he and others gave for the teaching profession and educational system.

While the Depression was the formative force in my parents' early lives, Alaska molded my life and the lives of my brothers and sisters. Unlike many U.S. landscapes that bear worn, tired faces, ones that express the uses and abuses that civilization often bestows, Alaska's vast fresh wildness was for a time a land unto itself. New, unsullied for the most part by "progress," it instilled in me an appreciation of its freedom and straightforward simplicity that Papa had taken to heart.

Alaska is referred to as "The Great Land," an insipid term these days, but if I dig beneath the crust of commercialism and political posturing, I still can feel the true depth and power of those simple words. It was a rare endowment that Papa and Mom gave to us children, but one that comes with an implacable irony: we, too, were—and even today still are—agents contributing to the changes sweeping across this land.

As I reminisce, I remember a part of their gift, the sunny days when our family walked down to the flats below our house, out to the edge of the inlet mud, to catch the turn of the ebb tide. I trotted out on the sun-baked areas of the silt to meet the bore tide surging up the bed of the steeply sloped channel. That low but inexorable wave of roiling water advanced up Cook Inlet under the broad cast of a blue sky, the Chugach Mountains, and our Knik homestead bluff, and as my family watched from the grassy bank the ocean traveled its time-told trail into the future, and I ran alongside that tumbling, rushing wave and reveled in the race.

IN FRONT OF THE WASILLA COMMUNITY HALL, JANUARY 1955:
George Harbeson Jr. with his second-grade report card.

Looking Back

Wasilla, Alaska—1954
(28 Below)

I was just to Wasilla in '54,
a seven-year-old East Coast boy
peering through December night glass.

My breath blew hot onto moonscaped frost
as my thumbs rubbed away the ice crystals
to reveal the shortest, and briefest, of tunnels.

Framed with silver, the Community Hall loomed,
shimmered, hazy and log-dark, over the restless
berms of Main Street's silent snow-cast currents.

Behind me, the sentient oil stove murmured
its warm, gently cautionary warning, while
my family stirred in Saturday slumber.

And, now, five fleeting decades later,
I wonder what I was looking for.

And if I have found it.

— *George Harbeson Jr.*

Index of People

EXCEPT FOR THE seven Harbesons who appear throughout the book—George and Katherine Bartholomay Harbeson and children George Jr., Lee Anna, Richard, Becky and Peter—this listing includes almost everyone named in *Homesteaders in the Headlights*. Not indexed are the newspaper captions for the Groton basketball photos on pages 201 and 202, the lengthy Wasilla community caption on page 212, and people referred to only by first name. **Boldface** numerals indicate photographs.

Abbott, Don, 272
Adcock, Danny, 210
Alexander, Jack, 237, 240
Alward, Lee, 260
Alward, Roberta, **72**, 260
Alward family, 260
Anderson, Mike, 228
Andrew, Karen, **37**, 223
Andrew, Linda, **244**
Armstrong, Bill, 228
Atkins, Wilbur, 109
Axtell, Roxanne, 34, **36**

Baker, Calvin, 224
Baker, Jess, 77
Baldwin, Billy, 90
Baldwin, Raymond, 17
Barlow, Bryan, 134, 277
Barlow, Jim, 134, 268
Barnes, Victor, 56
Bartholomay, Frank, 11, 35, 113
Bartholomay, Frankie, 11, 113, 131
Bartholomay, Hazel, 11, 71, 198
Bartholomay, Mary (Marshall), 11, 12, 92, 121, 275, 300
Bartlett, Bob, 78
Begich, Nick Sr., 78-80
Behnke, Peggy, 70, 71, **114**, 115
Behymer, Jerry, 237
Belden, Charlotte, 71, **72**, 83, 84, 115
Belden, Cheryl, 83
Belden, Christy, 83

Belden, Connie, 83, 84
Belden, David, 83, 84
Belden, Dennis, 83, 84
Belden, Floyd, 83
Belden, Joyce, **72**, 83
Belden, Kathy, 83
Belden, Melvin, 83
Belden, Melvin ("Gene"), 83, 210, **239**
Belden, Ronnie, 83
Belden family, 83-85
Bell, Tim, 247
Bergman, Judy, **37**, 210, 223, 240, 242
Betts, Alison. 164
Betts, Peggy, 70
Bezák, Ladislav, 289
Bliss, Mary Ellen, 176, 260, 277
Bliss, Roger, 150, 176, 260, 277
Blissard, Colleen, 296
Blissard, Cynthia, 296
Blissard, John, 296
Borden, Anna, 61
Borden, Mr., 61, 62
Bouwens, Jerry, **37**, **196**, 216, **226**, **239**
Bowers, Bill, 289
Brown, Dr., 163
Brudie, Phil, 240
Bryant, David, 131, 210, **235**, 242
Buchman, Gary, 247
Bunker, Bob, 245
Burrow, Sherry, **244**
Butler, Bill, 77
Byers, Margaret, 45, 73, 181

Byers, Orlando, 45, 73, 128, 176, 181, 183, 257
Byers residence, **44**, 46, 48, 57, 176, **254**, 257, 288, 291

Calhoun, Dan, 249
Calhoun, Dennis, 73, 185, 214, **226**, 231, 240, 249
Calhoun, Jimbo, 249
Calhoun, Nelda, 228, 249
Calhoun, Red, 228, 249
Calhoun, Sally, 249
Calhoun family, 237
Carl, Dicky, **196**, 214, 216, 221, 223, **226**, 228, **239**
Carney, Ed, 33-34, 162, 170, 218
Carney, David, 170
Carney, Doug, 34
Carney, Helen Carter, 33, **37**
Carney, Linda, **37**, 227
Carney, Mike, 170
Carney, Nick, 213
Carney, Pat, 168
Carney family, 33
Carr family, 56
Carryl, Charles Edward, 42
Carter, Colleen, 223, 242
Carter, Donnie, 38
Carter, May, 34, 59, 87
Carter, Pat, 59
Carter family, 33, 168
Chapman, Mark, 262, **278**
Chapman, Shanna, 262, **264**, 276
Cherneski, Vern, 247, 248, 249
Clark, Roger, 41
Claus family, 66, 68, 149
Clement, Chuck, **241**, 242
Collie, Jack, 237
Coghlan, Bonnie, **58**, 59, 64
Coghlan, Gene, **58**, 59-64, 87, 260
Coghlan, Gerald "Skip," 35, 59, 62, 63-64
Coghlan, Kathy, 59, 64
Coghlan, Violet, 59-64, 71, 93, 115
Coghlan family, 59-64, 73, 79, 85, 156, 181, 194, 195

Conway, Jimmy, 173
Conway family, 112
Cooper, Brigitte, 111
Cooper, John, 111
Cooper (Kenai Kardinal), 221
Corcoran, Thomas ("Tommy the Cork"), 18
Corrigan, Doug ("Wrong Way"), 211
Cottle, Rod, 218
Cottle's, 130, 155, 158
Crown's sugar house, 56

Day, Bob, 228, 237
Dean, Dizzy, 203
Decker, Mrs. (teacher/principal), 90
Devlin, Frank, 38
Devlin, Jack, 38
Dickerson, M. Ashley, 243
Dinkels' farm, 113, 186
Dr. Schultz' band, 43
Drumm, Ed, 55
Dulles, John Foster, 17
Dumas, T.D., 242
Dunphy, Bob, **235**

Eckhardt, Mrs. (principal), 284
Ede, Diana, 78
Ede, Ella ("Lori"), 78
Ede, Jim, **76**, 77-81
Ede, Julie, 71-81, **72**, **76**, 115
Ede, Stephen, 77, 78, 79, 172
Ede family, 77-81, 85, 260, 296
Edwards, Phyllis, 223, 242
Egan, Bill, 190
Erickson (Kenai Kardinals), 221
Erickson, Earl, **37**
Estelle, Jim, 237
Ettinger (law firm secretary), 18
Evenson (Kenai Kardinals coach), 217, 221, 222

Fennimore, Howard, **241**, 242
Ford, Sam, 93
Fowler, Dwayne, 245, 246
Franklin, Benjamin, 39

Garcia, Judy, **37**
Gehrig, Lou, 203
Gentile (fire warden), 92
German, Jeff, 131
Gershmel, Bob, 38
Gershmel family, 38
Gibson, Alan, 228
Gilbertson, Billy, 214, 216, 220, 223, **226**, 228
Gilbertson, Marilyn, **37**, 223, 227
Gillespie, Ray, **235**
Glidden family, 268
Goodwin, Sue, 39
Gore, George, 87, 173, **180**
Gore, Mrs., **180**
Gore family, 64, 73, 181, 260, 266, 267
Gose, Terry, 229
Gruening, Ernest, 78, 213
Gurtler, Bev, 113
Gurtler, Ed, 113

Hadfield, Ted, 245
Hagen's Playland, 34, 127
Haines, Ray, 68, 149
Haley, Bill (and the Comets), 198
Hansen, Ester, 113, 186
Hansen, Henry, 113, 186
Harbeson, Benjamin, 39
Harbeson, Bill, 118, 291, 293-294
Harbeson, Billy, 128
Harbeson, Davis, 12, 17, 18, 56, 118, 119, 120, 122, 168, 291, 293-294
Harbeson, Davis Lawler, 16
Harbeson, Dennie, 23
Harbeson, Dooner, 23, 134, 251-252, 277, 285, 289
Harbeson, Dorothy (Wilde), 17, 21, 91, 293
Harbeson, "Dotsy", 64, 134, 277, **278**
Harbeson, Ella, 121, 291, 293
Harbeson, Elmer, 203
Harbeson, Evelyn, 168
Harbeson, Louise (Drumm), 16, 25, 30, 42, 55, 122, 273-274, 294
Harbeson, Sterne, **14**, 16, 21, 23, 65, 91, 119, 121, 149

Hardcastle, Bob, 245
Harris, Brian, 134, 257, 277, 289
Harris, Florence—*see* Harbeson, "Dotsy"
Hartman, Jean, 240
Harvey, Donna, 296
Harvey, Rev. Wenter, 291, 294, 296
Heaven family, 56
Hendrickson, Jerry, **77**
Hickel, Walter, 268
Hill, Lary, **196**, 216, 227, 245
Hjellen, Gilbert, 38
Hjellen, Ida, **37**, 223-227
Hjellen, Pete, **196**, 214, 216, 223, **226**, 228, **239**, 245
Holliday, Henry, 135
Holly, Buddy, 50
Holtz, Ray, 218
Hoover (Herbert), 39, 299
Hubbell, Carl, 203
Hulke, Frieda, 105, 223
Hume, Dr. Vincent, 163, 214-215
Huston, Gene, 210
Huston, Jim, **241**, 242, 243
Hyde, Joe, 135
Hyde, Sallie, 135

Ingram, Richard, **196**, 214, 216, 223, **226**
Irish, Ed, 237

Jackson, Frank, 235
Jallen, Larry, 78, 79
Jallen, Ordeen, 79
Jameson family, 66, 149
Johnson brothers, 38
Jones, Bronwen, 33
Jones, Warren, 77, 218

Kalmbach, Fritz, 84
Kalmbach, Kathy, 164
Karnofsky, Danny, 210, 238
Keller, Jackie, 282
Kelton, Barbara, 112, 158, 223
Kelton, Claude, 112, 158
Kennedy, Gene, 78
Knutsen boys, 38
Kohler, Burton, 210

Kohring, Jim, 237
Kompkoff, Mike, **241**, 242, 243
Konner, Kevah, 273
Kritchen, Lynn, **241**, 242

Lamb, Chip, 237
Lambert, Bill, 38
Leone, Joe, 216, 220, **226**, **239**, 245
Levan residence, 45, 70
Lincoln, Bob, 45
Lincoln, Roger, 45
Longstreet, Dr., 16-17
Lorentzen, Bill, 39, 77
Lovejoy, Keith, 210
Lovejoy's Garage, 105
Lucas, Bob, 159, 171
Lum, Burt, 68, 149, 160
Lum family, 68, 149

Marshall, Jim, 172
Marshall, Jim ("Wrong Way"), 211
Martin, Al, 230
Martin, Charlyn, 71, 115, 255
Martin, Ray, 237
McCain, John, 247
McCavit, Dr. (dentist), 250
McDonald, Bill, 77
McDonald, Country Joe, 43
McSmith, Blanche Louise Preston, 190
Michelson, Janet, 210
Mielke, Bill, 237
Mielke, Bob, 237
Mitchell, Nancy, 223
Moon, D.J., family, 237
Murkowski, Frank, 78
Murphy, Monica, 90
Myers, Ann, 40

Neal, Shirley, 210, 223, 240, 242
Neilsen, Arnold, 210
Newby, Norma, **244**
Nixon, Brad, 237
Noonan, Katie, 218
Noonan, Patricia, 223, 227, **239**
Nunley, Jane, **37**, 240
Nunley, Joan, **37**

Olson, Karen, **37**
Olson, Edith, 70
Oswald family, 115

Page, Dorothy, 60, 71, 79, **82**, 87
Page, Vondolee, 79, **82**
Palin, Jim, 247
Palin, Sarah, 40, 247
Palmquist, Kelly, 223
Pate, Mike. 237, 240
Patrick, Dave, 247, 265
Patrick, Rip, 265
Patrick, Roland, 265
Patterson, Dennis, 219
Patterson, Joyce, 227
Patterson, Pat, **196**, 210, 219, **226**, **239**
Peck, Ernest, 33
Peltola, Ron, 228, 237
Petit, Mick, 237
Pinkham, Louis, 296
Platt, Ricky, 210
Porth, Carl Boston, 219
Polis, John, 41
Polis, Pete, 41, 131
Post, Hal, 21, 65-69, 110, 113, 143, 149, 160, 257
Post, Holly, 66
Post, Joy, 66, 68, 69, 110, 149
Post, Kim, 66
Post, Lee, 66, 69
Post, Sue, 66
Post family, 65-69, 85, 149
Potter, Louise, 33, 34, 49, **180**

Quill, Mike, 18
Quint family, 112

Redington, James Wesley, 135
Redington, Joe Sr., 87, 135
Redington, Ray, 135
Redington, Raymie, 147
Redington, Vi, 87
Redington family, 64, 87, 124, 169, 259, 275
Reeder place, 129
Reeder, Sharon, 101, 130, 230, **244**

Reigels, Roy ("Wrong Way"), 211
Rhea, Larry, 99, 270
Rhea, Vince, 99
Rhea family, 263
Richardson, Marvin, 230
Riddle, Betty Jo, 77
Riley, Fay, 216
Roth, Terry, **37**
Roth, Tom, 247
Rousey, Al, 165, 266, 275
Rowe, Schoolboy, 203
Ruth, Babe, 203

Schaeffer, Ross, 237
Schwartz, Kathy, 101, 176, 246, 277
Scrog, Garfield, 60
Selle, Jim, 237
Selle, John, 237
Sellens, Jay, 246
Senske, Ilah, 216
Serling, Rod, 71
Shaw, John, 243
Shellhorn, Dick, 228, 237
Shilber, Ray, **37**
Skutka, Tom, 35
Slee, Don, 21
Slumberger, Clara, 33-34, 45
Smith, Daryl, 159
Smith, Frank, 133, 137, 274
Smyth, Kathleen, 71, 77, **114**
Spencer, Mrs. (teacher), **114**
Spivis, J. Chauncey, 38
Starr, Bud, 247
Starr, Georgia, **37**, 223
Strang, Mike, 170
Swan, Janet, 224

Teeland, Larry, **37**, 194, **196**, 214, 216, **226**, 227, 228
Teeland, Wally, 38
Teeland's store, 41, 136, 141
Thomas, Clint, 154, 186, **188**
Thomas, Neil, 154
Thomas family, 178

Toomey, Melody, **37**
Toomey, Opal, 40, **76**
Toomey, Terry, 172
Totemoff, Marvin, 228
Tremarello, Joe, 242
Tucker, Robert L., 39
Turner, Bea, 39, 40, 70, 71, **72**, **76**, 77, 109, 115, 171, 221, 228
Turner, Dena, 71, **289**
Turner, Jim, 70, 109
Turner, Lee, **58**, 70, 74, 75, **76**, 77, 101, 109, 171, 192, **196**, 199, 217, 219-220, **226**, 230, **239**, 245, 258
Turner, Lin, 70, 109, **289**
Turner, Tom, 245
Turner family, 70-75, 79, 85, 109, 172, 181, 185, 193-194, 221, 227, 230, 231, 245

Vaska, Tony, **241**, 242
Vickaryous, Jimmy, 38
Vickaryous, Tony, 265
Vreeland, Eugene, 119

Wade, Rev. Donald M., 12
Wagstaff, Patty, 133
Wells, Jason, 237, 242
Wertz, Jay, 54
West, Esther, 40
Wetherington, Milton, 222, 230, 233, 235, 240
Wilde, Ed, 91
Wilde, John, 19, 79, 118, 119
Wilson, Jim, 56, 261, 268
Wilson family, 41, 56
Wiltrout, Bill, 245
Woodward, Peg, **37**
Woodward family, 33
Woody, Sybil, 34, 206
Wright, Gordon, Zachary, Parlin and Taylor (law firm), 17
Wykoff family, 85

Yadon place, 129

Acknowledgements

My family and I are grateful to all those within and without this book who have contributed in so many ways, for it has indeed been a group effort.

Praise be to the stellar cast of Hardscratch Press, whose work has made the book a reality: Jackie Pels for editing, author guidance, and publication leadership; David R. Johnson for multiple aspects of photography, design, layout and typography; Dickie Magidoff for composition and typography; and Leah Pels for digital imaging, photo retouching, and index proofing. Thank you for your effort and your patience.

Our gratitude goes also to Katie Hurley, truly an Alaskan treasure, and to her daughter Susan Derrera, equally generous.

Thanks and thanks again to the Wasilla-Knik Historical Society, the Dorothy Page Museum, Colleen (Teeland) Cottle, and Ray Gillespie, for last-minute photo assistance; and to the Coghlans, Posts, Turners, Edes, and Beldens, cousin John Wilde, and friends Skip Coghlan, Dennis Calhoun and Vern Cherneski, among others, for their many anecdotes, every one appreciated.

We send our regards as well to the people and town of Groton, Vermont, in recognition of that glorious in-between year of 1956-57.

— *George Harbeson Jr.*

GEORGE HARBESON JR. *at his present-day home in Ninilchik. The chainsaw carving is by artist J. Peverall.*

ABOUT *the* AUTHOR: George Harbeson Jr. graduated from the University of Alaska Fairbanks and UA Anchorage with B.A. and M.F.A. degrees in English and creative writing. His short story "Simeon's Anipaq" won the 1990 Grand Prize in the *Anchorage Daily News*/UAA Creative Writing Contest and was also published in the *North Dakota Quarterly*. George taught in the rural Alaskan communities of Selawik, Kivalina, Noorvik, Emmonak, Alakanuk, and Anchor Point, and is now retired and living on the Kenai Peninsula, devoting time to photography, writing, and contemplation of the idiosyncrasies of the human critter.

Homesteaders *in the* Headlights

Project coordinator and editor: Jackie Pels
Book design and production: David R. Johnson
Typography and composition: Dickie Magidoff
Photo work and proofreading: Leah H. Pels
CIP data by Rose Schreier Welton, M.L.S.

Harbeson family photographs, unless otherwise noted.

The back-cover photo is of the Harbesons in 1960, visiting the Olney family at Wasilla. From left, Katy Harbeson holding newborn Peter, Lee Anna Harbeson, family friend Margaret Byers, Richard, George Jr., Becky and George Harbeson Sr. (The vehicle in the background is the Byers' 1950 Packard Touring Sedan.)

Printed and bound at McNaughton & Gunn,
Saline, Michigan
Alkaline pH paper (Natural Offset)

[Hardscratch]

Hardscratch Press
2358 Banbury Place, Walnut Creek, CA 94598
Phone/fax 925/935-3422

www.hardscratchpress.com